JOHN OF THE CROSS AND TERESA OF AVILA

John of the Cross
and
Teresa of Avila

Mystical Knowing and Selfhood

EDWARD HOWELLS

A Herder and Herder Book
The Crossroad Publishing Company
New York

UNITY SCHOOL LIBRARY
UNITY VILLAGE, MISSOURI 64065

The Crossroad Publishing Company
481 Eighth Avenue, New York, NY 10001

Copyright © 2002 by Edward Howells

All rights reserved. No part of this book may be reproduced, stored in a retrieval system, or transmitted, in any form or by any means, electronic, mechanical, photocopying, recording, or otherwise, without the written permission of The Crossroad Publishing Company.

Printed in the United States of America

Library of Congress Cataloging-in-Publication Data   7/04

Howells, Edward.
    John of the Cross and Teresa of Avila : mystical knowing and selfhood
  / Edward Howells.
      xi, 212 p. cm.
    Includes bibliographical references and index.
    ISBN 0-8245-1943-4 (alk. paper)
    1. Mysticism—Catholic Church—History—16th century. 2. John of the
Cross, Saint, 1542-1591. 3. Teresa, of Avila, Saint, 1515-1582. I.
Title.
BX4700.J7 .H69 2002
248.2'2'0922—dc21

                                   2002001695

1   2   3   4   5   6   7   8   9   10   06   05   04   03   02

c. 1

Contents

List of Tables

Abbreviations

Works of John of the Cross

S   *Subida del Monte Carmelo* (Ascent of Mount Carmel)
N   *Noche oscura* (Dark Night)
C   *Cántico espiritual* (Spiritual Canticle) (B redaction)
L   *Llama de amor viva* (Living Flame of Love) (B redaction)
R   *Romances* (Romances)

For the redactions of C and L used, see note 1 to the appendix, p. 198.

Works of Teresa of Avila

CC   *Cuentas de conciencia* (in some other editions called the *Relaciones*; often translated as the *Spiritual Testimonies*)
CV   *Camino de perfección*, Valladolid manuscript (Way of Perfection)
Cta   *Carta(s)* (Letters)
E   *Exclamaciones* (often called the *Soliloquies*)
F   *Fundaciones* (Foundations)
M   *Moradas del castillo interior* (Interior Castle)
MC   *Meditaciones sobre los Cantares* (Meditations on the Song of Songs)
V   *Vida* (Life)
Vej   *Vejamen* (often called *A Satirical Critique*)

Citations are given in the following order:

(i) title of work; (ii) chapter; (iii) paragraph; (iv) page number in the English edition; (v) page number in the Spanish edition.

E.g., "L 3:30 (621/989)" means: *Llama de amor viva*, chapter 3, paragraph 30, page 621 in the English edition and page 989 in the Spanish edition.

The English editions used are those published by the Institute of Carmelite Studies: *The Collected Works of John of the Cross*, trans. and intro. Kieran Kavanaugh and Otilio Rodriguez (Washington D.C.: Institute of Carmelite Studies, 1979), and *The Collected Works of St. Teresa of Avila*, trans. and intro. Kieran Kavanaugh and Otilio Rodriguez, 3 vols (vol. 1: 2nd ed.; vols. 2 & 3: 1st ed.) (Washington D.C.: Institute of Carmelite Studies, 1980-87).

The Spanish editions used are those in the Biblioteca de Autores Cristianos series: *Obras Completas de San Juan de la Cruz*, ed. Lucinio Ruano (14th ed.; Madrid: Biblioteca de Autores Cristianos, 1994), and *Obras Completas de Santa Teresa de Jesús*, ed. Efrén de la Madre de Dios and Otger Steggink (9th ed.; Madrid: Biblioteca de Autores Cristianos, 1997).

In the case of Teresa of Avila's *Letters*, the translation by E. Allison Peers is used, as these do not appear in the Institute of Carmelite Studies edition: *The Letters of St Teresa of Jesus*, trans. E. Allison Peers, 2 vols. (Westminster, Md.: Newman Press, 1951).

Where the work is divided into a number of books (in addition to chapters and paragraphs) the number of the book precedes the title: e.g. "1S" means *Subida*, book 1; and "3M" means *Moradas*, 3rd Dwelling Place.

Occasionally, the chapter or paragraph numbering in the English edition differs from the Spanish edition, in which case the numbering in the English edition is given first and that in the Spanish edition second, in brackets: e.g., "CC 25(26)" means *Cuentas de conciencia*, number 25 in the English edition and number 26 in the Spanish edition.

Acknowledgments

I would like to thank the following for their help on this book: first, the Fulbright Commission, the Abbot of Elmore Abbey in England, and the Carmelites in Washington, D.C. (the Louis Herman and Susan Hamilton Rogge Endowment Fund), for generous grants; second, David Tracy and Susan Schreiner, my readers for the first incarnation of this book, as a University of Chicago Ph.D. dissertation, and also Denys Turner, Mark McIntosh, Iain Matthew, Steven Payne, Gillian Ahlgren, Rowan Williams, and Alois Haas, for informative conversations; third, my fellow students at the University of Chicago, Gordon Rudy, Patricia Beckman, and Constance Furey, for their advice and companionship; fourth, my Ph.D. adviser, Bernard McGinn, for his immense knowledge and close attention; and finally, Philippa, my wife, for too many other things to mention.

Introduction

IN SIXTEENTH-CENTURY SPAIN, two Carmelites, Teresa of Avila (1515–1582) and John of the Cross (1542–1591), working in the inauspicious circumstances of internal strife within the Carmelite Order and inquisitorial censure in the society at large, produced writings that have since been hailed as some of the greatest in Christian mystical theology. Their writings are important both historically, coming at the end of the rich medieval development of mystical theology in the West, and theologically, as statements of mystical experience and transformation. In this book, I ask a question of Teresa of Avila and John of the Cross that we might bring to any mystic: What is the "experience" that is called "mystical," and what makes this experience different from "ordinary experience"? Teresa and John turn the question around and ask, What kind of experience, if any, is possible when the mystical relation to God is attained—given how different this relation is from anything in our ordinary experience? The mystical is not primarily an experience but a relation: it is a change from our natural relation to God to a wholly graced, supernatural relation, which affects our very selfhood. They characterize the mystical relation in two ways. First, it is a purely "spiritual" and "supernatural" relation with God, in which all created intermediaries are bypassed, rather than a relation through creatures, as in our natural state. Second, it is "experienced" or felt, and becomes known, in the "interior" of soul, that is, in our own self-relation and in the act by which our "selves" are constituted, rather than in the "subject–object" relations to creatures which characterize our ordinary experience and knowledge. Such a relation requires considerable "transformation" and "deepening" of the self in order to be known. This book is about the type of self and the anthropological transformation required for mystical experience to become known, according to Teresa of Avila and John of the Cross.

The unusual feature of Teresa and John's mysticism, in the context of the late medieval mystical tradition, is the degree to which they "interior-

1

ize" the entire mystical journey and transpose it into anthropological categories. The final union occurs in the "center of the soul," a center that is reached after passing through other "centers" and interior regions on the path to union. God is found in the final center, in an infinite "capacity" in the soul, which has some similarities to the "ground of the soul" in the Rhineland "essentialist" tradition of Meister Eckhart and the Beguine mystics, except that Teresa and John take great care to differentiate the soul from God in this center, rather than simply pointing to their unity.[1] Combined with this attention to the "deep interior" relationship between the soul and God is a concern with epistemology, and particularly with the transformed epistemology attained in union.[2] Teresa is less systematic than John in her epistemology, as we would expect given their differences of education, but she too organizes the "interior" of the soul in terms of faculties and senses with which we feel and know God in "mystical theology," setting up a parallel epistemology to that of the natural faculties and senses in the "exterior" part of the soul.[3] The combination of these two elements from the tradition results in a highly developed mystical anthropology: on top of the relational "depth" between the soul and God in the interior of the soul is placed the epistemological detail of a faculty psychology, producing a complete theory of mystical experience and knowing.

This turn to the interior, added to the parceling out of different powers of the soul to different epistemological functions, is theoretically problematic. If the soul can feel and know God mystically in the interior part, in a distinct set of operations from those of ordinary experience and knowledge, while the ordinary operations are retained in the exterior part, can it be said to remain a single soul? Why would such a mystical interior continue to need the exterior part or wish to remain connected to it? The problem does not go unnoticed by either Teresa or John. Teresa says that, having progressed some way into the stage of mystical union, she feels divided like Mary and Martha, between the interior part which is "always enjoying quietude" in the presence of God, and the exterior part which is left "in trials, so she could not keep it [the interior part] company." She calls this a feeling of "division in her soul" (*división en su alma*).[4] Similarly, John says that in the deepest part of the "dark night," where the soul is closest to God, one part of the soul "seemingly has no relation to the other."[5] The problem for both Carmelites is that the creature–creator distinction has been broken down to some extent in the interior of the soul, while in the exterior of the soul it remains the same as before. Even though they are clear that both parts of the soul remain human, in establishing this immediate relation with God as uncreated in the interior, the soul finds itself closer to God in the interior part than this interior part is to its own exterior part. Thus, the ontological division between the soul and God enters into the soul, dividing the two parts—not to the same degree that the soul and God are naturally divided, but enough to dislocate the soul severely. The division in the soul is based on the traditional distinction between the spirit and the flesh in Christian anthropology, introduced by St. Paul, but goes further: the soul is not simply oriented to God as opposed to the flesh in the interior part, but has also lost all created intermediaries between itself and God, so that it is divided between two ontologically different types of relation to God.

In response to this problem of the division in the soul, commentators on Teresa and John have striven hard to show that there is not actually an *ontological* division in the soul. Henri Sanson, Georges Morel, and André Bord, in detailed treatments of John's anthropology, argue that it is merely a "psychological," as opposed to an ontological, division.[6] They correctly point out that, for John, the "darkness" and "annihilation" that the soul feels when it comes into immediate contact with God is a psychological *response* to the ontological difference between God and the soul rather than the reification of this ontological difference in the two parts of the soul. Also, "annihilation" has a positive ultimate goal, to renew the soul rather than to destroy it. Similarly, Teresa's "suspensions," which signify the separation of the interior part of the soul from the exterior part, are the *effect* on the soul of the ontological difference between God and creatures, and they are superseded in her later treatments of union, where she says that the two parts of the soul come to "work together." I do not, however, find this explanation of the division as merely psychological to be adequate: unless there were *something* of an ontological separation between the two parts of the soul, "mystical theology" would lose the unique status that Teresa and John fully intend to give it. The two Carmelites are careful not to go as far as to divide the soul into separate "divine" and "human" parts—both parts are *relations* between the human soul and God—but they intentionally develop a position where the *immediate* relation in the interior part is so different in kind and operation from the *mediated* relation in the exterior part as to threaten the unity of the single human person. Teresa and John cannot be accused of failing to demonstrate the unique nature of the mystical relation with God, but a question mark hangs over the ontological status of the interior part of the soul as a result of their strong distinction between the "mystical" and the "natural."

Commentators have pointed to Teresa and John's Christology as the means by which they reach a unity between the human and the divine in their anthropology. Rowan Williams says that we must not lose sight of the christological framework within which Teresa places her descriptions of "mystical experience." The "suspensions" and so on that she describes are part of the traditional difficulty faced by Christians "to be 'natural,' to live in the world as creatures bearing God's image."[7] In other words, the problem of the division in the soul is analogous to the relation of the divine and human natures of Christ in the incarnation. In an excellent study of John's Christology, Iain Matthew argues a similar case for John, saying that the division in John's anthropology is an attempt to understand Jesus "from the inside," reflecting the distinction in the hypostatic union between the human and divine natures.[8] As John says, the final union of the soul with God is a union "corresponding" to the hypostatic union.[9] To jump ahead to my conclusion to this study, my own finding is that Teresa and John arrive at this christological unity only through their understanding of the Trinity. They appeal to the christological analogy both on the journey to union and in union itself to make sense of the division in the soul, but they develop their anthropology *primarily* in terms of the Trinity. Teresa maintains a more "bodily" devotion to images of the humanity of Christ on the journey to union than John, but both Carmelites approach Christ, and their anthropology, first of all through the "interior" transformation of the soul into the form of the Trinity.[10]

In this book, I develop the view that it is the *dynamism* of the Trinity in its internal relations that solves the problem of the division in the soul and becomes the central feature of Teresa and John's anthropology. Indeed, the arrival at the "center of the soul," by which both authors characterize the final union, is the full appropriation by the soul of the dynamism of the Trinity in its internal relations, which then "overflows" into virtuous exterior acts. My analysis of this trinitarian view of the soul in union begins by making a distinction between the *structural* and *dynamic* aspects of the soul.[11] Structurally, the soul is divided into "interior" and "exterior" parts, and then into the various powers of a faculty psychology within these parts. Dynamically, the soul is the subject of transformation, being progressively drawn into the inner relations of the Trinity, such that in the final union the soul is positioned at the source of the divine "overflow" of the Trinity into creation, including the whole soul in both its "parts" in this divine dynamism. This distinction between structure and dynamism is used to organize the chapters of the book: there are two main chapters on each figure, the first on the structure of the soul, and the second on the dynamics of transformation. In each case, the division in the soul is considered first as the structural "problem," and then the dynamism of the soul in its participation in the Trinity is introduced as the "solution." This organization is not merely artificial but seeks to reproduce the order of events in the process of transformation, according to the two Carmelites. Teresa and John are treated separately until chap. 7, where they are compared closely and final conclusions are drawn, with some further comparisons in the epilogue.

Part of the difficulty in understanding the soul or "self" according to Teresa and John is that it is so different from the self of modernity. The aim in this book is to interpret Teresa and John's view in a way that is historically accurate. First, the self is "dynamic" in their view even before mystical transformation begins, in that it exists in a dynamic relation with God as its creator. Teresa describes how the soul attains self-knowledge by realizing that its "fount" is God rather than itself alone, and she contrasts the dynamism of this relationship with God to the stagnation of getting stuck in our own autonomous "misery."[12] She is describing an Augustinian idea of introspection, by which the soul sees its fundamental being as rooted in God, in the "image" of God in the soul. For John, this image of God in the soul is explicitly related to the Trinity from the beginning of the spiritual journey, in the "spiritual faculties" of memory, intellect, and will, as in Augustine's original treatment—though there are also some differences from Augustine's faculty psychology.[13] For Teresa too, the natural "image" is seen as the forebear of the supernatural center of the soul in union, but she does not link the dynamism of this interior relation with God to the Trinity until she starts to have visions of the Trinity in union. This idea of selfhood has been usefully contrasted with post-Cartesian ideas of the self by Jacques Maritain, in his *Degrees of Knowledge*. He calls it the "transobjective self," in that the soul requires relationships with others, and ultimately with God, in order to be a self.[14] There is no autonomous entity of selfhood, as in the Cartesian view, but only the relational ability or intentionality, rooted in the soul–God relation, by which our selfhood is continuously being constituted "on the move."

Second, in Teresa and John's understanding of the self, mystical transformation builds on the activity of this naturally dynamic self. In the natural state, the soul relates to God through creatures—through objects of beauty in the world and through its own interior beauty, when these things are seen as having their source in God—whereas in union, the soul's relation to God is known first, before creatures. As John says, in union the soul "knows things better in God's being than in themselves"—it knows its own relation to God from God's perspective, rather than through itself or through the world; it knows created things through their cause, a priori, rather than knowing the cause through the effects, a posteriori.[15] Here the soul's relation with God is truly intersubjective, in that it is not mediated through any created objects, and not even through ourselves as creatures. This is the relation that Teresa and John describe as the spiritual marriage. The spiritual marriage is given from God's side rather than from the side of creatures, introducing the soul to a relationship with God which *is* the mutual relation of the Son with the Father in the Trinity. The degree to which the soul must be transformed to reach this position is vast, but Teresa and John's dynamic view of the self means that they can regard it as a *reordering* of the soul rather than as a complete change of self. The thread of continuity between the divided parts of the soul is maintained through this fundamentally dynamic and theological view of the self.

The dynamism of the soul is used by Teresa and John to show how the soul can be raised to the level of the uncreated Trinity in union, while also retaining its individual identity and humanity. The soul shares in the inner life of the Trinity without losing certain key aspects of its created structure. First, the soul's created humanity is included in the Trinity through attaining a self-understanding within the mutuality of the relations of the Trinity: the soul not only knows God in the immediate relationship of union, but knows itself *through* this relationship, so that it attains a way of knowing which is at once both divine and human. Second, divinity is mediated to the full humanity of the soul through the Trinity's self-diffusion into creation: the Trinity "overflows" to all parts of the soul through the soul's center. "Overflow" is understood by Teresa and John as uniting the two parts of the soul in this trinitarian act of creation. Thus, the two parts of the soul attain the likeness of Christ's two natures in the hypostatic union: in the center, the soul's humanity is immediately united with divinity, while in the exterior part, the dynamism of the Trinity is mediated to the lower levels of the soul. The humanity of Christ is attained, with Christ, at the point of origin of all creation in the Trinity.[16] Third, the soul's humanity remains *distinct* from divinity within this union, without being *divided* as in the earlier stages of transformation. The difference from the earlier division in the soul is that the dynamism of the Trinity is no longer in excess of the soul's "capacity," sending it into "suspensions" and deep darkness, but through transformation the soul has been "expanded" and deepened to "contain" the overflow. The *same* dynamism that gives the soul "clear knowledge" of both God and itself within the Trinity is the motivation for its exterior actions in the world. John neatly summarizes this final unity in the soul by saying that now "the power to look at God is, for the soul, the power to do works in the grace of God."[17]

Teresa and John's final understanding of the soul is one in which the soul's perfected human structure is transparent to the dynamism of the Trinity. There is no longer a succession of acts by which the dynamism of the Trinity is mediated to the soul, as in the natural soul, but rather one continuous trinitarian act of "gazing" between the soul and God which produces concomitant "divine" activity in the world. The very act in which the soul looks at God is the act by which it does God's will in the world, in a single process of overflow. The final aim of this book is to provide an interpretation of mystical knowing and action that makes sense of this view. It should be noted that when the soul is united in all its parts in the final union, it is no longer the case that mystical knowing is merely an analogy drawn from ordinary knowing, by which a separate interior part of the soul is carved out and *likened* to ordinary knowing, but rather it is the fully incarnated human knowing and awareness with which the soul lives at all times. Teresa and John say that there are various degrees of "clarity" in the soul's perception of the divine, but it retains the mystical relation with God in the center permanently, performing all its acts without leaving union.[18]

One major question remains: On what basis can Teresa of Avila and John of the Cross be compared? The above represents my conclusions on one central aspect of their thought—their mystical anthropology—on which there is considerable agreement between them. Even here, there are differences, which are further explored in the epilogue. In particular, John is more negative in his theology than Teresa, being influenced by Dionysius and emphasizing the suffering and "darkness" of the mystical relation to God much more than Teresa, which leads to differences in their understanding of anthropology. But more widely, there is obviously the difference of gender, and as recent scholarship has shown, gender affected Teresa's life and thought in almost every detail. Alison Weber's thesis in *Teresa of Avila and the Rhetoric of Femininity*,[19] that Teresa used—and had to use—various forms of literary deceit to make her writings acceptable to the censor, clearly challenges the validity of any straightforward comparison between her writings and those of John of the Cross, who was not subject to the same restrictions. But rather than concluding that the writings of a man and a woman at this time simply cannot be compared, my view is that the recent studies of Teresa allow us to compare her thought with John more accurately than before, and no such detailed theological comparisons have been made in recent years.[20]

As Gillian Ahlgren has shown in *Teresa of Avila and the Politics of Sanctity*,[21] Teresa managed to overcome many of the disadvantages imposed on women at the time by teaching herself theology through her voracious reading, and entering the male world of spiritual writing through her careful use of language (following Weber) and her skillful handling of her opponents. Thus, in spite of her differences from John, we can regard their writings as belonging to the same intellectual context. John wrote in the same "vernacular spiritual" tradition of writing entered by Teresa. Indeed, our improved understanding of this tradition enables us to challenge some of the old stereotypes of both John and Teresa. John was not primarily the scholastic, university-trained theologian beloved of neo-Thomists early in the twentieth century but a vernacular writer in the "spiritual" tradition;[22] and Teresa was not the ill-educated woman with "experience" to supplement John's "learning," but a theologically literate writer in her own right.[23] In these circumstances, it is no surprise that there are close intellectual connections between the thought of Teresa and John, as expounded in this book. At the same time, it must be remembered that though John was Teresa's follower in the Carmelite Reform, the period for which they worked together was not more than two years, and otherwise their contacts appear to have been very few. To assert that there is a complete unity in their doctrine is clearly mistaken.[24]

CHAPTER ONE

Mystical Experience According to John of the Cross

J OHN OF THE CROSS uses a number of terms that come under the general heading of mystical "experience": "spiritual apprehensions," "mystical theology," "knowledge," and less often, "experience" itself. His aim is to give a detailed account of the epistemological transformation that the soul undergoes when it attains mystical union. The difficulty for readers today is that his understanding of experience is based on a different view of the self and the human relationship with God from that held in the modern period. At the outset it is therefore wise to look carefully at how he uses these experiential terms, before moving on to a deeper analysis of his epistemology.

John of the Cross's introduction of the term "experience" (*experiencia*) in the prologue of the *Subida del Monte Carmelo* contrasts both experience and human science with sacred scripture. On the way to perfection, John says that human science "cannot understand" the darknesses and trials that are encountered, and "nor does experience of them equip one to explain them."[1] The contrast of experience and human science with sacred scripture is indicative of the fact that here he is talking of the realm of faith. He concludes:

> I shall not rely on experience or science, for these can fail and deceive us. Although I shall not neglect whatever use I can make of them, my help in all that, with God's favor, I shall say, will be Sacred Scripture.[2]

John's negative assessment of experience as a means to knowledge of God within faith is very much that of Thomas Aquinas: human science, or philosophy, and human experience fail equally in the realm of faith, as faith is beyond human knowledge. There is some overlap between what can be known by reason and what is given by revelation, but for such knowledge to be *reliable* as a means to salvation, one must turn to *sacra doctrina*, as Aquinas calls it, or *sacra Scriptura*.[3]

John's mysticism is famously negative, but his treatment of experience is not nearly as negative as some commentators have supposed.[4] This is clear when one considers some of his positive statements about experience on the journey to union with God. John is adamant that there is a need for people who "have experience" (*tomar experiencia, tener experiencia, hay experiencia*) or who "are experienced" (*ser experimentado*).[5] This is the main criterion for spiritual directors, and indeed it is the prime qualification required—better even than learning, though that is an advantage too.[6] It is no use to be well versed in scripture, without having such experience. But what does this experience mean? The other phrase John uses for such people is to call them those who "are spiritual."[7] He is not referring to particular experiences but to a state of progress that has been achieved in which the person has been transformed spiritually. The culmination of this process, John says, is to receive an interior "habit" (Latin *habitus*; Spanish *hábito*), that is, a developed change in one's soul and knowing ability—the habit of divine union.[8]

But John also gives great importance to particular experiences in the mystical life which go to make up this state of spiritual experience. They become increasingly important as one enters the stage of union with God. The first, which he treats positively, is the "touch of union":

> A certain touch (*toque*) of divinity [is] produced in the soul, and thus it is God himself who is felt (*sentido*) and tasted (*gustado*) here. . . . I do not affirm that a person should be negative about this knowledge as he should be with the other apprehensions, because this knowledge is an aspect of the union toward which we are directing the soul.[9]

While many such apprehensions can be discounted as a distraction from the progress the soul is making toward union, at this point these "touches" begin to communicate God directly and reliably, and can therefore be received positively. John calls them "purely spiritual" (*puramente espirituales*) apprehensions, which fall into four categories—visions, revelations, locutions, and spiritual feelings—and he avers that they yield knowledge of God. They are purely spiritual in that they "are not communicated to the intellect through the corporeal senses,"[10] as all the previous apprehensions were; and further, some do not have any intelligible form but arise from the immediate contact of God with the "substance of the soul," and John says that these ones are "exceptionally advantageous and good."[11] These latter purely spiritual apprehensions build up to what John describes as a "science of love":

[A man will] feel he has been led into a remarkably deep and vast wilderness, . . . the more delightful, savorous, and loving (*deleitoso, sabroso y amoroso*), the deeper, vaster, and more solitary it is. . . . A man is so elevated and exalted by this abyss of wisdom, which leads him into the veins of the science of love (*la ciencia de amor*), that he realizes that all the conditions of creatures in relation to this supreme knowing and divine feeling (*supremo saber y sentir divino*) are very base. . . . He will also note the impossibility, without the illumination of this mystical theology (*mística teología*), of a knowledge (*conocer*) or feeling (*sentir*) of these divine things as they are in themselves through any natural means.[12]

"Mystical theology" is the criterion for John of this kind of feeling which is also knowledge: it is both the knowledge (*conocer*) and the feeling (*sentir*) of "divine things as they are in themselves"—a type of knowing that is formed in the soul through the reception of these apprehensions. Having entered the "abyss of wisdom," the soul is able to receive these apprehensions positively, finding them "delightful, savorous, and loving" and productive of "knowledge or feeling of divine things." At this point John could not indicate the positive value of this feeling more strongly, as well as of science—though it is not "human" but divine science, the "science of love" (*ciencia de amor*), which is science of "divine things as they are in themselves."

It is noteworthy, however, that here John does not actually use the word "experience" (*experiencia*) but rather the word which, literally translated, means "feeling" (*sentir, sentimiento*). He eschews experience (*experiencia*) in this sense, preferring *sentir* and its derivatives, and the words for the five senses (touch, taste, sight, hearing and smell). Often these *sentir* words are translated as "experience" in English translations because, as Trueman Dicken points out, the translators are trying to avoid the *emotional* sense that would be implied by using the word "feeling."[13] Trueman Dicken says, "the root meaning of the verb *sentir* is the perception of a tactile sensation caused by physical contact with the body."[14] To translate it as "feeling" would lead us away from this hard epistemological sense to the idea of an emotional feeling. As it happens, there is also an emotional sense included in this apprehension, as it is "delightful, savorous" and so on, but by using *sentir* John intends to convey not the emotional sense but the epistemological value of the apprehension for *knowledge* of God. As it is a *spiritual* feeling, it is also to be contrasted with physical sensation, but still John regards it as "feeling" in an analogous sense.[15]

We therefore have three possible meanings of the word "experience," the third of which arises only through a difficulty of translation—it is not to be found in the Spanish.

(1) experience, negatively evaluated by John, which is the merely human attempt to reach knowledge of God, short of mystical transformation;

(2) experience as a developing spiritual *habitus* in the soul—the result of specific events like the "touch of union" and other spiritual apprehensions, referring to the *effect* on the soul of such events, rather than the events themselves, as they change the soul inwardly—which is crucial for spiritual directors and for mystical union;

(3) apprehensions of God themselves, such as the "touch of union" and "spiritual feelings," which may be positively welcomed, termed "experience(s)" in translation, but which are in fact described by John as "feelings."

We must reject (3) as "experience," therefore, even though this is the meaning most familiar to us today, because it is not used by John and introduces confusion with the different senses used in (1) and (2). (1) and (2) may appear to be contradictory, but in fact they have the same sense: experience is not an individual apprehension but the *way of knowing* possessed by a person in that state. The difference is—and the reason for John's different verdict on each of them—that one is experience prior to union with God, and the other is part of union. John rejects all experience prior to "touches of union," because it requires a very advanced state of the soul before spiritual apprehensions yield the interior *habitus* of union described in (2). It must be admitted that John's negativity on this score is far more prominent—which is not to say more important—than his positive evaluation of the soul's capability. The reason is that he starts with a view of human nature as severely fallen, especially in the ability to know God, so that at this stage he says that "however impressive may be one's knowledge or feeling of God, [it] will have no resemblance to God and amount to very little."[16] Even when the soul begins to have "supernatural apprehensions" later on, he says that they must be rejected, as there is still the possibility that they are mixed with human error or may have their source outside God.[17] It is only when the soul enters the stage of union that it is deemed *capable* of receiving divine communications positively. This is not to say that true touches of union are not sometimes given to beginners, but that union with God must properly be understood as a state of transformation of the soul; union is not an exterior apprehension but a substantial change in the soul's very being. The soul is purified, transformed, and given a new *likeness* to God, and therefore the capability for apprehending God directly in the renovated "spiritual faculties." At this point, the apprehensions encountered by the soul change from having no value to being worthy of positive recognition. John's attention remains focused not on the apprehensions themselves, however, but on the inner development of the soul, and it is to this that he refers in speaking about experience. To "have experience" is not the same as having certain "feelings," but to be inwardly transformed and capable of *knowing* these feelings. Similarly, the experience that John rejected at the outset was not any particular apprehension but the *way of knowing* possessed by an ordinary human being, prior to mystical transformation. Therefore, there is only one sense of experience, referring to the *interior capability of the soul for knowledge of God.* When the soul has not developed this capability, it does not "have experience," but when it attains the interior *habitus* of union or is nearing it, it does "have experience." Apprehensions or feelings given to the soul have a distinct and different sense which, confusingly, is often translated as "experience" but in fact exists independently of the all-important interior development of the *habitus* of union in the soul.

What is the connection, then, between experience in this sense, as something possessed interiorly by the soul, and the important, but transitory, spiritual apprehensions? John here relates spiritual apprehensions to the interior structure of the soul, using a Neoplatonic/Aristotelian understanding of epistemology, which will be considered more fully in the next chapter. Briefly, the theory is that in ordinary knowing, to reach knowledge of an object, the soul *becomes what it knows* through understanding the form of the object; and John exploits this idea to the full to show how mystical knowing works. Ordinary knowing is based on sensory experience, providing the data, which is then abstracted into forms by the illumination of the intellect. Knowledge of an object is reached when the intellect is united with the object via the object's form (intentionally rather than really): then the object exists in the soul, as a form or mental likeness of the object's essence, uniting the intellect with the object. In mystical knowing—which John, and Teresa of Avila, often call "mystical theology"—the spiritual parallel of sensory perception occurs. In an analogous manner to the phantasms that pass from the ordinary senses to the interior of the soul, the soul receives "purely spiritual apprehensions," which in their "substantial" form are already in the form of God through an immediate "touch" with God's substance; they bring the soul into "substantial contact" with God, thus transforming the soul interiorly and finally achieving union.[18] The soul is then united with God by a participation in God's nature.[19] Purely spiritual, substantial apprehensions thus lead to a union of the subject with its object, setting up two parallel epistemological processes, the ordinary and the mystical, providing ordinary and mystical knowledge respectively. While mystical knowing may occur instantaneously, however, the difference from ordinary knowing is that it requires the gift of a new interior organization and orientation of the soul toward the objects it perceives. The soul must turn from the objects of the senses to those of the spirit. Consequently, the type of knowledge gained, though received by an epistemology related to that of ordinary knowing, is different from ordinary knowledge and indeed is recognized at first only by its contrast to ordinary knowledge. The word "mystical," as in the term "mystical theology," is used by John to refer to this contrast: "mystical" knowledge is "secret" knowledge, given within the darkness of faith, beyond ordinary knowledge—a knowledge given in grace, "infused," and part of the gift of love: it is "knowledge through love."[20] Furthermore, mystical knowledge has the character of breaking into the soul, so that for instance when "touches of union in the memory" occur, John says, "a sudden jolt is experienced in the brain . . . so sensible that it seems the whole head swoons and that judgment and sensibility are lost."[21] But these violent effects lessen as the soul advances toward union.[22] Still, even in union, mystical knowledge is very different from ordinary knowledge. First, while the relation of subject and object is clear in the case of physical objects presented to the body, in the case of divine contact with the soul, it is much less clear where the boundaries of subject and object lie. John says that the point of contact between God and the soul in mystical knowledge is in the substance or abyss or center of the soul, which breaks down the subject–object relation of ordinary knowledge. Second, there is the difference, alluded to already, that the "spiritual communication" to the soul that produces knowledge of God is the same communication that transforms the soul. The soul is constantly being changed by this grace, so that it is in a dynamic relation to the object of its knowledge, which again breaks down the subject–object relation of ordinary knowledge.

Thus, mystical "experience" is a complex term for John, with two main aspects to its meaning. First, the particular "spiritual apprehensions" felt by the soul in union, though important, are to be distinguished from the developed capacity for knowledge of God to which John gives the name "experience." Spiritual apprehensions are not knowledge in themselves but only the first moment of sensation, following which further cognitive acts are required to make them known. "Experience" is the overall cognitive process or *awareness* by which we know these apprehensions. Second, the difference between mystical experience and ordinary experience is that the ordinary relationship between subject and object no longer pertains, but there is a new kind of intersubjective relationship between the soul and God. Exactly what is meant by this and how the two kinds of experience and knowing are reconciled in John's epistemology remain to be considered in the next two chapters. Our central problem is how John maintains that there is *both* a strong difference *and* a deeper unity in the soul between these two kinds of experience and knowing.

CHAPTER TWO

The Structure of the Soul According to John of the Cross

JOHN OF THE CROSS seeks to understand mystical experience by developing an epistemology and anthropology within which mystical knowing is first strongly contrasted with ordinary knowing and then reconciled with it, by appealing to a deeper unity in the soul. John divides the soul into two "parts," the spiritual and sensory, or interior and exterior, which are used to differentiate the type of knowing attained in mystical experience. The purpose of this chapter is to examine exactly how he draws this contrast between the two parts of the soul. The focus is on the problematic separation between ordinary and mystical knowing in his anthropology, leaving the solution—his understanding of the deeper unity between the two parts of the soul—for the next chapter.

For John of the Cross, the components of the human person—body, soul, and spirit—operate differently in mystical knowing and ordinary knowing, and relate differently to one another. John uses this fact to explain the distinction between the two kinds of knowing. There are two epistemologies: one by which the soul knows "natural" objects, in the ordinary process of knowing, the other by which it comes to know "supernatural" objects, in mystical knowing. The soul is the same in each case, having the same components, but with these components in a different configuration and oriented to different objects. Most importantly, whereas ordinary knowing begins with the bodily senses, mystical knowing bypasses the bodily senses and is received in the spirit. This division of sense and spirit is the basis of John's separation of natural knowing from spiritual or mystical knowing.[1] But John is also keen to point out that mystical knowing, though not natural, becomes as integral to the soul as ordinary knowing: the soul develops capabilities within its structure that make it suited to mystical knowing. The soul is "deepened" into "an infinite capacity" through mystical transformation, so that "anything less than the infinite fails to fill [it]."[2]

The Sources of John's Epistemology

The sources of John of the Cross's epistemology are not at all clear. One thing that can be said is that attempts early in this century to match his view to that of Thomas Aquinas were misconceived.[3] John of the Cross differs from Aquinas on some key points, and it is likely that he is well aware that he is doing so. For instance, John does not leave our knowledge of God as a posteriori knowledge: he wants to go further toward an a priori knowledge of God.[4] Theories about which scholastic thinkers had most influence on John are based on the ideas he is likely to have come into contact with at the University of Salamanca, where he studied for four years (1564–1568).[5] Aquinas would certainly have been among these,[6] and it is likely that he studied the Carmelites' own John Baconthorpe and Michael of Bologna as part of the requirements of the order. Baconthorpe is the closer of these two to John's epistemology, using the same Aristotelian starting point as John—also used by Aquinas—that "nothing is in the intellect that was not first in the senses" (*nihil est in intellectu quod prius non fuerit in sensu*). But other differences are more pronounced, such as Baconthorpe's view that knowledge of God is possible without any supernatural light, which was not the view of John of the Cross.[7]

Another important feature of John's epistemology which cannot be explained by reference to Aquinas is his view that there are three spiritual faculties, memory, intellect, and will, against Aquinas's two (intellect and will). Augustine is the obvious source for this, but the similarity is only superficial. André Bord has shown that John and Augustine use memory very differently—most of all in the respect that memory for John is a power of recall but not a storehouse for images and forms as for Augustine.[8] In regard to scholastic thought, the best conclusion remains that of John's great biographer, Crisógono de Jesús Sacramentado, who suggests that John did not use Aquinas nor any other single scholastic authority for his epistemology but formed an original theory out of the various ideas he had learned, applying them to his thought in a pragmatic more than a technical or very systematic way. Crisógono points out that there was no single "line" taken in the theology faculty at Salamanca: the faculty had an eclectic make-up, with chairs in the thought of Aquinas, Scotus, and Durandus, and masters whose views covered a wide variety of positions from Thomist to anti-Thomist, Avicennian, Averroist, and Nominalist. In spite of the Inquisition, there was remarkable freedom of thought within the university.[9] We can only assume John made an original combination of those ideas he found most useful. He seldom cites his authorities, apart from the Bible, but his scholastic learning is clear and he appears to have taken a number of ideas freely from different scholastic sources.[10]

What about John's nonscholastic sources? Unfortunately, these are equally unclear but perhaps offer a more promising avenue of inquiry for explaining some of the sharp differences between John and the typical scholasticism of his day. A few studies in the 1920s and 1930s sought to liken John of the Cross to the Rhineland mystics, particularly John Ruusbroec,[11] but this line of thought was not taken up in any detail until the 1960s:[12] André Bord avers that this is the source, for instance, of John's idea of the center or substance of the soul, which relates to the three spiritual faculties not in the scholastic sense of substance but in the essentialist sense of the depth and root of the soul.[13] This indeed is one of the most prominent features of John's epistemology and one that I will be focusing on in understanding his view of mystical union, in that he places the transforming penetration of the soul into the "depth" of relationship with God ahead of the fine scholastic distinctions of his faculty psychology. But it is very hard to draw any clear connection to specific sources in Ruusbroec or other essentialist Rhineland mystics. It can only be affirmed that the works of John Tauler and Ruusbroec were commonly available in Spain at this time, particularly before they were banned in the Valdés Index in 1559—and even after then they seem to have been available—and it is quite probable that John read them and was influenced by them.[14] Again, the problem is that John seldom cites his sources, except in a few cases such as Gregory the Great, Dionysius, and Bernard of Clairvaux.[15] The prayer method of *recogimiento* taught by John's Spanish predecessor, Francisco de Osuna, is certainly assumed;[16] and Bernardino de Laredo's *Subida del Monte Sion* may be an influence.[17] William of St. Thierry is an obvious source one might look to for John's view of the spiration of the Holy Spirit and immediate presence of the Trinity within the soul.[18] But how much John actually knew of these mystical writers or drew on them remains unclear.

Henri Sanson, in his study of John of the Cross in 1953, made the important move of giving attention to John's style and genre as a key feature of his mysticism, describing it as "scriptural mysticism" (*mysticisme scripturaire*).[19] Colin P. Thompson's study of the *Cántico espiritual* takes a similar line in relation to the literary sources of John's poetry, showing that unlike his literary contemporaries John's sensibility and means of expression are formed almost exclusively from the Bible and from the Song of Songs in particular.[20] This is no surprise. Scripture, most of all the Song, was always a central model for mystical poetry and commentaries.

But where John's use of the scriptural model is unusual is in his adoption of the genre of scriptural commentary for his own reflections on his poetry. The poetry is set up as a quasi-scriptural text, on which John then comments.[21] Here he seems to internalize the world of the Song into his own language and experience to such an extent that some scholars, such as Michel de Certeau, suggest that he has raised personal experience to a level which competes with and actually destroys the theological tradition on which it is based.[22] My own view, however, is that of Max Huot de Longchamp, that John's placing of his own poetry in place of the biblical text is certainly an interesting reversal of the traditional order of monastic contemplation, but that it remains firmly within this tradition. It is not an attempt to put scripture below personal experience but to inhabit the scripture more deeply.[23] This use of scripture is indeed a mystical use in that it parallels John's attempt to enter into the interior relationship with God as far as is possible.[24]

The statements concerning epistemology that I shall be concentrating on in the remainder of this chapter are a part of John's thought which relates closely to his scholastic training, but the purpose of emphasizing his nonscholastic approach here is to show that his scholasticism is subordinate to a wider mystical context and formation. In particular, the mystical dynamic of immediate relationship with God is placed by John ahead of the scholastic distinctions that he seeks to make. Nevertheless, he works to integrate these two types of approach rather than to leave us with a simple contradiction between the scholastic and mystical aspects of his epistemology.

The Dichotomy of "Sense" and "Spirit"

The most problematic aspect of John of the Cross's epistemology, with which one must begin, is his stark opposition of sense and spirit. Early on in the *Subida del Monte Carmelo*, he states that the soul is a *tabula rasa*, which learns all knowledge through the bodily senses: the bodily senses are the only natural means to knowledge.[25] He follows this with a common scholastic principle, that *quidquid accipitur, accipitur secundum modum accipientis*, or as he puts it, "attachment to a creature makes a person equal to that creature" and "love effects a likeness between the lover and the object loved."[26] The soul, in order to know something, must become like the object of its knowledge. The consequence of this is that ordinary knowing, which must begin with the senses and with an orientation to creatures, renders mystical knowledge of God impossible: it makes the knower equal to creatures, while it obscures a mystical relation to God through the presence of creatures, as objects of sense, which are needed for knowing itself.

John's next move is more unusual, however, as he asserts the principle that "two contraries cannot coexist in the same subject,"[27] meaning that spiritual and sensory forms are mutually exclusive, and mystical knowledge of God is *wholly* prevented by the presence of anything sensory in coming to know.[28] Later on, he admits that a "remote" knowledge of God through creatures is possible,[29] but this is no use from the perspective of the goal he sets out, union with God, because "the means must be proportioned to the end" (quoting Aristotle) while God's difference from creatures "is infinite," and neither the intellect nor any creature can provide a "proportionate" means to God.[30] In union with God, which must be understood as a "union of likeness" (*unión de semejanza*) of the soul with God,[31] the soul will achieve a purely spiritual knowledge of God—in contrast with which even the beauty of creatures is ugliness.[32] Therefore, John sets up an extremely strong contrast between sense and spirit, and between creatures and God, because of the *exclusive* relation he sees between the two and in anticipation of the great height of the achievement to be reached in union with God.

It is the distance that the soul must travel to reach union with God which John is seeking to emphasize with these hyperbolic statements in the early stages of the journey to union with God; when the soul starts to approach union, he tones down the exclusive nature of the relation between sense and spirit. At the end of the *Subida*, for instance, he reiterates that "the sensory part of man can have knowledge of God through neither the senses nor the spirit,"[33] but goes on to say that if sensory joy, such as hearing music, seeing agreeable objects, or feeling the delight of certain tastes and delicate touches, is "immediately at the first movement" directed to God, then the soul "is doing something very good."[34] This, after all, he says, is the purpose for which the senses were created. The fact is that John does not believe that this is possible *before* the intense purgation of the "nights" in the *Subida* and the *Noche oscura* have done their work. He concludes:

> I deduce the following doctrine from all that was said: Until a man is so habituated to the purgation of sensible joy that at the first movement of this joy he procures the benefit spoken of (that these goods turn him immediately to God), he must necessarily deny his joy and satisfaction in sensible goods in order to draw the soul away from the sensory life. Since he is not spiritual, he should be fearful lest through the use of these goods he may perhaps get more satisfaction and strength for the senses than for the spirit.[35]

Until union with God is reached, the soul is not "spiritual," and hence must deny its joy in sensory goods entirely. But then, in union, it is possible "at the first movement" of such joy for the soul to elevate itself to God, rather than pause in its sensory satisfaction, which was its usual course, and so these sensory goods can be received positively rather than denied as was necessary in the earlier stages.

John therefore goes back on the position that there is *no* part for the senses to play in knowledge of God, which he maintains throughout the nights of purgation, to one in which the senses have a secondary role. He sees this as a matter of *orientation* of the soul to the spirit, rather than complete denial of the senses, and says that his distinction is the same as St. Paul's: the sensual man is the one who "occupies his will with sensory things," whereas "the other who raises his will to God he [St. Paul] calls the spiritual man."[36] Such a spiritual orientation of the will is what gives the soul true detachment from the senses and created things. The things that the senses are attached to are not *in themselves* an "encumbrance or harm" to the soul.[37] In other words, it cannot be said that John is a spirit/matter dualist; there is only a strong dichotomy between sense and spirit in his thought, like that between *pneuma* and *sarx* in St. Paul.[38]

John expands the sense/spirit dichotomy into a trichotomy of body, soul, and spirit—in the manner of Paul, Origen, and others in the tradition[39]—which corresponds with the progress of stages to union with God (purgation, illumination, and union). The *Subida*, for instance, is organized in its longest section according to the three kinds of vision first analyzed by Augustine—corporeal, imaginative, and intellectual—which are related to bodily knowledge (through the exterior bodily senses), interior knowledge (through the imagination and fantasy) and purely spiritual knowledge (produced directly in the intellect), respectively, corresponding to the tripartite structure of the soul.[40] In this way, John expands the simple opposition between spirit and sense to a gradual progression from sense to spirit in which the elements of both are frequently mixed and mutually involved.

Nevertheless, John's commentators find it necessary to distinguish between the psychological and ontological aspects of his opposition between sense and spirit to account for the psychological intensity of the suffering when the soul is undergoing purgation and illumination, which John likens to a war between darkness and light.[41] They maintain that there is no ontological dualism. The death that is undergone is patterned on the death of Christ, who was "annihilated in his soul, without any consolation or relief."[42] In the renovation of the soul, John says that God must accomplish more than in creating the soul from nothing, as nothingness raises no opposition, whereas the human appetites in their natural state present a much greater obstacle to the work of God.[43] Consequently, human nature must be "destroyed" in order to be rebuilt. In one of the examples of how his approach differs from Aquinas, John says, "[the objection will be made] that God does not destroy, but perfects nature . . . [but I answer] that the destruction of nature is a necessary consequence of this doctrine."[44] Yet it must be asserted that these statements only apply to the "night time" and purgative parts of the progress to union with God, which are superseded when the dawn arrives and union is reached.[45] Hence they have a psychologically dualistic ring to them but, these commentators argue, do not represent an ontological division, as the senses are included in the spiritual operation of the soul in union.

Epistemologically, however, the sense–spirit dichotomy is evident even in the stage of union with God, as John restricts the involvement of the sensory part of the soul to two areas. First, there is the possibility for sensory pleasure "in the first movement" to direct thought and the affection of the will to God, which directs sensory satisfaction to a spiritual fulfillment; and second, John speaks of the "overflow" from the spirit to the senses in union, which makes possible the "divine operation" of the whole soul and body.[46] In neither case do the senses impinge on the activity of the spirit, but they become involved in the activity of the spirit at a secondary level. In the first case, the senses act properly when they cease their operation and transfer to a spiritual operation;[47] and in the second case, the senses are directed in their activity by the spirit. Yet the overflow from spirit to sense requires an awkward crossover between these strongly contrasted poles. As we shall see, André Bord considers the separation of the soul into its spiritual and natural parts in John's epistemology to be his great achievement: "l'homme est double," he says.[48] But this also creates problems for the unity of the self. While the senses are not denied in mystical knowledge of God, neither are they integrated in mystical knowing adequately to overcome the tendency toward an ontological division in the soul in John's thought, even in the final stage of union, and this remains our focal problem.

The Natural Operation of the Soul

The whole soul, including the spiritual faculties of memory, intellect, and will, works together as one in natural knowing. The tendency toward a division in the soul arises only in spiritual knowing; but to understand how this comes about it is necessary first to examine the process of natural knowing. The soul is by nature designed for attaining knowledge of the world through the exterior corporeal senses—sight, hearing, touch, taste, and smell. John thinks that all natural human knowledge begins with the senses, as the senses are first in the human "order of knowing."[49] The senses are the "gates" of the soul to the outside world and the windows of its prison.[50] The apprehensions of the senses are collated in the interior senses or common sense,[51] which comprises imagination and fantasy.[52]

The interior sense then works in combination with the intellect to abstract forms from the information provided by the bodily senses. The imagination is a discursive faculty, which organizes the images and forms, while the fantasy stores and retains them.[53] The fantasy is an archive or receptacle of sensible forms, which are first abstracted with the aid of the intellect and then stored with the aid of the memory.[54] Once stored, the imagination can re-invoke the images stored in the fantasy, using the memory to recall them.[55] Imagination can also reorganize the images it uses: even though it has never seen "palaces of pearls" or "mountains of gold," for instance, it can imagine them. But such images are always "fashioned by the senses," in that the senses have previously provided the raw material of palaces, pearls, mountains, and gold, through objects seen, heard, and felt.[56] All the operations of the interior sense are thus based on the exterior senses, and together the interior and exterior senses comprise the "lower or sensory part of the soul."[57]

Although the interior senses require the aid of intellect, memory, and will to operate, they are not to be confused with these "rational" or "spiritual" faculties. Intellect, memory, and will are "capable of communion with God," and their "operations are contrary to those of the sensory part"[58]—though, as we have seen, there is only an *opposition* of the senses and spirit in the stages prior to union. The "spirit" is, however, distinguished from the "soul" as an "interior, secret chamber" within the soul,[59] and John works on the principle that the more interior a part of the soul is, the more spiritual and divine it is.[60] Thus, the interior senses are more capable of divine apprehensions than the exterior senses, but neither is remotely as capable as memory, intellect, and will. The tendency of the sensory part is always to "draw it [the rational part] out of its interior to a desire for the exterior things which they [the senses] crave," which first affects the will.[61] This tendency is part of the ordinary operation of the soul, produced by "the affections," which may be good or bad depending on whether they are directed toward God or the objects of sense, but they tend to be bad, because they are naturally directed to sensory gratification and selfish pleasure.[62] Similarly, "the appetites" seek to drag the will down to their level. The distinction between the appetites and the affections is that the affections are associated with the will, while the appetites necessarily pertain to the five senses ("appetites of seeing," hearing, etc.) and cannot be raised above the senses, though both affections and appetites have a similar effect on the will.[63] The appetites are divided into voluntary and natural appetites. It is the voluntary appetites that require one's assent, that are damaging to the will, whereas the natural appetites— hunger, thirst, and so on—cause no harm if one does not allow them to "pass beyond the first movement."[64] In general one *does* allow them to pass beyond the first movement, however, because of the human "passions," which are developed tendencies toward sensory gratification. They are four in number: joy, hope, grief, and fear.[65] "Hope" as a passion is clearly not the same as the theological virtue that is infused into the spiritual faculty of memory to purge and renew it: it is hope for created goods, not for God;[66] and similarly the other passions direct the soul to sensory objects and not to God. These passions bring satisfaction to the will in sensory objects.[67] In union, it becomes possible not to dwell in them, but raise sensory gratification "at the first movement" to affection of the will for God, though until then they remain deeply ingrained and must be wholly denied.[68]

The distinction that John makes between the voluntary and natural appetites indicates that he is using the word "natural" in two senses: most often it has a pejorative sense, meaning the natural tendencies of the soul to sin, that is, its state prior to union; but also it has a less frequently used, morally neutral sense, meaning the soul's operation with regard to merely natural *objects*. As regards his epistemology, in considering the "natural operation of the soul," it is the morally neutral sense that I mean here: the ability of the soul to know natural as opposed to spiritual objects. Of course, because of the Fall, John does not think that the soul will attain its full natural ability for knowing natural objects until restored to the pristine state of Adam's innocence, which requires grace.[69] But the soul is quite capable of knowing natural objects prior to union, even while it experiences the strong opposition between its sensory and spiritual parts. John repeatedly points out that the soul is "one supposit," and therefore works as a unity.[70] Memory, intellect, and will *also* have the ability to be oriented to spiritual objects, but their basic natural function is to work with the senses in order to attain knowledge of the outside world.

In "natural knowing,"[71] the intellect has priority over memory or will, though memory and will are both necessary.[72] The will is necessary as part of knowing, in order to direct the soul's attention to the objects it desires to know,[73] and the memory is needed to recall former objects of knowledge as part of the process of learning new knowledge; but it is the intellect that has the ability of perceiving reality or "being."[74] The will directs the soul to the object it seeks to know and then the intellect grasps the object through the forms and phantasms received in the bodily senses.[75] John appears to regard the intellect as working using the commonly understood method of an "active intellect"—"the intellect which the philosophers call 'active'"—and a "passive intellect," although he only refers to the passive intellect in the context of supernatural knowledge.[76] The active intellect "works upon the forms, phantasies, and apprehensions of the corporeal faculties," while the passive intellect receives these forms when they are illumined and elicited by the active intellect.[77] Here it is presumed that John sees the same relationship between the active and passive intellect in natural knowing as is found in Aquinas.[78] The process of knowing in John is therefore as follows: the active intellect illuminates the images or "phantasms" of objects which have first been sensed by the exterior senses and collated in the "common sense" (which John, unlike Aquinas, equates with imagination and fantasy), and having abstracted the forms of the objects—by which they are known—through this illumination, they are received in the passive intellect. Alternatively, to recall something to mind, the intellect works on the contents of memory in the same way. John has an original view of memory, however, as already noted: the memory has no storage function but serves only to recall what is stored elsewhere.

Here André Bord's assertion that the memory is only a power of recall for John, and not a receptacle or storehouse as in both Aquinas and Augustine, is important. Bord's study focuses on memory for the reason that it shows the originality of John's epistemology and highlights the nature of the distinction between mystical and ordinary knowing in John's thought. Bord sets out the three senses of memory according to Augustine and compares them with John:[79]

(1) memory as a power of recall. Both John and Augustine see memory as a power of recall. As Augustine says, sometimes memory spontaneously turns up memories not sought for. Thus, it has a *recalling* ability and not just a *storage* ability. John speaks of memory as a recalling ability in a similar way in advocating that memory turn away from recalling sensory information and toward God.

(2) "possessions" of memory. Both Augustine and John regard memory as "attending to" and "thinking about" its memories. Memory can get fixed on and obsessed with certain memories. Thus, memory can be filled with the possessions of memory.

(3) memory as a storehouse. John does not regard memory as having a storage ability, whereas Augustine does. How else could John insist so strongly that the memory be voided, while also asserting that natural knowing habits are not thereby removed? The "voiding" (*vaciarse*) of memory *reorients* the soul toward God but does not *remove* the contents of its natural acquired knowledge. It is easy to read John as meaning that the contents of memory are removed also, but he states quite clearly that when memory, intellect, and will are voided, "it should not be thought that because it [the soul] remains in this unknowing that it loses there the acquired knowledge of the sciences."[80] John has a simple reason for separating the recall from the storage function of memory: he wants memory to be entirely "dispossessed" when it comes to its spiritual operation so

that "at the moment it [the soul] recollects itself before God, it enters upon an act of general knowledge [of God]."[81] Memory has broken its bonds with the sensory faculties, including all the particular memories stored there, and becomes free for the "general knowledge" of God, but it has not lost access to its stored natural knowledge when it needs to turn back to objects of sense. When it returns to its sensory operation, it reconnects with the contents of its acquired knowledge. Bord shows that John separates the recall and storage functions of memory precisely in order to make the voiding of memory in its spiritual orientation feasible. When in its natural orientation, memory must work in tandem with fantasy, in which John locates the natural storage ability; he calls fantasy "the receptacle and archive" of forms.[82] Even in the case of purely spiritual forms received by supernatural means, Bord shows that John maintains this separation of functions by speaking of something called the "soul itself," which fulfills the storage function when nonsensible forms which bypass the fantasy and other corporeal faculties are received directly in the spiritual faculties. While the fantasy stores sensible forms that have come through the corporeal faculties, the "soul itself" stores intelligible forms that have bypassed the corporeal faculties and have come directly to the spiritual faculties. In either case, memory remains a distinct faculty with no storage function. Thus, John speaks of "memory *and* fantasy" as being required for the natural function of memory in regard to corporeal forms, and of remembering "through the form impressed on the soul itself," using memory *and* the "soul itself," in the case of spiritual reminiscence.[83]

John is not entirely consistent in this separation of the functions of memory, and Bord notes a number of examples where John speaks of images and ideas "impressed in the memory,"[84] suggesting that memory does have a storage function. But Bord regards these as "imprecision of expression" rather than inconsistencies. From the context, he shows that it is always clear that John means memory in combination with another faculty where he gives it another function.[85] Bord's analysis has been well received,[86] and it is extremely valuable not just in defining what memory means for John but in illustrating the exclusive relationship John sets up between the "spiritual" part of the soul—the faculties of memory, intellect, and will—and the corporeal part. It is not that the spiritual faculties are excluded from involvement with the corporeal faculties: the two parts of the soul work together as one in the natural epistemological process. Rather, Bord has shown that memory works in complete isolation from the corporeal faculties in its *spiritual* operation, when it is oriented toward God. As he says, "John safeguards the spiritual character of memory," in contrast to Aquinas, and much more thoroughly than Augustine.[87] The same goes for the other two spiritual faculties, intellect and will: all three spiritual faculties must be free of any involvement with the corporeal faculties as a precondition of mystical knowing. This will become clearer in considering the spiritual operation of the soul.

The Supernatural and Spiritual Operation of the Soul

In the *Subida del Monte Carmelo*, John of the Cross introduces a strong opposition between knowledge of the world and knowledge of God, which is the origin of the necessity he sees for separating the corporeal faculties from the spiritual faculties in order to achieve knowledge of God. It is not remote knowledge of God through creatures that he has in mind but essential knowledge—by immediate contact with God's essence.[88] He says:

> This divine knowledge of God never deals with particular things, since its object is the Supreme Principle. . . . It consists in a certain touch of the divinity produced in the soul, and thus it is God Himself who is felt and tasted here.[89]

Natural knowing, which begins with the body, is restricted to the particular, whereas knowledge of God is general knowledge, without particular ideas.[90] At this point, "[God] begins to communicate himself through pure spirit by an act of simple contemplation in which there is no discursive succession of thought."[91] John sees this reflected in the difference between the corporeal and spiritual faculties. While anything spiritual is "incomprehensible to the senses," by contrast "anything less than infinite fails to fill [memory, intellect, and will]."[92] The spiritual faculties have a capacity for the "infinite," "general knowledge" of God, which is in stark contrast to the finite, particular capacity of the corporeal senses. "They [the spiritual faculties] are as deep as the boundless goods of which they are capable," and the soul has "an infinite capacity," he says.[93] But initially this is only experienced as a lack. The problem is that the spiritual faculties are no more capable of divine knowledge in their natural state than the corporeal faculties, because the only kind of operation they know is through the corporeal faculties in their natural orientation to the outside world. The spiritual faculties are preoccupied with the objects of the corporeal senses, while "they cannot receive these infinite goods [of divine knowledge] until completely empty."[94] Two remedies are therefore necessary: first, to empty the spiritual faculties of all particular knowledge; and second, to stop all the natural operations of the bodily senses, so that the spiritual faculties cannot be distracted while being reoriented toward God.[95] Both remedies have a largely graced element in which the theological virtues, faith, hope, and love, "void" (*vacían*) and "darken" (*oscurecen*) intellect, memory and will respectively.[96] The infusion of this grace is already the infusion of the divine "light," but because it is so much in excess of the soul's capacity and because the spiritual faculties are full of "baseness and impurity," they experience it as darkness and purgation at first.[97] Only after some time, when "the sensory part is purified by aridity, the [corporeal] faculties by the void of their apprehensions, and the spirit by thick darkness,"[98] caused by the infusion of this divine communication, does the soul gradually attain the ability to see not just its imperfection but the spiritual light it possesses.[99] The spiritual goods received by the soul cease to be painful, but the knowledge received remains general and indistinct.[100] The fact that this knowledge can be known at all, however, entails a new epistemological process in the soul, which John goes on to analyze.

While John restricts the general, indistinct knowledge of God to the purely spiritual "substance of the soul," as it is knowledge of God by immediate contact with God's essence, as opposed to knowledge mediated through creatures, he allows a third category of knowledge, which is given by grace *gratis data*,[101] which has a divine source but is mixed with corporeal elements. His descriptions of this third kind of knowledge in the *Subida* are instructive concerning the relation of the spiritual and sensory parts of the soul. He bases his treatment on the three kinds of vision described by Augustine—corporeal, imaginative, and intellectual[102]—which he regards as designating the point of inception of these apprehensions into the epistemological process in the soul. In other words, corporeal visions enter the soul through the exterior bodily senses, imaginative visions enter through the interior bodily senses (imagination and fantasy), and intellectual visions enter through the spiritual faculties—the intellect in this case—bypassing the bodily senses.[103] His main point regarding these supernatural visions is that for a vision to be reliable, the bodily senses must be entirely absent from involvement, as "corporeal perceptions bear no proportion to what is spiritual."[104] (He gives further reasons, such as that the contrast between purely spiritual and bodily visions is so great that the bodily faculties must necessarily cease to work,[105] and where there is any use of the bodily faculties, the danger of deception by the devil always casts too great a doubt on the source of the vision for it to be considered reliable.[106]) In the case of corporeal and imaginative visions, there is always some involvement of the bodily senses, and hence they must be rejected; but in the case of *some* intellectual visions, it is different. All three kinds of visions may be regarded as *supernatural*, as even those that involve the corporeal senses have a supernatural source and must be received passively in the soul.[107] But here he makes a distinction of supernatural from spiritual visions: those that bypass the corporeal senses altogether are not just supernatural but spiritual.[108] As we noted earlier, he begins with the division of all spiritual apprehensions into two kinds. Those that use the same *forms* of representation as in natural knowing are called "distinct," because they use distinct intelligible forms, as in the case where one sees the same objects by such a vision as one might see in ordinary life, only by nonsensible means, such that the forms are stored in the "soul itself" rather than the fantasy.[109] The second kind of spiritual apprehensions use no intelligible forms, however, and therefore have nothing in common with knowledge through the senses whatsoever. They are felt in the "*substance of the soul*" and are indistinct; John says that they "cannot be unclothed and seen clearly in this life by the intellect, [but] they can nonetheless be felt in the substance of the soul by the most delightful touches and conjunctions."[110] John has thus distinguished three kinds of vision according to three levels of involvement of the corporeal senses: first, those that are represented through the exterior or interior corporeal senses (corporeal and imaginative visions); second, those that are represented solely through the spirit but that use intelligible forms of corporeal substances (the first kind of intellectual visions); and third, those that use no such forms at all because they are of "separate or incorporeal substances," remaining "general and indistinct," but are nevertheless felt by the part of the spirit known as "the substance of the soul" (the second kind of intellectual visions). Only the latter, John says, are to be associated with union with God.[111]

Thus the soul, to have knowledge of God in essence, must become divorced not just from its sensory faculties but from the entire epistemological process based on forms. John points out just how different these highest apprehensions are from all others:

> There is a difference in their objects, since the object of the spiritual goods is only the Creator and the soul, whereas the object of the supernatural goods is the creature. There is a difference too in substance, consequently in operation, and also necessarily as regards doctrine.[112]

When John says there is a "difference in their objects," he is not talking about the difference in the source of the visions (or "goods" as he calls them here, to refer to locutions and other apprehensions also)—he is assuming that both kinds come from God—but about the difference in the intention for which they are given by God. Those he calls "supernatural" as opposed to "spiritual" are graces *gratis datae*, which have no benefit for the one who possesses them but are only for "the profit of other men" in moving them to good works and the love of God.[113] Purely spiritual goods, however, are for the direct benefit of those who receive them, in advancing them toward a union of likeness with God as they transform the soul internally.[114] In this respect, there is a "difference in substance" also: they are given not in a manner suited to human knowing, through intelligible forms, but in the form that they exist in God. They are uncreated rather than created.[115] The soul must change its basic epistemological "operation" in order to know them.

The problem with John's position, which he appreciates, is that in excluding intelligible forms from the way in which spiritual goods are known he has now denied the basis of human knowledge. At the same time, he is clear that there is a symmetry between the two kinds of spiritual apprehension, in the way that they are received in the soul; and this seems to be because of his view that in order to deliver *knowledge* a parallel process to ordinary knowing must occur in the soul but using distinctly spiritual faculties and forms of knowledge, with no corporeal elements involved whatsoever. Thus, spiritual apprehensions of incorporeal substances are "sensed" by "touches of union" in the "substance of the soul." Though they do not use form, image, or figure as in apprehensions of corporeal substances, "they can nonetheless be felt in the substance of the soul by the most delightful touches and conjunctions."[116] John's phrases "bestowed immediately upon the soul" and "the substance of the soul" have the same sense, to denote that the medium used is far more immediate than in ordinary knowing. There is "substantial" or "essential" contact between the soul and God, "union of the soul with the divine substance," and "a touch of substances, that is, of the substance of God in the substance of the soul."[117] This ensures that it is God "in himself" who is known,[118] although there is still the need for mediation between God and the soul, as the substances remain distinct.[119] John describes how this mediation, while distinct from natural knowing and indeed lacking intelligible forms altogether, is also patterned on that of the bodily senses, in the *Llama de amor viva*:

> The feeling of the soul . . . refers to the power and strength that the substance of the soul has for feeling and enjoying the [incorporeal] objects of the faculties (memory, intellect, and will). . . . It [the soul] knows that its capacity and recesses [of the deep caverns of feeling] correspond to the distinct things it receives from the knowledge, savour, delight, etc., of God. All these things are received and seated in this feeling of the soul which, as I say, is its power and capacity for feeling, possessing, and tasting them. And the caverns of the faculties administer them [the incorporeal objects] to it [the feeling of the soul], just as the bodily senses go to assist the common sense of the phantasy with the forms of their objects, and this common sense becomes the receptacle and archives of these forms. Hence this common sense or feeling of the soul, which has become the receptacle or archives of God's grandeurs, is illumined and enriched according to what it attains of this high and enlightened possession.[120]

Here John invents a new vocabulary to describe the manner in which spiritual knowing resembles, but is entirely distinct from, natural knowing.[121] The "caverns of the faculties," taken from the line in the *Llama* poem, "the deep caverns of feeling" refer to the spiritual faculties (memory, intellect, and will) in their spiritual orientation. When memory, intellect, and will are turned toward God, their capacity is infinite, and they become capable of receiving communication from God, as we have seen; in this respect they are caverns. John likens these caverns to the bodily senses in natural knowing: first, because they relate to their object (incorporeal objects) in the same way that the bodily senses relate to corporeal objects, and second, because they administer these objects to the "feeling of the soul" in the same way that the bodily senses administer the forms of corporeal objects to the fantasy. The "feeling of the soul" is therefore the spiritual equivalent of the fantasy or "common sense."[122] It is also the "power and strength" that the substance of the soul has for feeling and knowing incorporeal objects. John has now developed *two parallel epistemologies*, one for natural (and supernatural) knowledge and the other for essential/spiritual knowledge of God. They bear an exact resemblance to one another, which may be pictured as follows:

**Table 2.1. Two Parallel Epistemologies
in John of the Cross's Anthropology**

	Sensory knowing	Spiritual knowing
Object	corporeal; created	incorporeal; uncreated
"Sensing" organ	exterior bodily senses	caverns of feeling (memory, intellect, and will in their spiritual orientation)
Storage faculty	interior bodily senses (fantasy/common sense)	feeling of the soul (common sense of spiritual faculties)
Knowing faculty	memory, intellect, and will in their natural orientation	power and strength of the substance of the soul

The two systems form a perfect symmetry, without overlapping at any point. John can therefore point to his epistemology as guarding both the similarity and the dissimilarity between natural and spiritual knowing. Spiritual knowing conforms exactly to the *structure* of natural knowing but uses neither the same senses nor the intelligible forms that are essential to natural knowing. Only the knowing faculties remain the same, though even they are said to operate quite differently in the two kinds of knowing: they are oriented to ontologically different objects, and spiritual knowing uses no intelligible forms. The similarity is solely in the *structure of the activity* of these higher faculties—in the pattern of cognitive activity running from sensation, to collation and storage of this sensory information, to full knowledge by the knowing faculty. Now the possibility of a breakthrough becomes clear: John will reconcile spiritual and sensory knowing in his anthropology by developing this understanding of continuity between natural and mystical knowing in the cognitive structure of the human subject while also retaining a strong contrast between the two epistemologies within this same structure.

The Role of the Memory, Intellect, and Will in Spiritual Knowing and Their Relation to "the Substance of the Soul"

John's understanding of the "substance of the soul" presents some difficulties in that sometimes it is said to be the same as memory, intellect, and will in their spiritual orientation, while at other times it is subsequent to them in the process of spiritual knowing. John's analogy between natural and mystical knowing will not succeed in unifying the soul unless the link between the two kinds of knowing is to be found *within* the higher faculties of memory, intellect, and will. Otherwise, there remain simply two separate systems of knowing that have no connection to one another. Thus, the "substance of the soul" must not be wholly separate from memory, intellect, and will in their spiritual operation but must be some kind of distinction *within* the operations of these three faculties.

Table 1 above shows that in the passage quoted, the substance of the soul is introduced as a stage *following* the "sensing" and "storage" or collation functions also found within memory, intellect, and will in spiritual knowing. The "caverns of the faculties" correspond to the exterior bodily senses, and the "feeling of the soul," which is closely related to the substance, comes afterwards, as the "receptacle and archives" of the spiritual forms received. There is, therefore, the suggestion that the spiritual faculties are secondary to the substance of the soul, as the bodily senses are to the interior senses, in the process of knowing. Another passage, however, in the *Cántico espiritual* likens the substance of the soul to the intellect as two equal aspects of the soul's ability to feel these spiritual apprehensions:

> This most sublime and delightful knowledge of God and His attributes . . . overflows into the intellect from the touch these attributes produce in the substance of the soul. . . . Two things are felt: knowledge and a feeling of delight. As the feeling of the breeze delights the sense of touch, and its whistling the sense of hearing, so the sentiment of the Beloved's attributes are felt and enjoyed by the soul's power of touch, which is in its substance, and the knowledge of these attributes is felt in its hearing, which is the intellect.[123]

John goes on to say that there must be knowledge in the substance of the soul, because "as the theologians say, fruition, the vision of God, is proper to the intellect."[124] In other words, there can be no strong distinction between the substance of the soul and the intellect, and likening the intellect to the bodily senses can only be a way of referring to it in its receptive capacity in spiritual knowing, rather than distancing it from the substance of the soul.[125]

What about the other spiritual faculties, memory and will? These have a similar reciprocal relationship with the substance of the soul, in which they relate to the substance of the soul on an equal level, very much as the spiritual faculties relate to one another. John allies the substance of the soul first with the will, as incorporeal spiritual apprehensions are felt in the will before they "redound" (*redunda*) to the intellect.[126] He adds that while the will feels them first, the intellect alone has the receptive capacity to take in the knowledge given.[127] Knowledge and love are therefore given together,[128] though one or other faculty may be more aware of the communication given on different occasions.[129] Elsewhere, in discussing the benefit of recalling spiritual communications of "uncreated" things, he shows that memory, also, has a similar relationship with the substance of the soul:

> As for uncreated things, I declare that . . . the memory does not recall these through any form, image, or figure that may have been impressed on the soul, for these touches and feelings of union with the Creator do not have any; it remembers them through the effect of light, love, delight, and spiritual renewal, etc., produced in it. Something of this effect is renewed as often as the soul recalls them.[130]

John denies that any image or form is impressed on the soul in the case of touches of union with the Creator; and yet the soul feels an effect produced within itself which may be recalled; this is the touch of union in the substance of the soul, which must be recalled using the memory. Memory and the substance of the soul must therefore function together in this spiritual reminiscence of uncreated things. Memory must work in tandem with the substance of the soul, just as memory and fantasy work together in sensory knowing, for uncreated things to be recalled. Thus, the substance of the soul is intended always to work in an equal partnership with memory, intellect, and will in their spiritual operation.

Still, these equal "partnerships" of memory, intellect, and will with the substance of the soul do not answer the question of whether the substance of the soul must be *added* to these spiritual faculties in spiritual knowing or is to be equated with memory, intellect, and will in their spiritual operation. Most commentators are agreed that the latter must be the case, as John never uses "the substance of the soul" in contrast to the spiritual faculties but to emphasize their depth and penetration into God.[131] First, "the substance of the soul" stresses the aspect of "substantial contact" between the soul and God which is crucial to spiritual knowing,[132] and second, it points to the cavernous capacity of the spiritual faculties for receiving divine knowledge as "abyss to abyss."[133] John focuses on the latter aspect in the *Llama*, in which he speaks of "the intimate substance of the soul's depth."[134] This is the point in which the soul has the closest possible contact with God, called the *apex mentis* in many earlier Western mystical writings.[135] Finally, at the end of the *Llama*, John sees the substance of the soul as *including* memory, intellect, and will in the threefold pattern of the spiration within the Trinity:

> It is a spiration which God produces in the [substance of the] soul, in which, by that awakening of lofty knowledge of the Godhead, He breathes the Holy Spirit in it in the same proportion as its knowledge and understanding of Him, absorbing it most profoundly in the Holy Sprit, [and] rousing its love.[136]

The mention of knowledge, understanding, and love at this ultimate point of the soul's earthly experience, of "absorption" in the spiration of the Holy Spirit in the Trinity, shows that intellect and will, and also memory,[137] are to be equated in their spiritual operation with the "inner working" of the substance of the soul, just as the three persons of the Trinity are also one in the Godhead. John sees a similar relation existing between the spiritual faculties and the substance of the soul as between the three persons of the Trinity and the Godhead. Most important is that the relationship between the faculties and the substance of the soul is that of a complex unity: the three faculties are distinct from the substance of the soul while also, at a deeper level, unified *in* this substance. The substance of the soul is "absorbed" by the Holy Spirit into the same spiration that occurs within the Godhead, and the extent to which this occurs is "in the same proportion" as the soul's spiritual knowledge and understanding. Thus, the substance of the soul is to be seen as including memory, intellect, and will as integral to it.

The soul is transformed in spiritual knowing into the pattern of the Trinity. John makes a further move here, no longer saying that the structure of spiritual knowing is simply the same as natural knowing but that *this structure is found first of all in the Trinity*, and it is into the pattern of the Trinity that the soul is being transformed on this journey. This assertion will permit him later to say that mystical knowing is both the perfection of natural knowing *and* "divine," rather than merely human knowledge *of* the divine. This is the interiority that he is aiming for, in which the soul's own structure becomes included in the structure of God's self-knowing through mystical transformation into the Trinity. But a fuller considera-tion of this "total transformation of the soul . . . in the three persons of the most holy Trinity"[138] remains for the next chapter.

To conclude, it must be asserted that all spiritual knowing occurs in the memory, intellect, and will—and that, most of all, it is proper to the intel-lect, as John says. The substance of the soul, caverns of the faculties, and feeling of the soul refer to the *depth* of memory, intellect, and will in their spiritual operation. Just as memory, intellect, and will work as a complex unity in natural knowing, so in spiritual knowing they are unified, but now according to a set of operations that are differentiated in relation to the soul's "substance." This substance becomes available to the soul through immediate contact with God's own substance. The soul comes to know God by appropriating, in relation to its own substance, God's self-differ-entiation in God's substance, in the internal relations of the Trinity.

The Role of the Corporeal Senses in Spiritual Knowing

The great achievement of John's spiritual epistemology, according to André Bord, is that he has separated the means of spiritual knowing from that of natural knowing while also preserving a symmetry between the two systems.[139] Even the spiritual faculties, which are ostensibly the same in the two systems, have a different mode of operation in spiritual knowing and are entirely "empty" of natural images and forms. Does this mean that the corporeal senses are excluded from spiritual knowing? If spiritual knowing works independently of the corporeal senses, as John has argued, the corporeal senses would seem to have no further use. But this is not John's final position. On the contrary, since the spiritual and corporeal parts of the soul remain as "one supposit" even after spiritual knowing has been attained, there is still an interrelationship between the senses and the spirit, and in union the relationship is to be regarded as stronger than it was before. This opens up two kinds of contact between the spirit and the senses in union: first, the ability of the soul "immediately and at the first movement" of a sensual gratification to raise itself to God, and second, the production of delight in the senses from an overflow of the spirit to the senses in union. The soul has two different orientations and capacities that correspond to the dichotomy of sense and spirit, but John also asserts that there is an interrelationship that holds them together.

The first state of the senses that John regards positively in the progress to union is that of being "stilled" or "put to sleep."[140] At this point the senses are divorced from the spirit so that very little of what happens in the spirit is felt in the senses. This has the advantage that spiritual experi-ences do not produce rapture or transport of the senses, and the spirit enjoys "freedom," "solitude," and "peace" from the senses, where before the senses caused "disturbances" to the spirit through their working.[141] But gradually, as the soul progresses further, the senses begin to be included in the experience of the spirit. In the *Noche oscura*, this occurs when the passive purgation of the soul moves from the senses to the spirit. John explains: "since these two parts [of the soul] form one *suppositum*, each one usually shares according to its mode in what the other receives," so that when the spirit alone is receiving, "each part of the soul can now in its own way receive nourishment from the same food and from the same dish of only one *suppositum* and subject."[142] The problem is that the senses do not have the ability for direct contact with incorporeal objects that the spirit has, so the best that the senses can do, according to the *Noche*, is achieve "quietude."[143] Even the intellect, in its natural operation, is led into error if it tries to work with the aid of the illumination received in the spirit: the whole sensory part of the soul must remain stilled and do no work.[144] On the other hand, the state of Adam's innocence is said to have been reached, in which the spirit and the senses in the soul are "put in order,"[145] so that, at the "first movement" of a sensory joy, it is possible to *raise* the senses to the spirit.[146] At this stage, the war that existed between the senses and spirit in their natural fallen condition is said to have ended, and they now have the close relationship that was intended for them at creation. But this represents no advance on the "stilled" state of the senses with regard to spiritual communications: even at the end of the *Noche*, John says that "in entirely spiritual activity there is no communication with the sensory part," and the bodily faculties are still "put to sleep and in silence regarding earthly and heavenly things."[147]

In the *Llama* and *Cántico*, however, a more positive view of the role of the senses in spiritual communications is presented—probably because here John is describing more advanced stages of union. He does not ignore the sharp sense–spirit dichotomy described in the *Subida–Noche*, but to a large extent he assumes his earlier treatment.[148] A new unity between the senses and the spirit is attained, described as the "fortification" of the senses so that they can also "participate" in the "savor and sweetness" given to the spirit.[149] John describes this as an overflow from the spirit to the senses:

> Sometimes, when the unction of the Holy Spirit overflows into the body and all the sensory substance, all the members and bones and marrow rejoice, not in so slight a fashion as is customary, but with the feeling of great delight and glory, even in the outermost joints of the hands and feet. . . . It is sufficient to say in reference to both the bodily and the spiritual experience, "that [the soul] tastes eternal life."[150]

The body becomes energized by the overflow from what is received in the spirit, even to its extremities, in the hands and feet. This leads John further, to point out the long-term benefit of such overflows for the doing of good works:

> The previous impulses of love were not enough, because they did not have sufficient quality for the attainment of my desire; now I am so fortified in love that not only do my senses and spirit no longer faint in you, but my heart and flesh, reinforced in you, rejoice in the living God [Ps. 83:3], with great conformity between the sensory and spiritual parts. What you desire me to ask for, I ask for; and what you do not desire, I do not desire, nor can I, nor does it even enter my mind to desire it. My petitions . . . come from you, and you move me to make them, and I make them in the delight and joy of the Holy Spirit, my judgment now issuing from your countenance [Ps. 16:2].[151]

Here John moves from describing transitory feelings of delight that overflow from the spirit to describing their overall purpose, which is to effect a general transformation of the soul so that it knows the will of God at all times and puts it perfectly into action.

For such action to result, however, more than a feeling of joy in the spirit is required: there must also be the "conformity" of sensory and spiritual parts, so that the impulse can be *directed* to bodily activity, and the soul can do the will of God in action. As John says elsewhere, at this stage the soul acts as "one perfect whole embodying in herself many perfect and strong virtues."[152] This makes the connection between John's understanding of union and the life of virtue. How do the senses receive this communication from the spirit? First, John asserts that the *whole* of the sensory part of the soul becomes involved. When the Bride in the *Cántico* says, "Now I occupy my soul/ And all my energy in His service," John interprets "energy" as referring to "all that pertains to the sensory part of the soul": "the body with all its senses and faculties, interior and exterior, and all the natural ability (the four passions, the natural appetites, and other energies)." Thus, the whole soul is oriented toward God so that even the body is conformed to God's will: "by directing the activity of the interior and exterior senses toward God, her [the Bride's] use of the body is now conformed to his will."[153] Second, John remains clear that the sensory part "has no capacity in this life, nor even in the next, for the essential and proper taste of spiritual goods"; so the senses, in regard to spiritual communications, "must discontinue their natural operations."[154] By this he no longer means that all activity of the lower part of the soul is excluded, as he has asserted that there is now bodily activity in conformity with God's will; rather, the senses, like the spiritual faculties, must turn from their old operation and be reoriented to a spiritual operation. Unlike the spiritual faculties, however, the senses cannot receive spiritual goods themselves but can only receive them through the mediation of the spiritual faculties:

> [The sensory part of the soul] can, though, through a certain spiritual over-flow, receive sensible refreshment and delight from them [spiritual goods]. This delight attracts the corporeal senses and faculties to the inner recol-lection where the soul drinks the waters of spiritual goods, and so they descend at the sight of the waters rather than taste them as they are.[155]

The idea that the senses "descend at the sight of the waters" is taken from the last stanza of the *Cántico*, which John interprets to mean that in order to participate in the spiritual goods that the spirit is enjoying, the senses are "attracted" and "recollected" away from their usual exterior orienta-tion and toward the inner, spiritual part of the soul, and from here they receive a taste of the spiritual goods through the mediation of the spiritual faculties rather than tasting them "as they are."

The senses are now turned toward the spiritual faculties, which ensures that they will receive the energy from the spirit and put it into use in doing good works. But do the spiritual faculties continue to operate as if the senses did not exist? This is still the strong implication, as the senses have come to the inner part of the soul to receive some of what the spiritual fac-ulties are enjoying, while the spiritual faculties continue in their operation regardless of the senses. Elsewhere John makes clear, however, that there is a double movement: not only do the senses turn toward the center, but the spiritual faculties turn to the senses in order to *direct* them to a spiri-tual goal:

> She [the Bride] employs the intellect in understanding and carrying out all the things that are more for His service, and the will in loving all that is pleasing to Him and attaching it to Him in all things, and her memory and care in what most pleases and serves Him.[156]

Here the intellect, will, and memory have turned to the consideration of how to serve God and do God's will in the world. This is not to say that they have left their spiritual orientation, but they must *also* have an orien-tation to the senses if they are to put God's will into action. In "under-standing and carrying out all the things that are more for his service" the intellect must not only remain fixed upon what it is receiving from God but also give attention to the world around it. Similarly, the will must be directed to the world around it in order to love "all that is pleasing to God and attach it to him"; and the memory must work to supply the intellect and will with the recollections of both spiritual and creaturely things. Thus, the spiritual and natural activities of the spiritual faculties meet at this stage. The spiritual faculties not only must receive spiritual knowledge but also must put it into practice in the world.

John adds to this picture of the soul freely and deliberately doing God's will in union by pointing out that the soul is not moved by God like a puppet but is a free agent which must exercise its own will. In discussing the agency of the soul, John makes the crucial point that "the soul reflects the divine light in a more excellent way because of the active intervention of its will."[157] His reason for this is that the relationship between the soul and God must be truly reciprocal, and therefore the surrender of each to the other must be voluntary: the soul must retain its freedom of will.[158] This cooperative relationship between the soul and God extends to the life of virtue: "the soul cannot practice or acquire the virtues without the help of God, nor does God effect them alone in the soul without her help. . . . God and the soul work together."[159] The senses do not, therefore, simply rely on the "overflow" of the impulses from the spirit, but are involved in deliberate action by the spiritual faculties, becoming *included* in the soul's spiritual operation.

These aspects of the connection between the senses and the spirit in union do not change the fundamental point made by André Bord that the soul possesses two separate systems for knowledge of the world and knowledge of God, but they show that the soul reunites with the body and senses in union. The sensory part of the soul is conformed to God's likeness by being first returned to the state of Adam's innocence and then fortified and made capable of receiving the overflow from the spirit, so that the whole is motivated to action in conformity with the will of God. John shows that the senses are reoriented to the spirit through "attraction" and "inner recollection." Furthermore, the spiritual faculties, though working independently of the senses in their spiritual operation, can simultaneously involve the senses to direct them in the service of God. Thus, there is a mutual meeting of spirit and senses in spiritual knowing, even though the spiritual character of this knowing remains "safeguarded," as Bord says.

The relation of sense and spirit in John's treatment of spiritual knowing has been the theme running through this chapter because it is the basis of John's own separation of spiritual knowing from natural knowing. John rejects the natural way of knowing *and* supernatural knowing—that is, knowing which involves any of the sensory or intelligible forms of ordinary knowing—because he regards these as excluding purely spiritual knowledge of God in substance. A distinction must be made, however, between the orientation to the senses and the presence of the senses themselves. John does not regard the presence of the senses as excluding spiritual knowledge; indeed, they are essential to putting the will of God into action. It is only the attachment to the senses that he excludes. Nevertheless, the actual *knowing* remains in the spirit alone, and this excludes even the memory, intellect, and will in their natural operation. The natural operation of these spiritual faculties is no longer sinful, as they have been purified and returned to the state of Adam's innocence, but John insists that it still has no part in their spiritual operation. Whereas natural knowing uses the forms and images of objects in the natural world, spiritual knowing uses "general, indistinct" "spiritual forms" which exclude natural forms altogether. Thus, memory, intellect, and will are bifurcated between these two kinds of operation, and this corresponds with the spirit/sense division.

For all the progress that we have made in this chapter toward seeing how John might unify the sensory and spiritual parts of the soul in his anthropology, there remains the stark fact that the soul possesses two separate epistemologies that exclude one another. Even though unity might be possible within the new, transformed state of spiritual knowing, we need to ask how the soul moves to this state *from* natural knowing, when these two kinds of knowing are so strongly contrasted. How can John say that it is the same person, indeed the perfected person, who reaches union, as compared with the person who started out on the spiritual journey, if they have two quite separate means of knowing? There remains a tendency to an ontological division in the soul between "natural" and "spiritual" knowing. In the next chapter, we shall see how John extends the element of *symmetry* between the two systems, in his notion of the "depth" of the soul, to show how the whole soul becomes united in a single depth or center in union, drawing both systems together into one unified way of knowing. This unifying depth will be found to be precisely that trinitarian dynamism that draws the soul forward in mystical transformation, instilling the structure of the Trinity in the soul without removing, but rather purging and perfecting, its natural cognitive structure.

CHAPTER THREE

The Dynamism and Unity of the Soul According to John of the Cross

I N THE LAST CHAPTER, we saw that John of the Cross's strong opposition of sense and spirit posed a threat to the unity of the self, as the soul gained a spiritual way of knowing God which bypassed the senses and the forms of natural knowing. In spiritual knowing, the senses were entirely excluded except by means of "overflow" from the spirit, and this seemed to divide the soul between its natural knowledge of the world, which remained through the senses, and its spiritual knowledge of God, which bypassed the senses and used no creaturely forms. Yet John also firmly maintained that in union the soul had a single "center" or "supposit" in which both the senses and spirit were unified. In this chapter, I intend to examine this claim for unity from a somewhat different perspective by taking greater account of the *dynamic* character of the soul in union.

Mystical transformation is the movement between two distinct kinds of organization of the soul, the ordinary and the mystical. As both Georges Morel and Max Huot de Longchamp have pointed out,[1] John's mystical itinerary is primarily described in terms of movement: the soul is constantly on the move from one spiritual state to the next, never standing still.[2] The purpose of this movement, imposed by grace, is to reorganize the soul by giving it what John calls a "great force of abyssal desire for union with God."[3] This desire is differentiated by the soul's transformed faculties, enabling the soul to know God in union. But the movement of transformation is not simply a change between two different states of the soul; it is the imposition of a new movement *in* the soul—the divine dynamism of the Trinity. The significance of John's emphasis on transformation is that he sets his epistemology *within* the dynamic of transformation. Transformation is a force for unity in the soul, changing it, but changing it by degrees rather than into something wholly unconnected from the state in which it started. Thus, John puts the division in the soul within this single trajectory and dynamism of transformation, so preferring unity ahead of division in his mystical anthropology and epistemology.

This "great force" of transformation which gives this desire for union with God puts the soul on a collision course with its other, natural drive to merely creaturely objects. Two fundamental orientations come into conflict, producing what John calls a "war in the soul": "contraries rise up at this time against contraries—those of the soul against those of God."[4] But while John placed the full weight of his emphasis on this stage in the *Subida–Noche*, in his two later works, the *Cántico espiritual* and the *Llama de amor viva*,[5] he turns from the *opposition* between the two "parts" of the soul to the possibility of reconciling these parts in an underlying unity or *depth* in the soul. The two parts of the soul do not destroy one another but fall ultimately into an ordered hierarchy in which the spiritual part is "deeper" than the sensory. As Louis Dupré has said in regard to this understanding of the self, "an altogether different layer of selfhood hides underneath the familiar succession of outward-oriented phenomena."[6] According to John, this "deep" level of selfhood is first experienced through "touches of union," and then excavated to still deeper levels through mystical transformation; and while there is an initial conflict between this and the "shallower" level of the soul's natural existence, John's emphasis on the increasing depth of the soul in the *Cántico* and the *Llama* builds toward the final unity of the soul in what he calls the center of the soul.

As we have seen, the soul is defined for John primarily by its attachments. "The soul lives where it loves," he says.[7] It is not the faculty of knowing, or any power of the soul in itself, which defines the self for John, but rather to what the soul is oriented, the "other" that it desires and tends towards. The "deepening" of the soul is the transformation of this self-other relationality. Two types of dynamism, that of the natural desire of the soul for objects in the world and the inner dynamism of the Trinity, come into contact in mystical experience, and after a period of conflict are reconciled through the process of transformation. The dynamism of the soul's natural relationality is deepened into the divine dynamism of the Trinity, and a new set of cognitive acts, structured within the Trinity, is introduced within this deepened relationality in the spiritual faculties. The two sets of cognitive acts, those directed toward natural objects, and those toward the supernatural in mystical union, are united in the soul as "shallower" and "deeper" levels of differentiation of a single, transformed relationality.

The "Transobjective Subject"

In spite of certain faults, Jacques Maritain's *Degrees of Knowledge*—still the most important attempt to relate John of the Cross's view of mystical knowing to the levels of knowing in the human subject—sets out very well John's relational view of selfhood and how this relationality is transformed by mystical experience.[8] Maritain contrasts his understanding of the self with the modern/Cartesian view. The mind is not first of all aware of its thought, as in Descartes' *cogito*, but is constituted first in relation to the objects that it desires and seeks to know. Though we are thinking subjects, we know ourselves only secondarily, in an awareness or "reflex intuition" *within* our knowing of objects.[9] Maritain calls this self the "transobjective subject" because it requires objects outside itself in order to discover its own selfhood.[10] The subject has a basic openness toward objects: this is the first fact about the self, before it is known.[11]

Maritain develops this idea of the self as fundamentally constituted in relation to the other in his final chapter on mystical knowing, "Todo y Nada." He says that in union God becomes present to the soul not as object but as another self: God becomes "spiritually present in the one (the lover) as a weight or impulse, becomes to him as another self."[12] Mystical knowing is therefore what we might call an intersubjective state between the soul and God. The soul is able to objectify this state without turning God into the object of knowing in the ordinary sense, because the soul relates to God, says Maritain, "inasmuch as by grace the soul is made capable of God and turned toward God to see and to love as He sees and loves Himself."[13] The "seeing and loving" of the soul remains its subjective prerogative, but now the soul sees and loves *through* God, in an immediate relation to God which has become part of the self, or to speak more correctly, in which the self participates in God. God as object is known *within* this act of participation, as the soul feels the touch of God "within the very depths of itself."[14] Thus, mystical knowing and ordinary knowing become a single act, as ordinary knowing is deepened into an intersubjective knowing and loving with God, *through* which both God and objects in the world are known. The very relationality which makes the subject open to objects outside itself, as a transobjective subject, is fulfilled by union with God.

Here Maritain correctly indicates certain features of the connection and distinction between ordinary and mystical knowing according to John. First, God is not known as an object like other objects but in an intimate relation with the soul's means of knowing, as a participation in God's own knowing. Second, this level of knowing becomes explicit in mystical knowing, as the soul is able to distinguish the "touch of God" within it, not in a reflective step, but within its own transobjective relationality. Third, there is no conflict with ordinary knowing, as the same relationality is involved, but mystical knowing is the fulfillment of all knowing because there is union with the source of the soul's self-constituting relationality in God. Thus, the two kinds of knowing are connected in that both belong to the subject's single relationality and yet distinguished by the fact that in mystical knowing the subject knows God within knowing—in what John calls the depth of the soul—not as an ordinary object of knowledge.

There are a number of ways in which Maritain's treatment of John's epistemology is inaccurate, principally because of his attachment to a certain kind of Thomism,[15] but in his emphasis on the relational nature of the self and the deepening of this self into God's own self-relationality, there is a firm foundation for the explicitly *trinitarian* understanding of selfhood and mystical knowing that I intend to develop in the remainder of this chapter.

Mystical Transformation:
From "Ordinary" Faith to Union

John's view of the separation of sense and spirit is accentuated by the immense distance that the soul must travel from its natural state to the high state of union. He has a very low theological anthropology—at least initially. In the *Cántico*, he divides the means through which God can be known not just into the two categories of natural and supernatural but into three: by mediation through creatures, through the incarnation and the mysteries of faith, and finally the immediate level of union with God.[16] Rather surprisingly, the main distinction here is not between the first and second categories, that is, between nature and grace, but between the level of grace on which the incarnation and the mysteries of faith are given in revelation and the higher level of grace, which is union, where God comes into immediate contact with the soul. John gives little consideration to the stage of nature prior to faith as this does not greatly concern him—even beginners on the mystical path are assumed to have faith, as his audience is the friars and nuns of the Discalced[17]—rather, the main issue is how the soul progresses from an "ordinary" faith to union. The soul exclaims,

> Oh, if only the truths hidden in your articles [the articles of faith], which you teach me in an inexplicit and dark manner, you would give me completely, clearly, and explicitly, freed of their covering, as my desire begs![18]

John is careful to say that the soul does not want anything other than the articles of faith in union but to have the "truths hidden in" these same articles more "clearly." The grace for union is not different in kind from that of faith, but nevertheless, it is an additional level of grace, beyond the articles of faith. At the level of "ordinary" faith, the soul's means of knowing is much the same as it was in the natural state: it is through the images and ideas of God given in revelation which, though they come from God, are accommodated to the human senses and use forms of knowledge derived from the senses. On the higher level of grace, that of union, these images and forms are entirely absent, as the soul attains a new means of knowing by direct contact with God. All of John's energy goes into explaining the vast difference between these two kinds of knowing and how to get from one to the other.

The first impression John gives is of a division in the soul caused by the huge change from ordinary to spiritual knowing. For instance, he begins the *Cántico* with a rejection of the kind of experiences which those with faith—who have an unreformed means of knowing—tend to associate with God. He says,

> However elevated God's communications and the presences of him are, and however sublime a person's knowledge of him may be, these are not God essentially, nor are they comparable to him.[19]

Because such experiences have a sensory component, it is clear that even "grand spiritual communications" are not the same as the possession of God or union with him, and equally, to experience spiritual "dryness, darkness and dereliction" is not a sure sign of God's absence. On the contrary, at the beginning of the path to union the soul must appreciate that God is hidden to it in faith, so that it feels a certain "dread and interior sorrow of heart" at God's absence. This feeling of absence shows that the soul possesses a "more authentic" light and the "necessary virtue of self-knowledge" in comparison with the one who identifies sensible awareness of God with the presence of God.[20] Indeed, the infusion of grace into the soul through the three theological virtues of faith, hope and love "voids the faculties,"[21] that is, the intellect, memory, and will respectively, so that "you should never desire satisfaction in what you understand about God, but in what you do not understand about him."[22] The contrast between knowledge derived from the senses and the growth of faith toward union becomes more intense after the soul receives its first "secret touch" of this God hidden in faith, which is properly called the "wound of love."[23] This is a transitory and brief experience in which the bridegroom (of the Song of Songs) first shows and then hides himself. The difference from previous experiences and even from the ordinary knowing of the articles in faith is immediately apparent, as the soul is taken "out of itself," which "wholly renews it, and changes its manner of being."[24] It does not just feel something new but is changed and renewed in its manner of *being*, throughout the soul and primarily in the rational faculties. This "wound of love" corresponds to the "touch of union," which profoundly changes the soul's way of knowing and is the beginning of union. Afterward, the suffering in the intellect, will, and memory is much more intense, as the soul has a new appreciation for the vision, possession, and memory of God that it lacks.[25] The essential change is that the soul's desire has been increased so that it is now "proportional" to the love of God. In the *Llama*, John says that memory, intellect, and will are now "capable" of God, in that "anything less than infinite fails to fill them": "their thirst is infinite, their hunger is also deep and infinite, and their languishing and suffering are infinite death." The finite, rational faculties which could only desire created objects have now been converted to spiritual faculties with an infinite capacity, "because the object of the capacity, namely God, is profound and infinite."[26] The soul has a single-minded desire for God which demands "that from henceforth he [God] no longer detain her" with mediated knowledge, including that through the articles of faith, scripture, and angels,[27] but give her the fulfillment that her infinite capacity now desires, which is the surrender of God to her "in complete and perfect love."[28] Unlike mediated knowledge, she wants the "communication of yourself [God] by yourself . . . that my entire soul may have complete possession of you."[29]

This stark opposition between the soul's ordinary capacity and infinite capacity, and between ordinary faith and union, suggests a division in the soul, as of two opposed functions. The distinction is between knowing God "remotely," in the manner of other things, and knowing God "in essence," by an immediate spiritual communication or "touch" of God's essence which is without images and forms. But in the *Cántico* John is careful also to note the continuity that exists at the subjective level between these two contrasting ways of knowing. He explains it in terms of the trinitarian *imago Dei* in the soul. Through a dim awareness of this image of God, the soul does not literally know nothing of God when it sets out on the path of unknowing in faith. Even though God is hidden, the soul can at least know the "place" of God's presence in its "innermost being." John says, "It should be known that the Word, the Son of God, together with the Father and the Holy Spirit, is hidden by his essence and presence in the innermost being of the soul."[30] John makes the distinction between two kinds of knowing: in its ordinary "object-knowledge" of the articles of faith, the soul does not know God "by his essence"; God is not known at the level of propositions or in any particular kind of knowledge, but only in unknowing; yet, the soul *does* know God's essence within it if it looks beyond *what* it knows to the *activity* and *orientation* of the rational faculties in their faith and desire for God, that is, to the deep level of its self-other relationality, which dimly reflects the activity of the Trinity. The paradox is stated by John as follows:

> Never stop with loving and delighting in your understanding and feeling of God, but love and delight in what is neither understandable nor perceptible of him. Such is the way, as we said, of seeking him in faith.[31]

Even on the level of ordinary faith, it is possible to appreciate that there is a distinction between the articles of faith, which accurately *point* us to God through images and forms but are in fact incapable of actually making God present to us in his essence, and the *activity* of knowing and loving God in faith, which makes God present to us interiorly in the fundamental movement of the rational faculties toward God prior to their grasping of any object. Thus, the "unknowing" way of faith is not intended to stop the soul delighting in its love and understanding of God; only, the soul should not identify the apparent objects of its love and knowledge with God "in himself." The image of God in the soul is to be found in the *activity* of the rational faculties in faith but not in what they know.

What then is the connection between faith as object-knowledge of the articles of faith and the activities of faith and love in the rational faculties? Are the articles as objects merely mistaken? John's point is that there is nothing wrong with the articles—they are the very best knowledge of God that is possible in human terms—but they fail precisely because they have been accommodated to human knowing. God is not an object like other objects but the cause and sustaining presence of all creation and so cannot be known "in himself" as an object of human knowledge. The articles *do* succeed in *directing* the soul toward God, such that the soul's rational activity is worthy of God in general terms, if not adequate in the particular object-knowledge that it supposes.[32] The soul is on the right track and can therefore trust in its knowing and loving as activities of the mind which form a pale internal image of what God is in himself. John speaks of the image of God in the soul at this stage as a "sketch" (literally, the "image of the first draft": *imagen de la primera mano*) in the intellect, memory, and will.[33] The truths of faith provide this sketch when they are infused, that is, when they activate the rational faculties. Most importantly, the sketch is to be seen not in the object of the rational faculties as something outside the soul in the manner of ordinary objects of knowledge but *in* the rational faculties themselves. This does not mean that God is seen simply in a different place, "within" as opposed to "outside" the soul, but that God is found to be in relationship with the soul's being, primarily in the *activity* of the rational faculties.

The rational faculties have yet to be "made spiritual" by mystical transformation and entering into union. This is achieved at the level of their inner activity: at this level, there is a continuity between ordinary faith and union. The sketch of God in the rational faculties reaches "completion" (*acabarse*) when the dynamism of the *natural* relation between the soul and God is raised to the *supernatural*, and spiritual,[34] dynamism of the immediate relationship with God in union, so that God becomes "clearly visible . . . like a perfect and finished painting in the soul."[35] Thus, though there is a considerable separation between ordinary faith and union, there is continuity in the soul's inner relationship with God.

It is with the background of this *connection* between ordinary knowing in faith and spiritual knowing in union that John enters into the intense oppositions of the stage of purgation. At the level of ordinary knowing, there *is* a discontinuity between the senses and the spirit in that the exterior orientation to the senses in ordinary knowing is opposed to the interior orientation to spirit, which is an orientation to the image of God within. This orientation to the senses is not just a matter of sin but the natural state of the soul, according to John's Aristotelian epistemology. Two opposing orientations thus come into conflict in the stage of purgation, but with the clear goal that the spiritual, inward orientation must win. The fact that they are opposed does not mean that they are irreconcilable: it is the *same* soul that is capable of *both* orientations. Beyond the fact of opposing orientations, at a deeper level in the soul, there is a unified origin of the two orientations in a single "center." It is to this underlying or deep level of selfhood that John wishes to turn our attention, rather than to let us remain on the level of opposition between the two ways of knowing.

Mystical Transformation:
The Depth of the Soul (*el fondo del alma*)

John's emphasis on the deep level of the soul is found in his frequent use of the phrase "the depth of the soul" (*el fondo del alma*) to signal the "voiding" or "hollowing out" of the "infinite capacity" in the soul, which is the level of the "substance of the soul" at which the soul feels the immediate touch of God in union. While John tends to speak of the "touch of union" in the substance of the soul in the *Subida–Noche*, in the *Cántico* and *Llama* he prefers the image of the "wound of love" in the "depth of the soul." As we have seen in the progress of the *Cántico* described above, apart from regarding the former sensory experiences as nothing in comparison with the wound of love that is now felt, the soul is left after the wound with an intensity of desire for God that is "proportional" to God and of an infinite degree. The soul has not only changed its orientation from creatures to

God but has found its desire to be extraordinarily intensified. The idea of "depth" is intended to signal this intensification of desire. This is the crucial moment for John, when the soul moves from meditation to contemplation and begins to enter into union. The "infinite" aspect of the soul is seen in a new single-minded desire for God alone, such that the soul can find no satisfaction in anything but God.[36] It has difficulty concentrating on ordinary objects of knowledge, including those used in spiritual exercises; it loses its grasp on all the object-knowledge that it had at the level of ordinary faith, because its ordinary knowing is exceeded by this infinite desire. It therefore enters into a "deep oblivion" in which "it knows only God, without knowing how it knows him."[37]

This deep oblivion cuts the soul off from its former knowledge through the senses, and it appears that it has destroyed the soul's old way of knowing altogether. But this is not the case. The soul has not lost its old way of knowing but only temporarily lost *touch* with it; the soul has been so *deepened* as to have become dislocated and cut off from the level at which it knows ordinary sensory and intelligible objects.[38] This is what John means by saying that the soul is made to "go out of itself" in the wound of love.[39] It has not ceased knowing altogether but has lost touch with *what* it knows, while its actual inner desire which is at the root of knowing has been intensified to an infinite level. Thus, it "knows God" without knowing God as a sensory or intelligible object, and so does not know "*how* it knows him." John is clear that for this reason "deep oblivion" is nothing like melancholy or some other humor of the heart—it is not psychological depression—as in melancholy there is a lack of application and yearning, whereas here the desire for God in the soul has been intensified.[40] Therefore, the soul's knowing has not been removed or superseded but rather intensified with a greater unknowing at the level of object-knowledge and a corresponding increase of activity at the deep level of the spiritual faculties.

John describes an especially intense touch of union in the memory which serves as an example of the effect of these touches on the soul at the beginning of union:

> Observing how we annihilate the faculties in their operations, it will perhaps seem that we are tearing down rather than building up the way of spiritual exercise. . . . When God on occasion produces these touches of union in the memory, a sudden jolt is experienced in the brain (where the memory has its seat), so sensible that it seems the whole head swoons and that judgment and sensibility are lost. . . . Because the memory is united with God . . . a long time passes without awareness or knowledge of what has thus happened. . . . These suspensions, it should be noted, occur at the beginning of union, and are not thus found in souls who have reached perfection, because the union is then perfect. . . . Someone will say . . . that God does not destroy, but

perfects nature and that the destruction of nature is a necessary consequence of this doctrine. . . . I answer that this is actually so.[41]

If anyone should object that he is "tearing down rather than building up
the way of spiritual exercise" by holding that "the destruction of nature"
is a necessary consequence of the doctrine that "God perfects nature,"
John simply answers that, yes, destruction is a necessary part of perfection.
He calls it the "annihilation" (*anihilar*) of the soul.[42] But the destruction
has a positive outcome. The someone who might object is presumably a
Thomist, as Thomists would deny that the destruction of the soul's nature
is a necessary part of its perfection, saying instead that it is only sin which
is destroyed in the soul, while the soul by nature is good and need not be
destroyed but only raised by grace to the supernatural level.[43] John agrees
that the destructive aspect of grace is primarily because of sin, but he differs from Aquinas in seeing the second reason for grace—to raise the soul
to the supernatural level—as painful and therefore as "destructive" also.
The soul experiences darkness not just because of its sin but "because of
the height of the divine wisdom which exceeds the capacity of the soul."
Until the faculties have been made infinite they are blinded like the naked
eye looking at the sun.[44] As the soul "feels within herself more the void of
God," she is "in great fear and trembling" at the supernatural light which
"darkens with its excess the natural light."[45] The difference from Aquinas
is largely because John goes much further toward likening the knowing of
union to the beatific vision than Aquinas does,[46] so that the extent of
transformation needed is far greater. Nevertheless, John's point is that
while the soul is being raised to the supernatural level, the ordinary knowing ability through the senses is not removed but *suspended*, while the
touches of union achieve the vital task of expanding the capacity of the
soul.

John goes on to say that the intended effect of these suspensions is
detachment, and once one has achieved detachment one can return to
ordinary knowing through the senses without being harmed.[47] Furthermore, these suspensions only "occur at the beginning of union"; later, it is
possible to receive the new communication of God in essence without
departing from the way of knowing through the senses at all. Thus, John's
view is that there *is* "destruction" of the nature of the soul on the journey
to union, but it is only temporary, being superseded later in union, and is
for a positive purpose.

The "wound of love" expands the soul at the deep level, but the soul is
temporarily divided, as the wound takes it "out of itself." This rapture is
essential to raise the soul to the supernatural level of union, but the soul
must "return to itself" to overcome this internal division. There is an end

to rapture in the next stage, "spiritual espousal," as the soul becomes more accustomed to the excessive, supernatural communication of union so that it is no longer internally divided by it. The communication from God continues to be by brief "touches," but the soul's "vehement yearnings and complaints of love cease," and "a state of peace and delight and gentleness of love begins in her."[48] The touches begin to be "in accord with the intensity of the yearnings and ardors of love that precede them,"[49] rather than vastly in excess of the capacity of the soul. The "void" in the three faculties is now becoming adequate to the supernatural communication which "fills" it. John expresses the change in terms of a new *mutuality* that is introduced between the soul and God at this stage. In the *Llama*, John describes the mutuality that now exists between the soul and God as an equality of *depth*, based on the mystical interpretation of the text from the Psalms (Ps. 41:8 [42:7]) that "one abyss calls to the other abyss":

> One abyss calls to the other abyss (Ps. 41:8), that is: An abyss of light summons another abyss of light, and an abyss of darkness calls to another abyss of darkness, each like calling to its like and communicating itself to it.[50]

The soul now has an *equal* capacity to God in its depth, an abyss as deep as God, so that whether it knows God as light or as darkness, there is fully mutual communication, "each like calling to its like."

Similarly, in the *Cántico*, the "wounded stag" now appears, the bridegroom from the Song of Songs, who is wounded because he now *shares* in the wound of love that he first gave to the soul. As in the Song, there is now a reciprocation of the wound that was formerly felt only by the bride, so that both share in the same wound. John says,

> Among lovers, the wound of one is a wound for both, and the two have but one feeling. Thus, in other words, He [the Bridegroom] says: Return to me, My bride, because if you go about like the stag wounded with love for me, I too, like the stag, will come to you wounded by your wound.[51]

Not only is the wound now shared reciprocally between the soul and God, in an equal depth, but the bridegroom, that is, Christ, appears explicitly for the first time, seen as "The wounded stag / In sight on the hill." He "comes to" the soul as a "stag wounded by your wound." Whereas before he wounded the soul and then departed, now he is drawn to the soul in a mutual movement, so that the soul *sees* him for the first time. This introduces a new turn in John's argument, as the mutuality and equality that exist between the soul and God are found to belong explicitly to the Trinity, beginning with the recognition of Christ in the figure of the wounded stag.[52]

The Trinitarian Argument

The appearance of the wounded stag is the soul's entry into the inner movement of the Trinity. As the wounded stag comes to the soul, he brings with him a "breeze": this breeze is a new "flight of contemplation" which the soul recognizes to be the very spiration of the Holy Spirit that proceeds from the union of the Father and the Son in the Trinity. Through the mutuality that the soul has recognized in its relationship to Christ in their shared wound, it also sees within its love and knowledge of Christ its own explicit participation in the same mutuality that exists between the Father and Son in the Trinity.[53] The soul is beginning to relate to God *from within*, in the internal relations of the Trinity, rather than looking to God as the external object of its desire who touches it and then departs. John says that, as a result of this love, the soul has "a glimpse of him [God as Trinity] from a great distance"[54]—an explicit knowledge of God in himself, where before it was in unknowing.

As we saw, the Trinity is already known as a pale reflection or sketch in the Augustinian *imago Dei* of memory, intellect, and will. But in its merely natural form, it could only be recognized through the mediation of creatures, and after the wound of love, it was felt as a greatly increased, supernatural desire, but only known as an absence and a thirst for more knowledge of God than the articles of faith could provide. Here however, the soul receives a positive apprehension of the Trinity's relation to the spiritual faculties. John calls it a touch of God in the "substance of the soul"—of "the substance of God in the substance of the soul"[55]—and says that it is the first apprehension that the soul should receive positively.[56] The "substance" of the soul is the "deep" level of the soul, also called its "infinite" capacity, which until now was divorced from the level at which the rational faculties could know, love, and remember *something*: the object of their activity was unknown and unknowable. Now, however, the object has become discernible at the deep level, not as other objects, but *within* the activity of the faculties. John uses the word "object" here of God in relation to the spiritual faculties, in spite of the possible confusion with the objects of the senses. He says that the spiritual faculties are perfected in regard to their spiritual objects (*objetos*),[57] which are the persons of the Trinity: the will in regard to the Holy Spirit, the intellect to the Son, and the memory to the Father.[58] By no means does he wish to suggest that God becomes known in the manner of ordinary objects of the senses; rather, he uses the word "object" in the sense of the *relationship* between these faculties and the Trinity which is now becoming explicit. The soul is beginning to recognize the persons of the Trinity as its partners in this relationship rather than as objects in the normal sense. Nevertheless, they are objects in that they are *other* than the soul and are now recognized in their essence for the first time: not just as the depth of the soul but as a *relationship* with God at this deep level which the soul is becoming able to differentiate more and more clearly. The substantial touch now fills the void in the faculties through the new mutuality of love,[59] and God is the object of the faculties and is found to be their *fulfillment*.

In the next stage, spiritual marriage, this explicit trinitarian image of God in God's immediate relation to the spiritual faculties becomes more clearly differentiated and also begins to be integrated with the rest of the soul. The periods of union with God become longer and hence the clarity of the trinitarian image grows. Union is no longer restricted to "touches" but becomes "habitual" in the soul. The transformation of the soul through touches brings it to a more stable state in which its exterior activity flows from the inner trinitarian activity of God in the dynamic relation with the spiritual faculties. The body also becomes included through an overflow of energy from the spirit to the senses, so that the soul does God's will perfectly in action while remaining in union.[60]

The most significant change, which brings a new clarity to the trinitarian image in the spiritual faculties, is an intellectual vision which John describes as an unexpected light in the soul and a new dawn following the former darkness:

> [The soul] very appropriately calls this divine light "the rising dawn." . . . The intellect is aware of being elevated, with strange newness, above all natural understanding to the divine light, just as a person who after a long sleep opens his eyes to the unexpected light.[61]

The touch of God in the substance of the soul now "overflows into the intellect"[62] so that there is a new clarity of knowledge of God, where before in spiritual espousal only the will was involved and the intellect was engaged secondarily.[63] The new knowing produces greater delight, "because it is pertinent to the intellect, and as theologians say, fruition, the vision of God, is proper to the intellect."[64] There is also increased involvement of the will and the memory. Before, the soul was still "weak" in its will, "dark" in its intellect, and oppressed by the weight of the touches of union in its memory, but now it receives added "strength" and "light" in all three faculties so that it has a positive knowledge, love, and memory of God in himself.[65] This does not mean that God is grasped by the rational faculties in the manner of other objects. John emphasizes again that this deep knowledge has no content: it remains general as opposed to particular knowledge, stripped of its accidents, knowledge "which in this life, as St. Dionysius says, is a ray of darkness."[66] The light adds nothing new to what was known *about* God in the darkness, because God in himself is simple, without accidents. Yet in being known with a new *clarity*, John says the soul is now able to receive "distinct things"[67] in God also. In the *Llama*, the soul attains a "clear knowledge" of God in God's attributes—that "he is almighty, wise, and good, . . . merciful, just, powerful, and loving, etc."— and "views distinctly" each of these attributes in the "very being" of God as Father, Son, and Holy Spirit. The attributes are likened to the "lamps of fire" which shine and burn within the soul in union, emitting light and heat and so giving forth knowledge and love of God.[68] The *distinct* nature of this knowledge comes as a surprise after John's repeated emphatic statements about the general as opposed to particular nature of knowledge in union. He does not go back on those statements, but the new clarity corresponds to the desire he expressed at the outset to know the articles of faith "completely, clearly, and explicitly, freed of their covering": they are now known clearly and distinctly at their very source in God.

John expands on this by describing the means by which the new clarity is possible. A new ability is formed in the soul called "the feeling of the soul," which is analogous to the "common sense" in ordinary sensory knowing, as we saw in the previous chapter.[69] The spiritual faculties are called "the deep caverns of feeling" because they have "the power and capacity for feeling, possessing, and tasting . . . [all] the distinct things" of God. Their ability to know these distinct things in God's being is on account of "the feeling of the soul," which is "the power and strength that the substance of the soul has for feeling and enjoying the objects of the spiritual faculties." The "feeling of the soul" gives "the substance of the soul" the power and strength to know, love, and remember God's being clearly and distinctly. The spiritual faculties, like the bodily senses, make immediate contact with their objects in God, and these objects are then collated and differentiated in the "feeling of the soul," which is like the common sense or fantasy in sensory knowing. John's essential point is that the deep level of the spiritual faculties, which is the "substance of the soul," is not itself capable of knowing God explicitly in union, but like the bodily senses requires the further stage of the common sense for storing, collating, and differentiating this information. The "feeling of the soul" thus provides the necessary extra faculty within spiritual knowing by which God becomes known explicitly. There is no *overlap* between sensory knowing and spiritual knowing: John simply uses the analogy to explain how God becomes distinctly knowable.

Yet the question remains: how is the soul able to reconcile this increasing ability of its spiritual faculties for distinct spiritual knowledge with its ordinary knowledge through the senses and its dealings with objects in the exterior world? As spiritual objects become better differentiated through the capability of the feeling of the soul, the divorce of this part of the soul from the sensory part seems to be increasing. There are two parallel capabilities which do not overlap. If spiritual knowing resembles sensory knowing but uses different faculties, are there not two selves? Here John returns to the *connection* between spiritual knowing and sensory knowing in order to show how they are integrated into a single self.

Spiritual knowing and sensory knowing only appear to conflict when we consider their objects as being similar in nature. But when God is known at the deep level of the soul, even when this level is highly differentiated and yields distinct knowledge, God is known quite differently from sensory objects. The nature of the soul's knowing at this level is like that within the Trinity. In the Trinity, the Son's knowing and the Father's knowing are precisely the same in essence; the Son and the Father cannot be distinguished according to their knowledge, as they *are* their knowledge, a single "activity" of knowing. But they can be distinguished by their relations: the Son processes from the Father and the Holy Spirit processes from them both together. Thus, the Son is the one generated by the Father and the Father is the generator of the Son, and they are one in the bond of the Holy Spirit. Perhaps the best way of describing the distinction in terms of knowledge is to say that Father and Son are the same knowledge, but this knowledge is not *static*: it passes between them in constant movement, as in the constant active procession of the Holy Spirit. It is thus a dynamic know*ing* without being knowledge "of" anything outside them; yet it is knowing in the true sense in that Father and Son know *each other*, according to their *relational* distinction. When the soul enters into this knowledge within the Trinity, therefore, it gains this relational *sharing* of knowledge with God. The soul must relate to God as *other* to have such knowledge, but it does not have knowledge *of* anything other than this relationship. There is no object in the normal sense, just a relation between two partners. This is the full sense of what I mean by an intersubjective cognitive relation and of what Maritain means by saying that God becomes present to the soul as "another self": the soul's knowledge of God is through God's own self-knowledge, in a shared subjectivity, rather than of an external object.

Thus, John says that the soul now "feels the Beloved within her as in his own bed."[70] God is "within" the soul in its "deep interior hiding place."[71] He goes on,

> With God, to love the soul is to put her somehow within himself and make her his equal. Thus he loves the soul within himself, with himself, that is, with the very love with which he loves himself.[72]

The soul is by no means able to "objectify" God through this relationship. It is wholly within God that the spiritual faculties know, love, and remember God. Yet "distinct" and "clear knowledge" is given through God's own knowledge of himself, with the soul standing to God as the Son does to the Father as two equal subjects that are distinct only in the sense of the relational distinctions within the Trinity. It is these very distinctions that make "clear" knowledge possible, as the soul knows God through becoming part of God's active internal relations. The soul receives this immediate participation in the Trinity as the differentiation of its own interior substance, apprehending God through the feeling of the soul. The soul knows God as the Son knows the Father, through the constant exchange in their mutual indwelling of one another. To have this knowledge of God is not therefore to have attained *another* knowing ability but to have deepened one's knowing ability in the sense of attaining a conscious participation in the dynamic structure of the Trinity and so receiving a new knowledge of God within the internal relations of one's knowing.

The Center of the Soul (*el centro del alma*)

As there is only one knowing ability in union, the soul's knowing ability through the senses must finally become *integrated* in this single knowing ability. John describes this final point of arrival in union as "the center of the soul" (*el centro del alma*). The center of the soul refers to much the same as the depth, substance, and feeling of the soul, but it has the additional sense of the place around which all the other parts of the soul are unified. It is another word for the single supposit which, as John previously asserted, united the sensory and spiritual parts of the soul, and which has now reached its goal. Everything has a power or force that brings it to its center or goal—for instance, the center of a stone is the center of the earth.[73] The soul has many centers "like the many mansions that the Son of God declared were in his Father's house," corresponding to each of the stages of transformation, but only one, the "ultimate and deepest center" is the goal of union.[74] From the moment that the soul received the "fathomless desire for union with God," which followed the wound of love, John says that it had a "driving force" like "a stone which is racing on toward its center."[75] The driving force was that infinite deep desire for God which we have seen gradually inculcated and then differentiated in the process of transformation in the three spiritual faculties, so that now the soul "understands, knows, and loves . . . in the Trinity, together with it [the Trinity]."[76]

The center of the soul is the deep trinitarian activity of the spiritual faculties in union, the fruitful relationship of union which lies at the root of all the soul's acts. But it is no longer restricted to the spiritual faculties. In addition, in the "ultimate and deepest center," John says that this divine activity has worked its way through the whole soul "to transform and clarify it in its whole being, power, and strength, and according to its capacity, until it appears to be God."[77] This must include the senses: there can now only be one center of the soul, that is, only one activity, both in the senses and the spirit. The spiritual part of the soul pervades and illuminates the whole soul:

> It should be known that, being a spirit, the soul does not possess in its being the high or the low, the more profound or the less profound as do quantitative bodies. Since it has no parts, there is no difference as to the inward and the outward; it is all of one kind and does not have degrees of quantitative depth. It cannot receive greater illumination in one part than in the other like physical bodies, but all of it is illumined equally in a degree of greater or lesser intensity, like the air that is illumined or not illumined according to degrees.[78]

This spiritual illumination is spread throughout the whole soul, but still the question remains as to how it is *mediated* to the senses. John uses the analogy of a brighter and a less bright light for the relationship between the spirit and senses:

> [The sensory knowing] habits are perfected by the more perfect habit of supernatural knowledge infused in her[;] . . . these habits do not reign in such a way that she must use them in order to know; though at times she may still use them, as this supernatural knowledge does not impede their use. For in this union with divine wisdom these habits are joined to the superior wisdom of God. When a faint light is mingled with a bright one, the bright light prevails and is that which illumines. Yet the faint light is not lost, but rather perfected, even though it is not the light which illumines.[79]

This makes clear that no violence is done to the former sensory knowing habits by the presence of the brighter light of spiritual illumination: the senses are not removed but simply outshone, while all the soul's acts are raised to the supernatural level. But what is the role of the senses, now that knowing properly belongs to the spirit alone? The question becomes more pressing when John stresses that the soul has become able to know God and all things a priori in this state, without the mediation of creatures. He says that the soul now "knows these things [created beings] better in God's being than in themselves. . . . The soul knows creatures through God and not God through creatures."[80] There is a profound reversal of the order of knowing in the soul, with knowledge no longer coming through the senses to the spirit, but precisely the reverse. The soul has been turned on its head so that God is known before creatures.

Yet John suggests that this "perfects" the soul. This perfection is clearly not that of the merely natural human creature. This has become very clear in the course of our analysis of the process of transformation. The soul has been returned to the state of Adam's innocence, but this is not the goal; beyond this, the soul has had its means of knowing and its relationship with God raised from the human to the divine level. The culmination of John's trinitarian argument is to conclude that "the soul's center is God."[81] At this point, he conceives of the soul's structure as conformed to *Christ* rather than being merely that of Adam. He says that the center of the soul is both God's "own" and the soul's "own," where God dwells "alone, not only as in your [God's] house, nor only as in your bed, but also in my own heart, intimately and closely united to it."[82] In saying that the center is the soul's "own," John means that it has full freedom in union, as God has raised the soul to the level of God's own active trinitarian mutuality. Thus, in the case of the will, "the soul reflects the divine light in a more excellent way because of the active intervention of its will."[83] There is an active cooperation between the soul and God, with no loss of the soul's freedom but rather its perfection. The soul can take full possession of its faculties while also remaining in union. This corresponds to the union of the divine Word with human flesh in Christ. The soul's created nature remains distinct from the divine nature of God—John says that in union "its being (even though transformed) is naturally as distinct from God's as it was before"[84]—but the relationship is one of immediate "contact," modeled on Christ's hypostatic union of human and divine natures. We do not enter into the Son's relationship with the Father "essentially and naturally," as Christ did, but nevertheless, "through the union and transformation of love" we become one with the Father "just as the Father and Son are one in essential unity of love."[85] In the "face-to-face" vision of union, our union "corresponds" to the "hypostatic union of the human nature with the divine Word," through the adoption of sons.[86]

There are two levels to this christological union in the center of the soul: the interior and the exterior. First, at the interior level, human and divine are joined in the inner-trinitarian activity of mutual love between the Father and the Son, through the relationship between the soul and Christ in the spiritual marriage. The soul says to her Beloved:

> *And let us go forth to behold ourselves in Your beauty.* This means: Let us so act that by means of this loving activity we may attain to the vision of ourselves in Your beauty in eternal life. That is: That I be so transformed in Your beauty that we may be alike in beauty, and both behold ourselves in Your beauty, possessing now Your very beauty; this, in such a way that each looking at the other may see in the other his own beauty, since both are Your beauty alone, I being absorbed Your beauty. . . . .This is the adoption of the sons of God, who will indeed declare to God what the very Son said to the Eternal Father through St. John: "All my things are yours, and yours mine" (Jn. 17:10).[87]

In this loving and seeing, the soul is "absorbed" in the beauty of the Son, not to the detriment of the soul's humanity but to its perfection in the "beauty" of the Son's exchange with the Father in the Trinity. The soul now *understands itself* as Christlike, that is, within the "loving activity" of the Holy Spirit which is shared by the Father and the Son. Second, through this interior possession of the spiritual marriage with Christ, sweetness "overflows" to the soul, not just interiorly in the will, but "exteriorly in works directed to the service of the Beloved."[88] The full humanity of the soul, not just interior, but exterior and bodily, becomes included in the spiritual overflow from the center of the soul where the marriage takes place. No additional activity is required to include the exterior of the soul, but through the fortifying of the soul's humanity, the same breeze of the Holy Spirit which earlier led the soul to the height of contemplation interiorly now extends to the body and senses.[89] John summarizes this unity of interior and exterior activity by saying that now, "the power to look at God *is*, for the soul, the power to do works in the grace of God."[90] Virtuous works proceed seamlessly from the interior union, as they did from Christ's own interior union with the Father.

Thus, the fact that the senses no longer come *first* in the order of knowing does not mean that they are rendered useless for John. His model for our perfection is the union of human and divine in Christ. Out of our inner-trinitarian relationship comes a clarity in our spiritual faculties and an energy for engagement with the world which *includes* all our sensory activity. The spiritual knowing that we have of God is a nonconceptual knowing, and as such, it presents no conflict with the concepts that we receive from the world through our senses. In this mystical state, the dynamism of the spiritual marriage is the immediate root and center of all our mediated cognitive activity. Indeed, our cognitive activity, extending to the body and to sensory and intelligible concepts, is united with the divine according to the same trinitarian structure that was first produced purely in the spiritual part of the soul in the process of transformation. The distinction of sense and spirit is now *included* in the soul's union with God, without being dissolved, according to the logic of distinction-within-unity found in the Trinity. The soul uses its senses and sensory forms within mystical knowing, while yet the origin, dynamism, and structure of this knowing is given not in relation to created things, as in the natural state, but in relation to the wholly divine source of the center of the soul, as is the case in Christ in the hypostatic union. As Iain Matthew puts it in his study of John's Christology, our knowing, like Jesus', is not given as "a catalogue of thoughts imposed from the outside, but as pure enhancement of his [our] truest self (*sustancia*)."[91] It is this "truest self" that the soul has attained, with Christ, in its final center, rather than a knowing in competition with the senses.

The final purpose of union, for John, is not to attain an "unfleshed," heavenly state but to enter fully into the incarnate life. He says that our union here "is not as essential and perfect as in the next life," and that the "sensitive veil" of the flesh remains between our present state and glory. Union gives us a taste and a longing for heaven. Yet God has fortified our sensory flesh to enable us to enter into the "consummation" of union and to be of service in the world.[92] John sees in Christ, incarnate and resurrected, the full possibility for human flesh, where the body becomes the perfect *expression* of the clarified spirit.[93]

John maintains that the two systems of knowing, the spiritual and the sensory, are independent of one another in union, but we have seen in this chapter that the deep penetration of the soul into God, culminating in the center of the soul, bridges the wide gap between these systems and establishes a single mystical selfhood in the soul. John appeals to the Augustinian image of God in the rational faculties to show that there is already in the soul, before mystical transformation, a relationship with God: this relationship lies at the heart of the soul's intentionality and constitutes its selfhood. The difference between this relationship and union is that God is known only remotely, through creatures, whereas in union in the center of the soul, God is known a priori, before creatures. Through the process of transformation, the dynamism of the soul's relationship to God is increased, as the "first draft" of the image in the soul is gradually brought to perfection. The soul is "hollowed out" and "deepened" until it no longer requires the mediation of creatures to know God but is fully accommodated to the immediate presence of God given in union. Initially, this provokes a "war in the soul" between the new kind of knowing and the former sensory kind, but as the new kind of knowing is possessed more deeply by the soul than the sensory kind, it becomes the source of all the soul's sensory acts, *including* the senses in the spiritual activity of union rather than destroying them. The senses are included in the single activity of union in the process of overflow from the center. Thus, the inner-trinitarian knowing of the spiritual marriage is mediated to the full humanity of the soul in a christological unity of sense and spirit.

CHAPTER FOUR

The Context of an Intellectual Comparison Between John of the Cross and Teresa of Avila

F<small>OR TERESA OF AVILA,</small> the questions of anthropology and epistemology are as important as they are for John of the Cross, and for the same reason. She uses distinctions in the structure of the soul to describe the nature of union with God and mystical knowing. Union with God is not an external relation with God, in the manner of our ordinary relations with physical objects, but an "interior" relation, which is formed in the inner structure of the soul. The difficulty in comparing Teresa with John on this issue, however, is that she had little formal education and did not develop a similar scholastic anthropology and epistemology. The differences between them, at a period in the history of the Spanish church when the Inquisition was especially repressive of women, raise the question whether there is a common context in which their ideas can be accurately compared.

The complicating factor in an intellectual comparison between Teresa and John is that, because of the restrictions on education and freedom of expression placed on women at this time, Teresa not only wrote but *thought* quite differently from her male contemporaries. If her view of expression was circumscribed on all sides by restrictions to which John was not subject, the view may be taken that a purely intellectual comparison between them is not possible. In this chapter, I shall examine how recent scholarship has changed our understanding of Teresa and her relationship with John and then consider the historical contacts between the two Carmelites. The discussion here cannot be comprehensive, but I shall argue that new studies of Teresa, far from removing the possibility of an intellectual comparison, allow us to make a more accurate assessment of

Teresa's thought and so to understand the connections between her thought and that of John of the Cross. The new information permits us to go more deeply into this comparison than was possible in the past.[1]

In the last ten to fifteen years there have been a large number of studies of Teresa focusing on the role of gender.[2] Gillian Ahlgren, in *Teresa of Avila and the Politics of Sanctity*,[3] makes the important point that Teresa's writing belongs to an identifiable intellectual tradition in late-sixteenth-century Spain of vernacular spiritual writing, so that however extraordinary it is in other respects, there is this key element of commonality between her thought and that of her—mainly male—contemporary writers.[4] From this it is possible to draw the connection to the thought and writing of John of the Cross.

Ahlgren makes use of the thesis of Alison Weber's *Teresa of Avila and the Rhetoric of Femininity* that Teresa used a "rhetoric of female subordination" to make her writings acceptable to the authorities,[5] but she argues that, at the same time, Teresa consciously "wrote herself into" the contemporary tradition of spiritual writing on prayer, using the intellectual forms and concepts that she had learned from her reading of the spiritual classics in order to authenticate her teachings. As Ahlgren says, "her extensive reading in classic spiritual texts gave her a theological background as strong as many of her male peers."[6] As the doctrinal investigation that followed soon after Teresa's death proved, her writings survived as a result of her sophisticated use of this intellectual tradition. Although there was much in her thought that remained suspect in the eyes of the inquisitors, the investigation concluded that her teachings were broadly orthodox, and they became the only spiritual writings by a woman to reach publication in the whole of the second half of the sixteenth century in Spain.[7] Thus, she succeeded in entering the intellectual tradition of spiritual writing generally inaccessible to women at this time. This happened for two reasons, the second of which is of special concern to us here. The first centers on her rhetorical techniques, including her "rhetoric of subordination" in relation to her confessors and the church authorities; the second concerns her doctrinal sophistication in handling theological ideas. It is in the latter respect that we can see the similarities of her thought with that of John of the Cross. The great difference between her and John was that, as a woman, she had to fight to enter this tradition and to use a wide variety of techniques to make her writing acceptable. These place her writing in a different genre from John's.[8] Despite her lack of scholastic training, she effectively used the knowledge gained from her reading to formulate her ideas and to give herself a theological voice. In this respect, though she exercised a different voice from John of the Cross, she did so in the same context in which John became her follower, as a writer for the education of the friars and nuns of the Discalced and a fellow-worker on the Carmelite Reform.

The background to Teresa's battle for orthodoxy shows how she was formed in this vernacular spiritual tradition of writing. In the early sixteenth century, religious reform had been spurred by the great Franciscan archbishop, Cardinal Cisneros (1415–1517). Cisneros was instrumental in opening up Spanish universities to humanism, particularly in his foundation of the University of Alcalá. Teresa's reform of the Carmelites sprang from Cisneros's influential religious reforms among the Franciscans, stressing a return to a simpler form of life and the practice of "interior" or "mental" prayer.[9] This method of prayer was formulated most popularly by Francisco de Osuna in his *Third Spiritual Alphabet*, with an emphasis on *recogimiento*, "recollection," in which the soul is advised to withdraw from exterior things and enter the heart, detached from the world and rational thought, usually beginning with a meditation on the Passion.[10] As the century progressed, however, the period of openness came to an end, and the activity of the Inquisition, first set up in 1478 to combat the threat of Jews and Moors within the Christian realm following the completion of the reconquest,[11] was turned increasingly against suspect Christians. The first victims were the *conversos*, the Jewish converts who were suspected of having been re-judaized; the second were the *luteranos* (Lutherans), particularly at the time of the Council of Trent, when the Protestant threat from Northern Europe was considered to be most immediate. The third group were the *alumbrados* (illuminists), who were mostly uncloistered women (*beatas*) teaching about visions and passivity before God. These became regarded as a threat to the sacramental mediation of the church in much the same way as Lutherans. This progressive clamp-down reached its peak at the time Teresa was writing (1560–1581). In 1559 the inquisitor general, Francisco de Valdés, published an Index of Prohibited Books of unprecedented length, 253 titles, including many popular Spanish spiritual writings, such as works by Luis de Granada and Juan de Avila, and fifty-four books of hours.[12] This was precisely the kind of religious material used by women, who could not generally read Latin, and Teresa describes its loss as a major reason for her decision to write on prayer: she wanted to provide a replacement for teaching her nuns.[13]

Teresa was forty-four at this time and had herself already read many of the books that were now forbidden to her nuns, and therefore would have been confident that she could replace much of this teaching in her own words.[14] The question we must ask is how in this climate of fierce repression, which applied especially to women's writings, she managed to get her writings past the censors or to obtain permission to write at all. Two broad factions had arisen within the religious orders by this time: the *espirituales*, the "spirituals," heirs of Cisneros's reforms, who resisted the increasing prohibitions on mental prayer and the gradual exclusion of practices like *recogimiento*; and the *letrados*, the "learned," who were in the ascendant as the leaders of the Inquisition and the party favored in the reforms of Trent. The *letrados* taught that the unlearned and women should stick to "vocal prayer"—using authorized words and forms of practice—and to active forms of spirituality, as opposed to passive recollection before God. Otherwise, their intellects would succumb to devil-deception. There is no question that Teresa was on the side of the *espirituales*, and it was through her perceptive assessment of the division between these factions that she was able to win support for her writings from sympathetic spiritual confessors.[15] These confessors appreciated that there was a serious lack of teachings on prayer available to women religious following the Valdés Index, and they permitted Teresa to fill this void for the benefit of her nuns. At the same time, Teresa took care to remain obedient to her confessors in order not to attract the attention of the Inquisition. She kept within the authority structure laid down by the church. It was only after her death, when her teachings became more widely known following their publication in 1588, that a number of *letrados* sounded the alarm regarding her teaching as far beyond the bounds of orthodoxy.

Teresa was denounced to the Inquisition no less than six times during her lifetime, including three separate occasions on which her *Vida* was investigated, but Ahlgren points out that it was Teresa's work of reform and her character that was under suspicion during her life more than the orthodoxy of her teaching, as it was her foundations rather than her writings that first attracted attention.[16] Only after the posthumous printing of her works in 1588 did these writings become the focus of attention, and then she was judged not on her character, which by then was popularly established, but on the soundness of her doctrine.[17] The main opponent and first to denounce her teachings was Alonso de la Fuente (1533–1594), a Dominican who had worked assiduously through the 1570s and 1580s against the *alumbrados* and who brought similar accusations against Teresa. He accused her of speaking with an authority beyond that given to women by nature; of teaching *dexamiento*, "passivity" or "abandonment" to God in prayer; of drawing too close an equality between God's nature and the center or depth of the soul in union; of equating justification with union with God in the manner of the Lutherans; and of teaching that one can be certain of salvation. He also claimed that she belonged to a heretical tradition going back to the Messalians and, more recently, to Tauler. Alonso had not failed to read Teresa's works in arriving at these statements, but he used the common Inquisitorial technique of taking her statements out of context and without attention to the whole of her thought. Thus her supporters, principally the Augustinians Antonio de Quevedo and Luis de León, were able to refute Alonso's charges with a more thorough reading of Teresa's teaching, showing for instance that she did not go as far as the *alumbrado* doctrine of *dexamiento* but maintained that the soul's faculties and senses remained active in union. Most importantly, Teresa's supporters rejected the accusation that she belonged to a "heretical tradition" of the Messalians, Eutyches, and Tauler by showing that her teachings could in fact be better likened to and derived from orthodox authorities. Luis de León cited the examples of St. Brigid, St. Gertrude, and St. Catherine of Siena as women who had taught on the basis of their visions, and Quevedo cited Jean Gerson's teaching on rapture. León and Quevedo also cited the mystical teachings of Dionysius, Bernard of Clairvaux, Richard of St. Victor, Bonaventure, and Francisco de Osuna as precursors to her doctrines. Ahlgren makes the important point that this was not simply a refashioning of Teresa after the event: it was the line of argument Teresa had made herself, particularly in her *Vida*, where she had cited traditional authors or their example in profusion to bolster her arguments—Jerome, Osuna, Gregory, Augustine, Alonso de Madrid, Francis, Anthony of Padua, Bernard of Clairvaux, Catherine of Siena, Bernardino de Laredo, "the Carthusian" (Ludolph of Saxony), and Cassian.[18] She had used their terminology wherever she could to make her case, such as her threefold division of visions along Augustinian lines, her use of the term "mystical theology," and of Osuna's terms of "recollection," "the prayer of quiet," "suspension of the faculties" and so on.[19] As a result, Teresa's supporters were able to furnish more than adequate replies from her writings to Alonso's and others' accusations, and the charges against her were successfully refuted.

The opposition that Teresa faced was especially harsh on account of her sex, but there was a wider set of circumstances, wider than the issue of gender alone—one in which John of the Cross would have shared. John also wrote to fill the void of teaching on prayer in the vernacular available to the friars and nuns of the Discalced, as stated in his prologue to the *Subida*, although the prohibition on many vernacular writings is not mentioned.[20] In joining Teresa in this work of education on prayer, John was clearly on the side of the *espirituales* rather than the *letrados* in the wider religious debate. Further, John recommended Teresa's teaching on visions and expressed the hope that her works would be published in his "B" redaction of the *Cántico*, which was written in the mid-1580s.[21] The difference between John and Teresa was that he neither required a "rhetoric of subordination" nor felt bound to cite his traditional authorities as Teresa did in her *Vida*. Their writings, however, occupied the same intellectual space in terms of their motivation and background. They were linked both positively and negatively to the religious climate in the sixteenth-century Spanish church. Positively, they were part of the movement for religious reform inspired by Cisneros; negatively, in an attempt to educate nuns and friars in "mental" prayer and the higher states of "union" as well as in its merely vocal forms, they were leaders of a countercurrent in the later part of the century against the clamp-down on spiritual writings. Thus, their writings share a similar theological agenda and can be said to belong to the same tradition. None of this denies that Teresa was an original thinker whose particular position as a woman puts her writings in a different literary genre from John's. She also differed from John on some points of teaching. But this does not negate the common intellectual background to their writings in the spiritual tradition, which is the context of my comparison of their thought.

The Historical Connection between Teresa of Avila and John of the Cross

Concerning the actual contacts in life between Teresa and John, I shall confine myself to the evidence provided by their own writings. The sources are numerous, but there is not space to consider them all here and, in any case, only their own writings can be regarded as entirely reliable.[22] A sufficient picture of the relationship between John and Teresa emerges from these writings to show the main facts regarding their joint work on the Reform and the likely extent to which they shared their ideas and influenced one another.

For two contemporaries who are so often spoken of together and who became regarded jointly as the great proponents of Christian mysticism in the subsequent tradition, it is surprising to find how small a proportion of their working lives they spent together. As the following brief account makes clear, they were certainly friends who were engaged in the same work of the reform of the Carmelite order, but the subsequent tradition has tended to make more of the closeness of their partnership than the evidence indicates. In fact, Teresa had closer companions in the reform than John, even closer male companions, notably Jerónimo Gracián, to whom she wrote hundreds of letters, in contrast to perhaps a few dozen to John (which have not been preserved),[23] and Gracián's position as apostolic visitator to the Carmelites in Andalusia and then in Castile in the mid-1570s gave him an authority over Teresa's foundations that John never had. Nevertheless, in matters of spiritual teaching, the contacts that did exist between John and Teresa were enough for them to have influenced one another considerably.

John was first introduced to Teresa by the prior of the Carmelite friars in Medina in 1567, when he was twenty-five and she was fifty-two, during the period that he was studying theology in Salamanca.[24] John and this prior were the first Carmelite friars to join the reform, and they followed Teresa's model in making new foundations for men, as Teresa was doing for women, according to a stricter version of the Carmelite rule than that used by the rest of the order, calling themselves "discalced" Carmelites.[25] The following year, 1568, Teresa invited John to participate in her new foundation in Valladolid as a kind of apprenticeship in discalced practice, before he set out to found the first house for friars in Duruelo a few months later.[26] Teresa mentions that while they were waiting for the workmen to finish the house in Valladolid, before the enclosure was made, there were "some days" in which she had the "opportunity to teach Father Fray John of the Cross about our way of life so that he would have a clear understanding of everything."[27] After these few days, the rules of enclosure and the amount of work to be done in organizing the house brought this close discussion to an end.

Teresa's next meeting with John was on a brief visit to Duruelo in February 1569, in which she professed herself "astonished to see the spirit that the Lord had put there," but she was also alarmed by the severity of the friars' penitential practices, and she begged them to be less severe—to which they "paid little attention."[28] Teresa was impressed by John's fervor and always complimented him highly to others,[29] but his asceticism, for which he already had a reputation when they first met, clearly disturbed her on this occasion.[30] Her worries must have abated, however, because in 1572 she arranged for John to be sent to the discalced friars in Pastrana with the task of moderating the excessive practices that the prior was imposing on the novices there.[31] In the summer of 1572, after several years apart, Teresa succeeded in persuading the visitator to the Carmelites, Pedro Fernández, to send John to join her on the reform of her original monastery in Avila, the Encarnación, where she had recently been elected prioress. John remained there for the next five years, until he was captured and imprisoned by his Calced brethren, in December 1577. Teresa finished her term as prioress in October 1574, so their time working closely together was about two years.[32]

Teresa ascribed the success of the reform of the Encarnación largely to John's work of spiritual direction among the nuns, both for imposing external disciplines and for helping them "interiorly,"[33] and she said that he was responsible for keeping the community in shape after she left.[34] In her strongest recommendation of John, in a letter to Madre Ana de Jesús in 1578, she said:

> Since he left us [at the Encarnación] I have not found another like him in the whole of Castile, nor anyone else who inspires souls with such fervor to jour-

ney to heaven. . . . See that all the sisters in your house talk to him and tell him about their souls. They will see what good it does them and will find themselves in every way greatly advanced in spirituality and perfection, for Our Lord has given him a special grace for that purpose. . . . He is indeed the father of my soul and one of those with whom it does me most good to have converse. . . . He is very spiritual and has great experience and learning.[35]

John's strength, therefore, was in spiritual direction—precisely the area that Teresa considered most important in the work of the reform. He may not have been a friend of Teresa on the scale of Gracián, but he possessed the two great qualities Teresa required in directors: he "had experience"— that is, he was "spiritual"—and he was also learned in doctrine. Her mention of his ability to inspire the "fervor to journey to heaven" also indicates that he could teach the higher stages of prayer and union, something that she considered rare in confessors. She rates him as "the father of my soul" in response to a complaint made by Ana de Jesús that John had called her "my daughter," which Ana had found offensive. Teresa disparaged Ana's concern for honor and dignity and suggests here that John had earned the title of spiritual father in her estimation for the authority that he had clearly demonstrated in spiritual matters. John did not occupy a unique position in Teresa's life in this respect, by any means, as she developed close friendships with many of her confessors, but he was someone she found valuable to talk to on spiritual matters and no doubt this went back to their time together at the Encarnación.

While receiving the sacrament from John on November 18, 1572, Teresa had an imaginative vision in which she attained spiritual marriage.[36] Ironically, considering how much she valued his opinion on spiritual matters, she describes the vision as a kind of compensation from God for John's meanness on this occasion. In handing out the host, John had broken it in front of her in order to give some to another sister when, according to Teresa, there was no lack of hosts. She thought he had deliberately mortified her, as shortly beforehand she had told him that she liked large hosts. Judging by John's strict attitude to self-mortification, which is evident in his own writings, there is no reason to doubt that Teresa was right in her suspicion. Teresa expressed a similar exasperation with John when she was asked to judge his submission for a competition on the meaning of the words, "Seek yourself in Me." John wrote an answer that called for such perfect self-mortification as a preliminary to seeking God that Teresa commented: "Seeking God would be very costly if we could not do so until we were dead to the world. . . . God deliver me from people so spiritual that they want to turn everything into perfect contemplation."[37] But there is no reason to read a great rift between Teresa and John into this comment, or even a significant difference in their teaching.[38] Like John, Teresa was strict in her doctrine of detachment, and both emphasized that true self-knowledge and humility were dependent on a prior knowledge of God; self-mortification would be pointless if exercised without a divine goal, as true knowledge of self proceeds only from knowledge of God.[39] Teresa's frequent compliments regarding John did not diminish after this date, as we would expect if there had been a falling out between them. The fact that John could annoy Teresa on this issue was a result of their different and to some extent opposing personalities—which was also what kept them from becoming the best of friends—but did not extend to the level of basic teaching.

Teresa's most frequent references to John in her letters come during the time that he was in prison in Toledo. In addition to her friends, she wrote to those she knew in authority or thought could help, including the King of Spain, in a desperate attempt to secure John's release. She achieved little, and in the end John escaped himself, but the letters, with frequent references to his being a "saint," are further evidence of her admiration and concern for him at a time when, as she said, everyone else had forgotten him.[40] After his escape, John did not return to Northern Castile but went to Andalusia. He probably saw Teresa only once more in the remaining four years of her life, when he visited Avila in November 1581 to try to persuade her to come to Granada to make a foundation there. She declined, but the foundation went ahead under the direction of another discalced nun, Ana de Jesús, and John and Teresa corresponded further over the foundation.[41] In the same year, the year before she died, Teresa wrote to Gracián that she was still trying "to get him back here"[42]—to get John to return to Avila or somewhere nearby. Thus, the picture is of a sometimes awkward but nevertheless close working relationship developed over a period of fifteen years—close in spite of the fact that other than two years together at the Encarnación there were only a handful of meetings and contacts between them.

There is little doubt that John read some of Teresa's writings, as he refers to them in his own writings. The differences between them on visions and ecstasies must be balanced against this citation and clear approval by John of Teresa's treatment of these spiritual apprehensions.[43] Teresa, however, could not have read John's writings, as all but a few of his early poems were written after her death.[44] The relationship between their writings is typical of their whole relationship: John was supposedly the one in authority, but Teresa was the elder and more experienced, and John learned from her. The help was also mutual, however, as John probably enabled Teresa to work through some of the conflicts in her thought, as we see them in the *Vida*, during their meetings at the Encarnación, toward producing her more developed position of the *Moradas*. The most crucial element in this development was undoubtedly Teresa's own reflection and changing experience in prayer, but it is likely that John clarified some of the complex distinctions that she sought to make.[45] We have the testimony of both writers of their admiration for the other's teaching, so that it is fair to assume that there was a cross-fertilization of ideas. At the same time, it must be remembered that they could not have conferred on the bulk of what they wrote, given the small length of time they spent together and the fact that John's main writings date from after Teresa's death.

CHAPTER FIVE

The Structure of the Soul
According to Teresa of Avila

M Y APPROACH TO Teresa of Avila's anthropology in the present chapter will be to focus on her fundamental distinction between the "interior" and "exterior" "parts" of the soul. In order to distinguish mystical knowing from ordinary knowing, Teresa separates the interior part of the soul, where supernatural objects are "felt" and "understood," from the exterior part, where merely natural sensation and knowing occurs. While she is unable to develop her faculty psychology to the extent that John does, she makes her own distinctions to show how the two kinds of knowing are related. In particular, she treats the question in terms of the figures of Mary and Martha, the types of the contemplative and active lives, and this theme will form a prominent part of my analysis of her anthropology in this chapter. Teresa explores the relationship between Mary and Martha as an analogy for the two parts of the soul, first emphasizing the division in the soul caused by mystical transformation, but also, like John, looking forward to the final unity of the soul, in a unity patterned on Christ's union of natures and the distinction-within-unity of the persons of the Trinity. Her discussion focuses on the question of how the soul is to combine exterior activity in the world with the interior union with God.

In the next chapter, I shall turn to the detailed consideration of the most important element in Teresa's anthropology, the center of the soul. The center of the soul is the dynamic element that unites the two parts of the soul in mystical knowing, which Teresa developed only in her final major work, the *Moradas del castillo interior*. This division of chapters will reflect that of chaps. 2 and 3 on John of the Cross, with the first on the structure of the soul and epistemology and the second on the underlying *dynamism* that draws together the separate elements in this anthropology. A comparison of the two writers will be saved for the final chapter.

The works of Teresa that will be considered are her autobiography or *Vida* (1562–1565), the *Camino de perfección* (1566–1569), the *Meditaciones sobre los Cantares* (1566–1575), and the *Moradas del castillo interior* (1577).[1] In addition, I shall refer to her *Cuentas de conciencia*, a set of about sixty brief spiritual testimonies which she wrote in the form of a diary between 1560 and 1581.[2] Unlike John of the Cross, who wrote his major works mostly within a period of about five years, Teresa's works span over twenty years (1560–1581), and there is a marked development in her thought. She presents much of her thought in autobiographical terms but it is not simply autobiography: though it is clearly less systematic in presentation than the thought of John of the Cross, it is theological discourse, written for the education of her nuns in "mystical theology."

The Dichotomy in the Structure of the Soul: The Interior and Exterior Parts

Teresa bases her anthropology on an interior/exterior division of the soul which she uses to show which operations are to be considered natural, and which, beyond that, are supernatural and mystical. She uses this division to differentiate ordinary knowing of the world from mystical knowing, as pertaining to different regions of the soul, called the exterior and the interior respectively. The origin of this division is to be found in the early stages of her *Vida*.

In her *Vida*, Teresa ascribes her first breakthrough in prayer to a time in her early twenties, shortly after her profession, when she took some time away from her monastery of the Encarnación in order to recover from a serious illness. While staying at the house of her uncle, Don Pedro Sánchez de Cepeda, during her convalescence, she was given Francisco de Osuna's *Third Spiritual Alphabet*, which taught her the "prayer of recollection (*recogimiento*)," as mentioned in the previous chapter.[3] In this popular vernacular work, Osuna (ca. 1492– 1540) describes three stages of prayer: first, "vocal prayer," which uses the "Our Father" as its model; second, reflective and meditative prayer, based on holy and devout thoughts of the Lord, the church, and so on; and third, "mental" and "spiritual" prayer, when the soul attains *devoción* and moves beyond words, withdrawing to a point in the interior of the soul where there is "quiet" and ultimately "union" with God. Teresa appears to have taken her basic vocabulary of prayer from this account of recollection and says that, at this early age of about twenty,[4] she began to practice Osuna's method with all her strength, attaining the prayer of quiet and sometimes even union. In spite of her initial progress, however, she characterizes the entire period of twenty years after her profession as a failure in **prayer**. With hindsight, she analyzes the cause of this failure as her inability to make an adequate distinction between the interior life of prayer and the exterior pleasures and pastimes of the world:

> On the one hand God was calling me; on the other hand I was following the world. All the things of God made me happy; those of the world held me bound. It seems I desired to harmonize these two contraries—so inimical to one another—such as are the spiritual life and sensory joys, pleasures and pastimes. In prayer I was having great trouble, for my spirit was not proceeding as lord but as slave. And so I was not able to shut myself within myself (which was my whole manner of procedure in prayer); instead, I shut within myself a thousand vanities.[5]

Teresa understood the prayer of recollection as concerned with an area "within" the soul which belonged to God, the place of her spirit, where she could enjoy "the things of God," while the contrary, "sensory joys" were to be kept firmly outside this interior region, in the "world." She blames her failure in prayer—of "not proceeding as lord but as slave"—on the fact that she confused these two contraries, so that instead of shutting herself in the interior of her soul with God in prayer, she introduced "a thousand vanities" from the outside instead. This is her first statement of the dichotomy that is to be found throughout her subsequent teaching on the structure of the soul: her starting point is a correlation of the contraries of God and the world, the spiritual life and sensory joys, with the interior and exterior parts of the soul respectively.

Teresa's next breakthrough in prayer reinforced this dichotomy between the interior and exterior of the soul, when she had what is known as her second conversion at the end of the period of twenty years, in the Lent of 1554.[6] One day on entering the oratory at the Encarnación she saw a statue of the wounded Christ, which made her reflect on the wounds, and her "heart broke . . . with the greatest outpouring of tears."[7] As a result, she found that if she represented Christ to herself at the start of her prayer, concentrating on the scenes where he was "alone and in need" such as in the garden of Gethsemane, she could habitually become recollected.[8] The change was from feeling inadequate, like a "slave" in prayer, to relating to God in "an intimate sharing between friends," which was how she now defined mental prayer.[9] Teresa saw the change as following the pattern of Augustine's conversion, which she read about in the *Confessions* at about this time.[10] She had received the gift of tears, which she likened to Augustine's tears in the garden at his conversion; and elsewhere she comments on how Augustine sought God in many places but ultimately found God "within himself"[11]—which was her experience now. Her second conversion made clear to her that the new prayer of "an intimate sharing between friends" involved a double homecoming, like Augustine's, in which she was drawn both to God and also to herself. She realized that the interior that she had sought for years based on her reading of Osuna was properly found only with God's help, as Augustine had found it, in the mutuality of a relationship with God which had brought him "to himself" after a long time of confusion with the exterior world.

In spite of this new mutuality between herself and God in prayer, Teresa found that the *passivity* of the state increased rather than lessened her sense of the dichotomy between what was happening in the interior of her soul and her exterior life in the world. Even before her second conversion, she had observed that her success in prayer had little to do with her own desires, including her desire to pray, but rather depended on how much God "helped" her.[12] As she progressed, she noted that there was a considerable difference between the occasions on which the favor of grace in prayer was "in part acquired" and when it was given by God irresistibly.[13] When given irresistibly, she found herself reaching a higher level of prayer than she had previously experienced, characterized by a state of "suspension" (*suspensión*) in the soul. She found herself "within" the interior of her soul in this prayer, but now also strangely "outside" it:

> It used to happen, when I represented Christ within me in order to place myself in his presence, or even while reading that a feeling of the presence of God would come upon me unexpectedly so that I could in no way doubt that he was within me or I totally immersed in him. This did not occur after the manner of vision. I believe they call it "mystical theology." The soul is suspended (*suspende*) in such a way that it seems to be completely outside itself.[14]

Teresa uses the term "mystical theology" for this state, and goes on later to explain that mystical theology entails certain important changes in knowing, which will be pursued further below,[15] but she begins by relating it to the state of "suspension," in which her soul "seems to be completely outside itself." Clearly, she does not mean that her soul has returned to its exterior activity in the outside world, as she has entered into the presence of God "within" her and is "immersed" (*engolfada*) in God. She stresses the contrast between this interior state and her exterior activity by saying that the prayer is not "after the manner of vision": she does not use her exterior bodily eyes or any other exterior senses.[16] On the contrary, she has entered more completely into the interior of her soul; and yet, *within* this interior, she encounters a "suspension" which divorces her from the interior that she has entered. While she remains within God, she is not fully in herself, in that the suspension has taken her to a place "outside" her natural center of *agency*. The *passivity* of the state thus puts her "outside" herself, without returning her to the exterior in the sense of worldly activity.

Teresa therefore complicates the interior/exterior division somewhat at this stage by mixing two different senses of interiority and exteriority: in the first sense, the "interior" means the part of the soul where spiritual activity occurs, in contrast to the "exterior" where worldly joys occur; whereas at the same time, in a second sense, she speaks of being "outside" herself, not meaning outside in the world, but the exact opposite of this, of being more deeply in God and still further removed from the world. Later, though not until the *Moradas*, Teresa clarified the distinction between these two: she characterized the state of suspension as occurring in the superior part of the soul as distinct from the interior;[17] but in the *Vida*, it remains unclear precisely which region of the soul is to be identified with suspension. The point to notice here, however, is that mystical theology increases rather than decreases the basic interior/exterior division in Teresa's view, as the soul is immersed in God and removed further from the exterior world. The total immersion in God signals an even deeper penetration into the interior of the soul than was found in mental prayer.

The Interior and Exterior Faculties and Senses

The fact that the soul is deeply immersed in God in mystical theology and removed from its ordinary senses and means of knowing makes it an especially difficult state to describe, but Teresa says that her aim is "to explain what the soul feels (*siente*) when it is in this divine union."[18] The soul both feels nothing, according to its ordinary senses, and yet receives clear sensations and knowledge of God by some other means. In her first description of mystical theology, Teresa says that these feelings are known in the faculties (*potencias*) of memory, intellect, and will: "the will loves; the memory, it seems to me, is almost lost; . . . the intellect does not work, but it is as though amazed by all it understands."[19] While the memory is "lost," the will and the intellect achieve a positive involvement in union by being drawn into the interior of the soul, though this involvement is very different from the ordinary.

Teresa goes a long way toward developing a formal doctrine of the spiritual senses in the 59(58)th of her *Cuentas de conciencia*, written in 1576 in Seville. It is not clear whether she knew about the tradition of the spiritual senses going back to Origen,[20] but in this *Cuenta* she takes the view that there are two sets of senses in the soul, by which the soul "feels" natural things and supernatural things separately. The distinction is between what the soul feels in the interior and what it feels materially (*material*) in the bodily senses. What the soul feels in the interior in this case are "impulses" which "wound" the soul "as though an arrow is thrust into the heart" and, she goes on, these feelings of pain have no resemblance to bodily (*corporal*) pain.[21] This closely resembles her description of the transverberation in the *Vida*, which will be considered further below,[22] but here the important development to note is that there is an additional set of senses in the soul:

> It appears that just as the soul has exterior senses, it also has other senses through which it seems to want to withdraw within itself, away from the exterior noise.[23]

When the soul "withdraws within itself," which Teresa calls "interior recollection" (*un recogimiento interior*), it uses "other senses" as distinct from the "exterior senses." Through these other senses "within itself," she says, the soul attains "communication with God in solitude." This is to be contrasted with the use of the eyes and bodily senses; indeed, the soul cannot "hear or see or understand anything other" than this communication with God when it occurs, which indicates to her that there must be a separate set of senses providing hearing, seeing, and understanding in a distinct set of operations from those of the bodily senses.[24]

Thus, the soul possesses *two* sets of senses, and not only this: there are two separate epistemological abilities associated with each of these sets. There is the ordinary sensory knowing ability through the exterior senses, and a parallel spiritual knowing ability through the interior senses. Just as the soul comes to feel and know things through the exterior senses, so it attains communication with God through a similar but distinct set of interior senses and operations. These two sets of senses operate exclusively of one another, because they reflect the strong distinction that Teresa sees between the natural and the supernatural levels of prayer. Teresa here defines "interior recollection" as the first supernatural level of prayer, in the sense of "what cannot be acquired by effort or diligence, however much one tries."[25] Hence the importance of the word "other" in speaking of the interior senses: they operate exclusively of the exterior senses, receiving only the communication from God, while the exterior senses have no ability to feel this supernatural communication. The other senses do not therefore refer simply to the nonbodily senses but to a separate set of senses providing a distinctly supernatural kind of knowing. They are interior because they are oriented to *supernatural* objects, while the exterior senses are those oriented to *natural* objects.

Teresa runs into a difficulty of terminology over these interior or other senses. She does *not* mean what John of the Cross means by the interior senses. As we have seen, John calls the imagination and fantasy "interior senses" because they are more interior to the soul than the five exterior bodily senses, but they belong equally to the natural process of knowing. For Teresa, the other senses are interior because they belong to the *supernatural* process of knowing as opposed to the natural: they have no connection with the natural process of knowing—in the same way that, for John, natural knowing and "purely spiritual" knowing have no connection.

Teresa introduces something closer to John's "interior senses" in another context, where she is making distinctions between the three main categories of visions—intellectual visions, imaginative visions, and bodily visions.[26] The need to introduce such senses arises in the context of imaginative visions, because imaginative visions involve the soul in a middle state *between* the exterior senses of natural knowing and the other senses of supernatural knowing. In the *Vida*, she says that imaginative visions require some special senses called the "eyes of the soul," because they are not seen with the bodily eyes but nevertheless have created images and forms.[27] Imaginative visions have a supernatural source, but their form is natural: they bypass the bodily senses, but they are mediated through created images accommodated to the ordinary knowing process in the soul. Consequently, they are sensed not by the bodily senses but by a level of senses between the natural and the wholly supernatural, which Teresa calls the senses "of the soul." She contrasts these senses of the soul with the situation in intellectual visions, where all images and forms are absent, so that neither the bodily senses nor these senses of the soul are required.[28] Thus, Teresa's senses of the soul fulfill a role similar to John's interior senses. John uses the interior senses as a convenient middle term *between* the bodily senses and the spiritual faculties. Similarly, Teresa's senses of the soul are midway between the bodily senses and the other senses.[29] Returning to the *Cuenta*, it is clear that Teresa's other senses are not the same as these senses of the soul. The other senses do not involve mediating elements between the natural and supernatural, but are supernatural to the exclusion of these elements. The fact that Teresa calls them "senses" does not mean that they require created images and forms, but simply that even in the absence of such images and forms the soul is able to "feel" the purely supernatural communications given by God. Her position is summarized in table 5.1 on the following page.

Teresa's attempts to describe the involvement of the faculties (*potencias*) of memory, intellect, and will in relation to the other senses of supernatural knowing cause her considerable difficulty, and she changed her view in the course of her writings. The soul in its ordinary operation uses the "faculties and senses" together,[30] but as the senses of the body and soul are bypassed in purely supernatural knowing, the faculties alone both sense and know the supernatural communication. The problem for Teresa is how to distinguish the operation of these faculties in supernatural knowing from their merely natural operation. She has particular difficulty in regard to the intellect, as she seeks to describe how the soul receives an extraordinary kind of understanding which is distinct from ordinary

Table 5.1. Spiritual Sensation and Knowing According to Teresa of Avila

Account	Type of knowing or vision, and senses used		
	natural	supernatural (with created images)	supernatural (with no created images)
Vida 27–28	bodily vision	imaginative vision	intellectual vision
	bodily eyes	eyes of the soul	neither bodily eyes nor eyes of the soul
Cuenta 59(58)	exterior senses	[*no middle term*]	other senses
John of the Cross	exterior senses	interior senses/ soul itself*	"caverns of feeling"

* John makes an additional distinction not found in Teresa between the interior senses and the soul itself. See n. 29.

understanding of the world and yet occurs in the same faculty. It was not until the *Moradas* that she reached a satisfactory distinction. The *Moradas* will be mainly treated in the next chapter, but it is worth noting three key developments here.

First, Teresa had a frequent experience of being in union in the interior part of her soul while her faculties appeared simultaneously to "wander" in the exterior part, and this raised the problem of the distinction between the interior and exterior activities of the faculties with particular clarity. How could the faculties be both in union and not in union? In the *Vida*, her answer was to say that *some* of the faculties were in union while others remained "outside." She said that the will was drawn into union first, while the memory and intellect remained "free" and concerned with worldly things; then the intellect was also drawn into union with the will, while the memory remained outside with the imagination; and finally, all three faculties entered into a full "union of all the faculties."[31] In the *Moradas*, she changed her view in order to take account of the fact that the *same* faculties often appeared to be simultaneously in union and wandering outside union. She said that *each* of the faculties could be both in union *and* wandering outside, as they each had *two kinds of operation*. She first realized this in relation to the intellect. She made a distinction between the "mind" (*pensamiento*) and the intellect (*entendimiento*), which came as a breakthrough in her understanding.[32] The mind (*pensamiento*) was the exterior part of the intellect which wandered outside union while the interior part, the intellect proper (*entendimiento*), was in union. This explained how not only the intellect but all the faculties could be divided between their interior operation and distinct exterior operations in the world. Similarly, she found that the "imagination" (*imaginación*) worked with the faculties in their exterior activity to produce mental fabrication and devil-deception.[33] Thus, Teresa regarded the lower faculties of mind and imagination as defining the three higher faculties in their exterior operations and distinguishing them from their interior operation in union.

Second, Teresa expanded on the interior operation of the intellect in the *Moradas* by making a distinction between the intellect (*entendimiento*) and what she called the *conocimiento*. As we shall see in greater detail in chap. 6, Teresa named the *conocimiento* as that part of the intellect that entered into union, while the rest of the intellect remained outside.[34]

Third, in the final union, Teresa saw the gap between the interior and exterior operations of the faculties as bridged by "overflow" from the interior to the exterior faculties, and even to the senses and body. She developed this view considerably between the *Vida* and the *Moradas*, and this will be a major part of my analysis in the rest of this chapter. She maintained a strong distinction between the interior operation of the faculties and their exterior operations, but the overflow included the exterior part of the soul in the activity of the interior, at a secondary level.[35]

Teresa develops her view of the use of the faculties in union slowly, as she does not begin with a scholastic faculty psychology already in place, as John does. Rather, she begins simply with the idea that union introduces a division into the soul, particularly in the higher faculties of memory, intellect, and will, between the interior part that enters into union and the exterior part that remains outside. We must now look further at the development of this basic distinction in Teresa's anthropology.

The Division of the Soul: The Nature of the Problem

The change from natural to supernatural prayer is the distinctive feature of mystical theology, as the soul attains a new way of knowing through the other senses. The problem that arose for Teresa was to show how two such different kinds of knowing, which she distinguished according to the interior and exterior parts of the soul, could remain parts of a *single* soul, connected within a single self. In relating these two kinds of knowing to the mutually exclusive interior and exterior parts of the soul, she appeared to have divided the soul into two opposing halves. There was a superficial unity in the soul in that both kinds of knowing used the same components of the human person—the higher faculties of memory, intellect, and will. But there was no room for overlap between the two kinds of operation in Teresa's account: they were mutually exclusive. As a result, the question that I asked of John of the Cross is raised with equal force in Teresa's case:

How can the soul remain a single soul in Teresa's anthropology, when she has introduced such a strong division between the interior and exterior parts?

It is well known that Teresa changed her view of union during the course of her writing career, presenting a markedly different position in the *Vida* from the *Moradas*: the most important change was that she allowed for the involvement of the body in the final union of the *Moradas*, whereas in the *Vida* she associated union with physical paralysis. What is less well known is that this change reflected a profound alteration in her anthropology, which Teresa intended as an answer to the division that I have just described. Teresa's early position that the body was excluded from activity in union came directly from her view that the interior part of the soul where union occurred excluded the body, by definition. As the soul was oriented to God in the interior, it could not be simultaneously oriented to the outside world. Between the *Vida* and the *Moradas*, however, she developed a more subtle view of this interior orientation, to allow for the inclusion of world-directed bodily acts *without* the loss of the exclusive orientation of the soul to God in the interior. This required a change in her understanding of the nature of the interior operations of the soul: she needed a way to account for the ability of the soul to be exclusively oriented to God in union and yet, simultaneously, to be deliberately and consciously directed to activity in the world. The inclusion of the body was a relatively minor part of this larger development in her understanding of the interior. In a revealing passage in the *Moradas*, Teresa alludes to her experience of the "division" in the soul and pinpoints this as the division that she is seeking to overcome. Using the image of Mary and Martha, the traditional types of the contemplative and active lives, she says:

> It seemed to her that there was, in a certain way, a *division in her soul*. . . . She complained of that [interior part of the soul], as Martha complained of Mary, and sometimes pointed out that it was always enjoying that quietude at its own pleasure while leaving her in the middle of so many trials and occupations that she could not keep it company.[36]

This "division in her soul" was an accurate reflection by Teresa on the inherent conflict in her anthropology between the interior and exterior parts of the soul in union. The interior is separated from the exterior by the ontological gap between its divine life of union with God and the merely human "trials and occupations" that beset the exterior in the world.

Significantly, Teresa introduces the figures of Mary and Martha here to refer to the anthropological problem of division in the soul rather than simply to the ideas of contemplation and action—and this is the case in all her major works. In speaking of Mary and Martha, her aim is to show that the two types of operation, relating to the interior and exterior of the soul respectively, are distinct, and *also* to point to the possibility of their reconciliation: as she goes on to say, gradually the world-directed activity of Martha becomes fully consistent with the interior life of Mary, so that there is one unified operation of the soul in union, in which Mary and Martha "work together." She does not remove her strong distinction between the interior and exterior of the soul, but she allows for a cooperative relationship of the whole soul and body to develop *within* the interior region, in which the virtuous activity of Martha becomes *part of* the interior life of Mary. Teresa develops a position in which the body and worldly activity become subsumed under the interior operation of the soul, in one united soul. In her final view of union, the exterior is taken into union and united under the single head of the interior. This was not a sudden development in her anthropology but is to be found occurring gradually between the *Vida* and the *Moradas*. Teresa's own progress and her experience of union must have played a part in determining the stages of this development. It was not just dependent on her increasing theological reflection.[37] The seeds of this breakthrough are already present in the *Vida*, Teresa's earliest work, and it is to this that I shall now turn. After that, I shall examine the significant "Mary and Martha" passages in all four of her major works, to show the gradual development of her anthropology from division in the soul to unification.[38]

Elements of Division and Continuity in Teresa's Anthropology in the *Vida*

Teresa's early understanding of union with God is contradictory, particularly in the *Vida*. By "union with God" she means the same as mystical theology: a brief and transitory change in her way of knowing in which she has the "feeling of the presence" of God, giving her an extraordinary feeling and knowing of God in the interior of the soul by purely supernatural means.[39] On the one hand, the soul becomes increasingly divided between its interior and exterior parts as it progresses in this union, and yet, on the other hand, Teresa wants to assert that this makes it increasingly fit for virtuous works, while *also* maintaining that works are "exterior" to union. She cannot reconcile these two positions: works cannot both be stimulated by progress in the interior of the soul and belong *exclusively* to the soul's exterior operations. The important point, however, is that both positions are present: she is aware of the tension between her views, and from the start is already working toward her later resolution of the problem.

As we saw, in introducing mystical theology in the *Vida*, Teresa regards "suspension" (*suspensión*) as a central feature of union resulting from the shift from "acquired" to "supernatural" prayer. Suspension occurs when the shock of receiving irresistible grace removes the soul from its center of agency, at the same time as "immersing" it in God in the interior. Teresa continued to hold that this shift to supernatural prayer tended to be marked by suspensions even in the *Moradas*, as the initial change in the soul's operation was sudden and extreme. But the difference in her later position was that she no longer saw suspension as an essential part of union. In the *Vida*, the progress in suspension structures the fourfold theory of prayer, which Teresa included in her second draft of the work in chaps. 11–22.[40] In the first stage, of preparation for supernatural prayer, the soul uses practices like the active "recollection" described above, representing scenes from Christ's life to itself by the discursive work of the intellect, in order to quiet the intellect and to inflame the will with love for God.[41] In the second stage, "the prayer of quiet," the prayer shifts from active to passive, as the soul is suspended and becomes unable "to move or stir" for the duration of the prayer, but the memory and intellect remain free to wander.[42] In the third stage, "the sleep of the faculties," the intellect is increasingly drawn into the interior with the will, until in the fourth stage there is a full "suspension of all the faculties" in which "all the external energy [of the soul] is lost."[43] In other words, from the prayer of quiet onward, when the prayer shifts from active to passive, the soul becomes suspended such that the body and one or more of the faculties are "unable to stir," and all three faculties are progressively taken into this suspension until there is no "external energy" left at all. The only exception to this is a brief "Mary and Martha" stage that Teresa describes as occurring in part of the third stage, when the suspension is lifted, although she regards this significant phase as a kind of aberration in the *Vida*.

Why does suspension persist and increase throughout the stages of union in the *Vida*? We must presume that Teresa's experience was behind this view, as she clearly regarded "raptures" and other "elevations," "flights of the spirit," and "transports" as the highest kind of union at this time. She says that she regards rapture as the highest kind of union because it produces "stronger effects than union" and "many other phenomena" (not in contrast with union, but showing that it is a higher kind of union than the kinds she has just described).[44] After introducing the fourth and highest stage of prayer in chap. 18, she follows it with a section on raptures in chap. 20, and further descriptions are to be found through the remainder of the book. Most famously, she describes her "transverberation" experience, which became the exemplar of her view of union:[45] she had a vision of an angel plunging a golden dart into her heart and felt him "carrying off with him the deepest part of me"; this "carrying off" was a painful suspension, in which the body "did not fail to share" some of the "sweetness" of the experience, but was nevertheless "paralyzed" and "unable to stir."[46] The ability of the body to participate in union would become her means of showing in later works how the stage of suspensions could be surpassed as the body became reconnected to the life of the interior of the soul in union. But in the *Vida*, suspension is to the fore and bodily participation is marginal. In fact, the transverberation is characterized by Teresa as an "impulse" rather than a rapture: in impulses, the body participates in the supernatural feeling in the soul, but in raptures, which are superior, the soul ascends "far above itself and all creatures," so that there is no bodily participation at all.[47] Rapture is a state in which "the soul is not in itself, but on the roof or housetop of itself and of all created things because it seems to me to be above even the very superior part of the soul."[48] As the soul is "far above itself and all creatures" there is no possibility of engaging in virtuous works while the rapture is taking place, and even afterward there is no strength left in the body, and the faculties may remain absorbed for several days.[49] Indeed, afterward she feels only antipathy for her earthly life and companions and a "longing to die" in order to see God.[50] Although rapture itself is short and should lead to progress in virtue,[51] her soul is clearly disabled by it. Further, she says that rapture "is what my soul is now always experiencing" and that it is her aim for it to last longer and longer, because like conversation with a saintly companion, it is not "as beneficial when it lasts only a day as when it lasts many."[52] Thus, her final position in the *Vida* is to emphasize suspension at the expense of virtuous works and involvement in the world, culminating in her position that rapture is the highest kind of union.

Yet it is clear that Teresa was not happy with this position, even in the course of writing the *Vida*, and realized that it presented a false dichotomy between union, on the one hand, and virtuous works, involvement in the world, and the life of the body, on the other hand. Hence in her ordering of the added section in chaps. 11–22, she included a chapter on the continuing importance of the humanity of Christ in prayer and put this after her treatment of rapture as a corrective to the anti-incarnational tendencies in her position. In the penultimate chapter, chap. 21, she refers to the soul's "poorly harmonized life" in being divided between raptures and the converse of bodily needs such as sleeping and eating;[53] she feels this as a "continual martyrdom." She excuses this internal conflict of desires as a "captivity that we endure because of our bodies,"[54] and she points to the "royal prophet" and other great persons in the desert who also felt such an "extreme sense of solitude":[55] like them, she has a special calling to this state, as shown by the words that she heard in her first rapture, "No longer do I want you to converse with men but with angels."[56] But in chap. 22, she opens up a different line of argument, to counter the implied suggestion that humanity itself is excluded from union. She makes a distinction between two kinds of attachment to corporeal things. When the soul reaches the most advanced stages of prayer, though not before, she says that it should turn from creatures to God, but it should not turn from the humanity of Christ, as "the most sacred humanity of Christ must not be counted in balance with other corporeal things."[57] Attachment to the humanity of Christ is of a different order from attachment to other corporeal things, and this is the point of continuity in the soul between its interior and its corporeal activity. She contrasts her position with the advice given in "some books written on prayer" that one should rid oneself increasingly of all corporeal things including the humanity of Christ.[58] This would make it wrong to go on using images of Christ as an aid to the higher levels of prayer, whereas she says, "I wanted to keep ever before my eyes a painting or image of him."[59] The humanity of Christ is after all the goal of our own humanity, which we cannot exceed this side of death. Through the humanity of Christ the soul in rapture is not "left floating in the air"; rather, "it is an important thing that while we are living and are human we have human support," as "we are not angels but we have a body."[60] Teresa is suggesting that by focusing on Christ's humanity, rapture is given the support necessary to keep our human nature intact while we enter briefly into "heaven" in union. It is no surprise that the humanity of Christ is the means to this end, as Christ contained the union of human and divine natures in one supposit, or person, that is the meeting point of heaven and earth for us. Thus, using the humanity of Christ is the way to appropriate the union of Christ's human and divine natures in our own practice of prayer.

But Teresa does not expand on these ideas in the *Vida* and leaves them at the level of inference: the humanity of Christ is the key to sustaining our own humanity in rapture, but it is not fully clear how this works, and she does not yet extend this to her view that "Mary and Martha" can "work together." She continues to put the stage of Martha *before* that of Mary at this point, saying that the soul must avoid "wanting to be Mary before having worked with Martha"—implying that when Mary is reached, the stage of Martha is left behind.[61] Nevertheless, it is this incarnational move in the *Vida* emphasizing the continuing role of the humanity of Christ in the higher levels of prayer that later filters through to her anthropology and permits her to unite the soul and bring the roles of Mary and Martha together in union.

Overcoming the Division in the Soul:
The "Mary and Martha" Passages in the *Vida*,
the *Camino de perfección*, and the *Meditaciones sobre los Cantares*

The Mary and Martha image serves the purpose for Teresa of showing how *two* types of operation associated with two distinct parts of the soul can become unified in *one* soul while retaining their distinction. She uses Mary and Martha in their contemplative and active roles to describe the different activities of the interior and exterior parts of the soul respectively. Increasingly, through her reflections on the humanity of Christ, she became aware that what she was dealing with was the christological problem of the hypostatic union of divine and human natures.[62] But she used the roles of Mary and Martha as a more familiar image than the classical and scholastic terms commonly used in Christology, of which she had little knowledge and which, in any case, she could not discuss without attracting unwanted attention. In the following, these correlations should be borne in mind:

Table 5.2. The Two Sides of Teresa of Avila's Division in the Soul

Correlation with Mary and Martha	Mary	Martha
	interior part of soul	exterior part of soul
Increasing christological reference	divine nature	human nature
	God	soul

As we saw, in the *Vida*, Teresa introduces the possibility of Mary and Martha working together simultaneously for the first time in the third stage of prayer, the "sleep of the faculties." She says that the soul can find itself "rejoicing in that holy idleness of Mary" at the same time as being "Martha in such a way that it is as though engaged in both the active and contemplative life together."[63] But she denies that this is a full union: she says that the soul "isn't master of itself completely," as "the best part of the soul is somewhere else," namely, in the interior union, while the ability to do works is a function of the part of the soul that remains outside this union.[64] The soul is divided between the "will," which is held in union in the interior of the soul, and the "intellect" and "imagination," which are outside this interior, being "free" to engage in "business affairs" and "works of charity."[65] Because the faculties are divided in this analysis, Teresa concludes that this is a transitory stage and a kind of aberration on the journey to full union. Temporarily, the soul does not suffer from suspension, which permits the uniting of Mary and Martha, but the interior/exterior division in the soul remains. Soon after, and within this same stage of prayer, the intellect is also drawn into the union with the will, leaving the soul powerless and unable to engage in further activity.[66] Thus, Teresa appears to make a breakthrough in combining the roles of Mary and Martha, but in the same breath she denies that this is a genuine possibility for union. Nevertheless, she has opened up a possibility that she develops further in later works.

The *Camino de perfección* was written only about a year after the *Vida* was completed and was intended to replace it,[67] so it is not surprising that Teresa's position on Mary and Martha has developed little over the *Vida*. As in the *Vida*, the active and contemplative lives join together only briefly, and there remains a division in the soul between the will, which takes the part of Mary, and "the other two faculties," which "serve in the work of Martha."[68] But though Teresa's language of Mary and Martha has not advanced on the *Vida*, in the background she is clearly progressing on the issue of how the soul can combine heavenly or interior activity with earthly/corporeal activity in union. Unlike in the *Vida*, where her emphasis was on her individual experience in relation to God, she now speaks as the prioress of St. Joseph's with the care of a community: there is more concern for how communal life becomes part of union with God. For instance humility, which was given a high value in the *Vida* as the "groundwork of prayer," is now also regarded as the foundational ethic in the community: it is the means for holding communal relationships in balance with a single-minded orientation to God.[69] The community, as a united human community and not just as a group of individuals, becomes the place where heaven is found on earth.[70]

Teresa understands the connection between these two dimensions, the heavenly and the earthly, as being based, first, on the imitation of Jesus. Here she develops the christological relation between the interior and exterior dimensions. Contemplatives do not shun suffering for others but are more ready to give than to receive, in imitation of the love of Jesus; their "standard" is the "flag of humility," the cross of Christ, which they "hold high" in battle.[71] Second, in her exposition of the Lord's prayer (chaps. 27–42), she uses a trinitarian argument for the way in which the soul participates in the life of Christ: in this prayer the soul presents the Son to the Father and receives the Son from the Father in return, becoming Christ in itself. In the first stage of "recollection" the soul offers the Son to the Father by representing Christ in scenes from his Passion,[72] while in the blessed sacrament the Father gives Jesus to us so that he "doesn't make any difference between himself and us": at this point Christ's presence is not merely pictured, but "he is in our house," and this "is happening now and is entirely true."[73] Thus, the soul is joined to the Father in heaven and also joins Christ on earth. Teresa says that at this time, during communion and immediately afterwards, the highest stages of union are attained.[74] But still she associates union with rapture, and she continues to hold that "nothing will occupy" the soul in this state.[75] She cannot therefore work out a way of combining virtuous works with union *simultaneously*: works are something we do "in return for such great favors," when the raptures have ceased.[76] Nevertheless, in comparison with her treatment in the *Vida*, she is more successful in showing how heaven and earth intersect. The Almighty "becomes one with our lowliness, transforms us into himself, and effects a union of the Creator with the creature."[77] There is an intimation of Teresa's later descriptions of spiritual marriage at this stage: the Lord "begins to commune with the soul in so intimate a friendship that he not only gives it back its own will but gives it his. . . . The Lord takes joy in putting the soul in command."[78] The soul is now beginning to regain its *agency* in the highest stage of union, and this points directly to the possibility of an active union and to overcoming the division in the soul.

Teresa's breakthrough comes in her *Meditaciones sobre los Cantares*, written at some point between 1566 and 1575, probably in two drafts.[79] She begins by noting that in the words from the Song, "let him kiss me with the kiss of his mouth," the Bride asks for the union of "two natures" that is found in Christ, "for that union so great that God became man, for that friendship that he effected with the human race." But she says that she does not intend to dwell on this, "because my intention is to speak about what I think can be beneficial to us who engage in prayer."[80] This does not mean that she intends to avoid the problem of Christ's two natures, but rather that she will tackle it under a different guise. She turns immediately to the "war" in the soul between two types of "peace" belonging to the world and to God—a war that reflects the division between the exterior and the interior of the soul. She makes a new suggestion, that in the highest stage of peace the soul is able to "venture out to war against all worldly kinds of peace, while remaining in itself completely secure and tranquil."[81] There need be no loss of the interior state of union when the soul becomes involved, simultaneously, in worldly activity: this is the crucial change over her previous position. How can she now reconcile these interior and exterior activities? Using the imagery of marriage from the Song, Teresa describes the active works produced by the soul in union as the "offspring" of a fruitful marriage. The soul is like a "peasant girl" who marries the "king," and their children have "royal blood": these are the "heroic deeds" produced cooperatively by God and the soul out of union.[82] The pieces in Teresa's final position on union are therefore now in place: first, there is a simultaneous joining of action and contemplation, in that world-directed activity does not remove the soul from its interior peace; and second, the actions produced from this union belong properly to union, as they have "royal blood"—they are produced by God and the soul together, and not by the soul alone or by some part of the soul "outside" the union.

The underlying change here is in Teresa's understanding of the categories of interior and exterior in union, as is seen in her treatment of Mary and Martha. She says that "in the active—and seemingly exterior—work the soul is working interiorly": "active works rise from this interior root."[83] Mary and Martha remain distinct but now share a common unified activity: the works of Martha are only "*seemingly* exterior"—they involve the exterior parts of the soul, the body and the faculties directed to the body, but their activity now belongs to the interior of the soul. Before, Teresa had insisted that active works were confined to the exterior of the soul, whereas now she allows that they can be produced in the soul out of the "interior root." Thus, the faculties need not be divided between those in the interior and those which remain "on the outside" in order to combine the roles of Mary and Martha, as in her earlier position, but can be in union in the interior *and* directed to active works. The distinction is not entirely removed, however: Mary and Martha remain two in the sense that there are *two* partners in the marriage, but they share *one* single activity. This, she implies, is a christological solution, in which the interior and exterior parts of the soul are united in a single activity, in a manner analogous to the divine and human natures in Christ. But this christological aspect of her argument does not become explicit until the *Moradas*. Here we see Teresa's solution to the long-running division in the soul in her view of union: there is now interiority *without* suspension, as works spring wholly from the "interior root." The orientation of the faculties to God in the interior does not exclude their simultaneous activity in the world and the involvement of the body. The two sides of the correlations noted above are now united in a middle term, as shown in the table:

**Table 5.3. The Solution to the Division in the Soul
in the *Meditaciones sobre los Cantares***

Mary	work together	Martha
interior part of soul	share same "root"	exterior part of soul
divine nature	joined in Christ	human nature
God	marriage and offspring	soul

What then is the relation between this new kind of union and the old kind? The *Meditaciones* also contain Teresa's emerging view of the relationship between her former view and her new view of union. She does not abandon her old view: she regards the state of rapture as a valid part of union but inferior to the new union. She reiterates her old theory of union as characterized by suspension in describing the prayer of quiet in chaps. 4–6: the faculties become "totally engulfed" in divinity so that the soul "would not want to stir or speak or look lest the blessing go away."[84]

But then she confronts the problem inherent in this view of union head on: she asks, if the soul "is so outside itself and so absorbed that it can do nothing with the faculties, how can it merit?"[85] The problem of merit points to the underlying problem in her old view: if there is a suspension, how can the soul be the genuine subject of the union, and how can it attain merit if it is not active in works? Teresa's answer is to hierarchialize the two types of union. She does not deny that rapture is a beneficial state—it is a time when God refines the soul like "gold he has prepared and tested so as to see how many carats the soul's love is," and when God "sets love in order" in the soul[86]—but this is a transitory phase which is superseded in the new union. The new union is "another good so as to escape from the one that is so huge": rapture is "so huge" (*tan grandísimo*) in that it causes the soul to suffer by operating "with such force that it rules over all the powers of the natural subject,"[87] whereas in the new union the soul is purified and the "suffering doesn't consume it and waste it, as would this suspension, if very frequent, of the faculties in contemplation."[88] Thus, rapture loses its position as the highest stage of union, and all the states involving suspension become mere preliminaries to the highest union.

It is typical of Teresa's approach to allow that both kinds of union are compatible: "union" was always a flexible term for her, meaning a number of different states, and now the new union is simply added to these as the highest state. But there is still a considerable conflict between the two kinds of union. The progression in degrees of suspension has been interrupted and reversed. The new kind of union involves a rejection of raptures in favor of active works. Teresa speaks of this climb-down from raptures as involving the experience of pain: it is a "cross," because it requires souls to give up their special "delight and satisfaction" in rapture in favor of working for "the benefit of their neighbor, [and] nothing else."[89] These souls are now "weaned" from the divine breasts of rapture so that they can go out in active works for the benefit of others.[90] But by speaking of weaning Teresa neatly includes not only the change in the soul's state but also the idea of progress: weaning indicates progress in maturity, as the suffering of leaving rapture behind does not remove the benefit that was gained but allows the soul to *build* on that stage. When the soul is weaned, the nourishment of the "milk" of the old union becomes a "gain" that can be shared with others—now the soul's "gain will not just be for herself" but also for others.[91]

The Final Unity of the Soul
in the *Moradas del castillo interior*

In the *Moradas del castillo interior*, written in 1577, maybe as little as two years after the final draft of the *Meditaciones*, Teresa formalizes her new theory of union using the whole structure of the work. The *Moradas* will be the main subject of chap. 6, but here it is worth noting her final developments in the arguments that we have been considering. The itinerary to union is now reduced to a journey from division in the soul to unity, from the exterior part to the interior part, until finally union occurs in the undivided center of the soul.[92] The focus of the mystical itinerary is on the anthropological issue of overcoming the "division in the soul" inherent in Teresa's old view of union, to reach the goal of spiritual marriage in the center of the soul. The idea of the center of the soul reflects the marriage relationship of the soul with God described in the *Meditaciones*: the two partners are united, not in a simple unity, but in the shared *activity* of their love. All the correlations that we have seen in the *Meditaciones* are to be found in this center: Mary and Martha "join together," the interior and exterior parts of the soul are united in a single "root," and the soul joins in an explicitly christological union of natures.

The mechanism by which works are produced out of union is considerably developed over the *Meditaciones*. Teresa no longer uses the image of works as the offspring of the spiritual marriage but sees them as the immediate product of "loving expressions" between the soul and God.[93] Spiritual marriage is described as the moment in which Christ tells the soul, in his humanity, that it is now "time that she consider as her own what belonged to him and that he would take care of what was hers."[94] The soul then "understands clearly" that it is has entered into union with God, and from the "loving expressions" between itself and Christ, "secret aspirations" proceed to the rest of the soul, including the body: "streams of milk" flow from the "divine breasts . . . bringing comfort to all the people of the castle."[95] This is not simply the overflow of some of the "sweetness" of a transitory union to the body, as in the old kind of union—as in the transverberation, for instance, described above—but an overflow in which the soul's self-understanding of its mutuality with Christ enables it to *direct* its actions in deliberate works of service.[96] The words of mutual self-surrender that Christ spoke to the soul lead her to want to do active works which will "help the Crucified," and she is given the ability to do them using the motivation of the "loving expressions" produced in union, which extend to the whole soul and body.[97] Here, Mary and Martha join together in the sense that "messages" are sent "from the interior center to the people at the top of the castle and to the dwelling places outside the center," that is, to the "faculties, senses, and all the corporeal" part, so that they cannot be idle, giving the soul the "strength to serve."[98] As a consequence, the purpose of spiritual marriage is fulfilled, which is "the birth always of good works, good works."[99] Teresa concludes that the soul's "life is now Christ."[100]

Teresa uses the image of the soul as a "castle" with many "dwelling places" (*moradas*), in which union takes place in the "bridal chamber" at the center.[101] This image was based on some previous images she had used. In the *Vida* she described the soul as "a brightly polished mirror" with Christ in the "center," and this mirror was also "engraved upon the Lord himself by means of a very loving communication" in union;[102] and in the *Camino* she saw the soul as "an extremely rich palace" in which the "mighty king" dwells, whose throne is our "heart."[103] The most important feature of the center of the soul in the *Moradas* is the idea taken from the *Vida* that in looking at ourselves in the mirror of union, we see ourselves as Christ. Teresa understands spiritual marriage as enabling the soul to have the self-understanding of Christ, seeing his union of natures in its own union with God. We see our image in God at the same time as seeing "ourselves placed inside his greatness."[104] There is clarity or *awareness* of the relationship between the soul and God where before the relationship itself was not known.[105] The loving expressions of the spiritual marriage then flow from this consciously appropriated "company" that the soul is enjoying in its interior center: in this "wine cellar" the soul drinks the wine of God's company, which "gives it much greater strength than ever," just as "in the company of saints we become saints."[106] This company enables the soul to take hold of its own agency, first, by having the self-understanding of Christ, and second, by mediating the loving expressions in the interior of the soul to the exterior part, so that it can engage in active works of service.

Teresa shows that the awareness that the soul has of both God and itself in union is an explicitly *trinitarian* awareness. Through Christ, the soul has the same relationship to the Father as the Son to the Father in the Trinity. She describes an intellectual vision of the Trinity in the highest state of union in the *Moradas*. Unlike in the old union, this intellectual vision neither causes suspension nor is transitory: the actual vision of the persons passes, but the mutuality of the inner-trinitarian relations remains within the soul, and this characterizes the full spiritual marriage.[107] Teresa follows her description of the intellectual vision with the image from the Gospel of Jesus appearing to the disciples after the resurrection in the upper room: God enters the "center of the soul without going through any door, as he entered the place where his disciples were when he said, *pax vobis*."[108] There is no longer any need for God to break in to the soul as God did in the old union, as God is already in the soul as in a mirror, such that when it looks at God in union it also sees itself. The absence of a "door" means that human nature no longer hinders the soul: the full humanity of the soul has been accommodated to union, so that there is a very deep "peace" in the soul which the sufferings encountered in our human nature cannot reach.[109] Thus, the soul is able to enjoy the same trinitarian relationship with God that the Son has with the Father: Teresa quotes the famous trinitarian text for union, that the soul is one with the Father just as Christ is in the Father and the Father is in him (Jn. 17:21).[110] Most importantly, through this inner trinitarian mutuality the soul attains an intellectual clarity of God's will, as we shall see more fully in chap. 6.

Teresa achieves a more effective synthesis between the old union and the new union in the *Moradas* than in the *Meditaciones*. The new union follows after the old union, as in the itinerary of the *Meditaciones*, but she subjects both kinds of union to the same criterion and goal. All the experiences of suspension and rapture are assessed in relation to the center of the soul from start of the *Moradas*. First, she downgrades the old union further than in the *Meditaciones*: she refers to raptures as a "delightful union" in contrast with the new, "true union,"[111] no longer regarding them as the weaning of the soul but as a purely gratuitous stage that we "needn't care about," as our first attention should always be to "being resigned to God's will."[112] Raptures, however, are genuine unions in the sense of the "betrothal" (*el desposorio*) or a "meeting" (*una vista*) that precedes full marriage: brief meetings characterize this stage, in which the soul sees God for the first time, which "greatly helps one to die."[113] This is not full union, but it is a glimpse of union, and the suffering given is in order "to purify the soul" for the subsequent marriage.[114] Second, Teresa extends her view, first stated in the *Vida*, that raptures occur in the superior part of the soul.[115] She brings out the distinction between this superior part and the interior of the soul: the true union is contrasted with suspensions as occurring in the deep interior or center of the soul as opposed to the superior part.[116] The states of union are now judged *only* for their effects in the deep interior of the soul, so that suspensions are no longer regarded as an essential part of union, but only as a side-effect, and one which is superseded in the higher unions. Third, it is here that Teresa arrives at her distinction between the mind (*pensamiento*) and the intellect (*entendimiento*) that we saw above, by which she explains how the faculties can simultaneously be in union and wander outside union, and how they can have both interior and exterior kinds of operation.[117]

Let us now summarize the argument of this chapter. Teresa introduces a problematic distinction into her anthropology between those operations of the soul associated with the "purely supernatural" state of union or mystical theology and those belonging to the soul's merely natural operations. The intense difference between union and the ordinary state of the soul becomes fixed in her anthropology in terms of the interior and exterior parts of the soul. She insists that the two parts of the soul are distinct, to reflect their mutually exclusive objects of God and the world. But she succeeds in working out a solution to this "division in her soul" without compromising the strength of her distinction. She uses the model of Mary and Martha to show how the two parts of the soul can work together, and develops an idea of distinction-within-unity between the soul and God based on the marriage relationship of the Song. She brings these elements together in her final view of the center of the soul in the *Moradas*, which makes explicit that this is a christological union of natures. In the next chapter, I shall examine Teresa's idea of the center of the soul more closely, considering particularly her christological and trinitarian arguments for the type of knowing of God attained in union.

CHAPTER SIX

The Dynamism and Unity of the Soul According to Teresa of Avila

IN THE *MORADAS DEL CASTILLO INTERIOR*, Teresa of Avila made a new development in her anthropology, which was to identify what she called the "center of the soul" as the goal of mystical transformation. As in John of the Cross, the idea of the center of the soul in Teresa's thought provides us with the best answer to the question at the heart of this book, which is how the extraordinary life of mystical union can be combined in a single soul with ordinary knowing and action. In chap. 5, some of the structural solutions to the "division in the soul" that Teresa developed in the course of her writings were considered. Here, I turn to the *dynamism* of the center of the soul as the crucial unifying force in the soul, and to Teresa's understanding of the type of knowledge of God that is possible in this center. The center of the soul is the attainment of the dynamic structure of the Trinity, in the mutual exchange between God and the soul of the spiritual marriage. Further, it is the conforming of the rest of the soul to this trinitarian structure, enabling the whole soul to work together in performing good works in accordance with the divine will. In the *Moradas*, Teresa provides her only treatment of the formation of this center in the soul and sustains this focus on the center throughout the stages of transformation, including the early stages before mystical theology intervenes. She reaches a greater unity in her anthropology by considering closely the transition from the natural states of the soul to the supernatural and by discussing the mystical transformation of the cognitive faculties *within* this understanding of unity rather than as a conflicting, separate development.[1]

Teresa of Avila's Understanding of "Experience"

Teresa's understanding of mystical experience is based on her wider view of experience in general, and it is worth briefly examining how she uses this term. Like John, Teresa makes a distinction between the terms for sensation or feeling (*sentimiento, sentir,* and the five senses) and experience (*espiriencia, esperimentar*). By experience she does not mean sensations or emotions but a field of knowledge, which in mystical union is the field of supernatural or immediate knowledge of God. For instance, she says that her confessor García de Toledo "has had much experience in spiritual things in a short time,"[2] referring to his advancement in the spiritual life rather than to any particular spiritual sensations or feelings that he may have had. Teresa's earliest uses of "experience" in her writings concern spiritual directors and confessors, whom she says must "have experience" (*tener espiriencia*) or "be experienced" (*haber/ser esperimentado*) in spiritual things above all else, if they are not to be of danger to their charges.[3] By this experience she means a developed knowledge or familiarity with the field of prayer. She contrasts this with the learning that comes from books: "I pity those who begin [prayer] solely with books because it is strange how different what one understands is from what one afterward sees through experience."[4] Experience is the skill brought by one who knows not just something *about* the object under view but how to orient and position oneself in *relation* to this object in order to grasp it accurately. Teresa's sense of experience is that of "being experienced in" something or "having experience of" something, as opposed to the more commonly used modern sense of the sensory apprehension of an object.[5]

In addition to this broad sense of experience, Teresa refers to the more specific levels or states of development by which experience is gradually transformed from the natural way of knowing to the mystical way of knowing God. For instance, she says that her experience of "spiritual delights" (*gustos*), the first mystical state in the *Moradas*, is "great" (*la espiriencia es mucha*), explaining that her ability for knowing has been "expanded" in relation to the divine object encountered, enabling her to know God in a new way.[6] Here, experience is ranked according to different levels of "expansion" of the soul as the soul comes to know God mystically.[7]

In the last of her *Cuentas*, Teresa describes the final state of understanding that is attained by the soul at its most highly developed level of experience. She says, "this presence of the three persons is so impossible to doubt that it seems what St. John says is experienced (*se esperimenta*), that they will make their abode in the soul."[8] Here the soul's experience is its possession of the three persons of the Trinity within the soul, such that it can differentiate and know the persons in its mutual indwelling with God in the soul. This represents a profound change from the level of experience with which it began: the soul does not know the persons as an object like other objects in the world but knows them within itself, as part of its own self-understanding. This indicates that for Teresa "experience" is a dynamic term which not only has a number of stages of development but can include the changing relationship between subject and object implied in the process of mystical transformation, reaching the intersubjective relationship between the soul and God in the final union.

In summary, experience has three aspects to its meaning according to Teresa, which closely parallel those aspects of John's understanding of the term. First, experience refers not to apprehensions or sensations, which she calls feelings, but to the developed, habitual ability by which we *know* such feelings. Second, experience is, at root, a dynamic relational ability, a self-other relation, which is expanded by mystical transformation, such that we attain a new ability for knowing God in union. Teresa sets out the stages of transformation according to the various levels or states of expansion to which experience is developed. Third, experience has its ultimate goal in an inner-trinitarian, intersubjective union with God. Here experience is as much God's self-experience in the Trinity as our own experience of God: experience is the human dynamic and structure of knowing, but it is now constituted within God's own dynamic structure of the Trinity. Thus, experience is the focus of Teresa's attention in the *Moradas*, beginning with our natural state in the image of God, and being expanded through mystical transformation to the final state of the center of the soul.

The Process of Mystical Transformation: The Image of God in the Soul

Teresa makes a new departure in the *Moradas* by beginning with the image of God in the soul in order to point toward the goal of transformation at the center of the soul. Her aim is to identify at the start a point in the soul which will provide a perspective from which her anthropology and the process of transformation can be seen as a unity with a single goal. It is a unifying *perspective* that she seeks, as opposed to finding something in the soul that is already in union, either explicitly or implicitly. She does not begin with the contrast between the pleasures of the world and the spirit or the division between the natural and supernatural operations of the soul, as in previous works, but rather first sets out the unifying perspective of the creation of the soul in the image and likeness (*imagen y semejanza*) of God.[9] Teresa understands this image in the Augustinian tradition of the point of closest contact in the soul to God, as is clear from the fact that she regards it as a forebear of the center or middle of the soul where the "very secret exchanges between God and the soul take place" in union.[10] The difference between the image and the center is that the image is a reflection of God's likeness in the soul which is present from creation, whereas the center is the *goal* of this likeness when it is restored from the damage of sin *and* raised above the level of nature, specifically in mystical union. Thus, the image and the center are the same in that they both refer to the point of highest contact and likeness to God in the soul, yet different in that this point of contact with God, and the relation of the rest of the soul to this point, changes as transformation proceeds. The soul becomes more like God and is raised above nature to the level of God, so that a far greater likeness to God is found in the center than in the natural image. Yet in asserting the similarity between the image and the center at the outset, Teresa signals that continuity will be placed ahead of discontinuity in her anthropology in the *Moradas*—not denying the powerfully divisive effects of union when it arrives, or the separation between nature and supernature, but showing that the *possibility* of both union with God and unity in the soul is present from creation in the image of God.

The initial difficulty with this starting point is that the image of God is not evident in the soul from the start, given our fallen state, but we require God to help us find it. Teresa says that the effect of sin is to place a "black cloth" over the soul, which obscures the light from the "shining sun that is in the center of the soul."[11] Furthermore, the soul cannot see the future importance of this image in its relation to the center, because "our intellects, however keen, can hardly comprehend" the "marvellous capacity" of the soul, given the great difference "between the Creator and his creature."[12] The combined effect of these two restrictions, of sin and nature respectively, is that at this stage "we don't understand ourselves or know who we are."[13] In the first instance, therefore, Teresa can only appeal to the authority of scripture for the presence of the image of God in the soul: God "himself *says* that he created us in his own image and likeness," she says.[14] Second, she appeals to her own understanding: "I know there were certain things I had not understood as I have understood them now," she says, referring to the development of her understanding of union, which has grown with her experience since the time of the *Vida*.[15] Like John of the Cross, she regards the starting point of transformation as understandable only from the perspective of union—as John says, "the latter parts will explain the former"[16]—and this is why she fixes on the image of God: not because it is plain to see or the obvious place to start but because from the perspective of union she can see that it is the forebear of the center of the soul. Because of sin and nature, the beginner, unaided, is unable to discern the image of God or to know that it is the place to begin transformation. It can only be recognized with the benefit of hindsight.

The beginner starts with the image of God on the basis of faith, and not only is faith required, but Teresa says that it must be a *living* faith in order to gain what she calls self-knowledge. Here Teresa introduces the two elements that she will develop throughout the remainder of the *Moradas*: first, the *dynamic* element of relationship with God, in which the soul is growing in each successive stage of transformation, and second, the *cognitive* element of knowledge of God, which is similarly growing, in relation to knowledge of self. The first stage or "dwelling place" of the *Moradas* is the "room of self-knowledge" (*el propio conocimiento*).[17] This is acquired by the *active* practice of prayer, rather than by simple assent to the proposition that the soul is created in the image of God. If we are involved in the vanities of the world rather than in prayer, Teresa says, "our faith is so dead that we desire what we see rather than what faith tells us."[18] To fail to practice prayer is to have a "dead" faith, "like people with paralyzed or crippled bodies"—like the man who waited at the side of the pool for thirty years before Jesus healed him. Changing the image, she adds, "if these souls do not strive to understand and cure their great misery, they will be turned into statues of salt."[19] Teresa likens the sinful state of the soul to being static and failing to move, so that we are "tied down" to our own misery. Prayer, on the contrary, is an activity, the activity of faith: we "ponder the grandeur of the majesty of God" and come to self-knowledge by active self-reflection in exploring our relation to God, "dealing in turn now with self and now with God."[20] Teresa says that she made this first step of self-knowledge through receiving a "mirror for humility" in a favor from God: in this mirror she saw that all her good deeds had their "principle" or "fount" not in herself but in God, which made her realize her complete dependence on God.[21] Self-knowledge is therefore first of all to realize our "lowliness" in comparison with God's "grandeur."[22] But there is a crucial difference between this sense of lowliness and the misery produced by pure introspection without God. The activity of prayer *relates* the soul to its source, the fount where it is "planted" in God, and this gives it a great positive sense of its "capacity" for God, in spite of the simultaneous feeling of its lowliness.[23] This leads Teresa to say that the soul has a "magnificent beauty" and "marvelous capacity": not because of the soul alone but because of its relationship to God.[24] She says, "the things of the soul must always be considered as plentiful, spacious, and large; to do so is not an exaggeration. The soul is capable of much more than we can imagine."[25] The capacity of the soul *looks forward* to what it is capable of in its relationship with God in union: it is capable of whatever God chooses, because God is its source, and it therefore has a potential limited not by its own nature but extending as far as God's greatness. This is what it is to see the image of God within: the principle and fount of the soul is found in God, so that it knows its dependence on God at the same time as it sees its vast capacity for likeness to God.

Teresa differentiates the first three "dwelling places," which are the preparatory or premystical stages, according to the level of activity with which the soul practices its faith in prayer. The first dwelling place is concerned with wrenching the soul away from its "absorption" in the world as it first enters into an active relationship with God.[26] Teresa sees this activity in terms of "walking through" the soul, instigating movement where before there was stagnation.[27] Even once the soul has begun the movement by entering into the first room of self-knowledge, devils seek to "fight off souls when they try to go from one room to another."[28] Thus, a "war" (*guerra*) develops between two contrary movements in the soul: the activity of faith, on the one hand, and the deadening activity of devils and our attachment to the world and sin, on the other hand.[29] At no stage, including the first stage, does the soul have the strength to defend itself in this war without help from God.[30] The grace that the soul receives here is remedial, to restore it to its prelapsarian state of nature—it is given because "here . . . the vassals of the soul (which are the senses and faculties) do not have the strength God gave human nature in the beginning"—rather than the grace which raises the soul *above* nature to the supernatural level in the mystical stages.[31]

In the second dwelling place, the activity of faith is greater and the soul makes more "effort" (*trabajo*). "The intellect is more alive and the faculties more skilled," Teresa says.[32] The primary difference from the first dwelling place is that the soul now fights with the "cross."[33] The activity of the soul becomes explicitly christocentric, and this becomes a major part of Teresa's argument for the continuity between these first stages and the later, mystical stages of transformation in the *Moradas*. A further benefit is that the soul finds peace within. By "peace" she does not mean the end of activity, but rather that the soul now directs its activity more effectively to goals beyond itself, to God in prayer and to external works of charity, rather than to its own internal warfare with the world and the devil, as it is more fully restored from sin and is less absorbed in the world.[34] In the third dwelling place, there is still greater activity in these two respects, prayer and works of charity.[35] But the main change is that the soul has now achieved "nakedness and detachment" (*desnudez y dejamiento*) and is "stripped" (*desnuda*) of its own will.[36] The soul has fully surrendered its will to God, and this gives it peace in the sense of "freedom of spirit."[37] It is no longer circumspect in its activity but abandons itself to God.[38] Taking courage from the example of those who are "free from illusion about the things of this world," it is "made bold to fly."[39] "Flight" is what will happen in the next, mystical stage, and in this stage the soul has been stripped of its worldly attachments so that it is free and prepared to fly in mystical union.

In setting up these first three stages of transformation, Teresa has in mind the extreme discontinuity that is about to be introduced into the soul in mystical union, in the difference between the natural and the supernatural activities of the soul. She therefore structures the soul's activity in these stages with a view to union, pointing to certain small ways in which the soul can prepare for its later supernatural operation, even though it cannot anticipate what the supernatural state will be like. Teresa's treatment in the *Moradas* is unique in making four such connections between the preparatory stages and union. She summarizes the effect of these four preparatory acts by saying that the soul "disposes" itself for union in the sense that wax is prepared to receive the impress of a seal by being "softened."[40] The importance of these connections is that they prepare for the unifying of the interior and exterior operations within the soul in the later stages of transformation.

First, the dynamic or active nature of prayer in the early stages, as against the stagnation of absorption in the world, distantly anticipates the dynamic mutuality of union in the spiritual marriage. The "mirror for humility" (*espejo para la humilidad*) which Teresa uses to explain how self-knowledge is attained, "dealing in turn now with self and now with God,"[41] looks forward to another "mirror" which she describes in the final union—the mirror (*espejo*) of perfect mutuality between the soul and God in the spiritual marriage.[42] The first apprehension of true self-knowledge, which is the first knowledge of the relationship between the soul and God, is thus shown to be an imperfect yet real preview of mystical knowing, possessing something of the same mutual dynamism between the soul and God. Even though the preparatory stages cannot *anticipate* that mutual dynamism of union, an underlying pattern is established in the soul's activity which will be taken up in union.

Second, the element of the "cross," introduced in the second dwelling place, transforms the lowliness that the soul feels in comparison with God in the first dwelling place into suffering shared with Christ, which looks forward to the soul's Christ-like activity in works of service in the final union. The introduction of the cross signifies that, even before union, the soul's activity is being conformed to Christ's, and here a genuine bridge or continuity—indeed, the *only* continuity—is formed between the preparatory stages and union. Teresa says,

Embrace the cross your Spouse has carried himself and understand that this must be your task. . . . The whole aim of any person who is beginning prayer . . . should be that he work and prepare himself with determination and every possible effort to bring his will into conformity with God's will. Be certain that, as I shall say later, the greatest perfection attainable along the spiritual path lies in this conformity.[43]

The fact that this way of embracing the cross is the "greatest perfection attainable along the spiritual path" is a clear signal by Teresa that it anticipates, even if distantly, the conformity with Christ of the final stage of transformation. In the *Meditaciones*, as we have seen, Teresa put the cross *within* union for the first time, in the sense of the soul "serving and working" in union, as opposed to the position in the *Vida*, where she regarded the cross as outside union.[44] Having made the cross continuous with the final union, in the *Moradas* she now shows that this continuity extends back to the active stages of preparation, in the Christ-like activities of conforming the will to God's will and doing virtuous works. There is thus an underlying christocentric thread between the natural and supernatural stages of transformation, in spite of the intense differences, which is ready to be taken up in union to reconnect the exterior part of the soul to the divine activity of the interior.

Third, the "detachment" and "freedom of spirit" introduced in the third dwelling place, though again they cannot anticipate the state of union, are intended to reflect the discontinuity between the soul and created things that is attained in union. Teresa says at this stage that, unlike in union, "love has not yet reached the point of overwhelming reason. But," she goes on, "I should like us to use our reason to make ourselves dissatisfied with this way of serving God, always going step by step. . . . Wouldn't it be better to make the journey all at once?"[45] Detachment is designed to remove anything from the soul that might be thought of as an *intermediary* to God, including the idea that we can reach God step by step. The stages of transformation are indeed steps by which our humanity is conformed to God, but in detachment we must realize that there is no *continuity* between the premystical and mystical stages: there is an infinite gap, which can only be traversed from God's side. Because there is an infinite gap, our efforts at making the journey step by step are futile: we must remove all intermediaries and prepare to "make the journey all at once." Detachment does away with any idea that we can build our humanity toward God but rather aims to strip away our human will and all other impediments to union. Thus, we prepare for the discontinuity between the natural and supernatural operations of the soul in union, and paradoxically, in doing so we reduce the conflict between the natural and supernatural stages which contributes to reuniting the divided parts of the soul in union.

Finally, it should be noticed that Teresa has removed a prominent point of contrast between the preparatory and mystical stages of transformation from the *Moradas* in comparison with her early works: this is the contrast between activity and passivity. In the works prior to the *Meditaciones*, union was regarded as a wholly passive state and the preparatory stages as wholly active. This introduced a problematic discontinuity between divine and human activity in general. As Rowan Williams says of the *Vida*, "Teresa makes a rather sharp disjunction between divine activity and planned or conscious human activity, with nothing much in between."[46] Divine activity in union overruled human activity altogether, and so there was little room for the cooperative activity of spiritual marriage and still less for the involvement of the body in union. Having put this right in the *Meditaciones*, Teresa now shows in the *Moradas* that activity and passivity are combined not only in the final union but right from the start in the preparatory stages. The elements of the dynamism of self-knowledge and of the cross in these stages include both activity and passivity together: in self-knowledge, the soul is active in its relationship to God in prayer, while at the same time being passive to God as its "fount." Similarly, the soul's embracing of the cross both lays it open to God, passively, and is an active working, with determination and effort, to do the will of God. Thus, there is a structural similarity not present in Teresa's previous works between the soul's activity in the preparatory stages and in union precisely in the combination of activity and passivity which reflects the state of union. This again lends a pattern to the soul's natural operation which later helps it to overcome the division between the interior and exterior parts of the soul.

Teresa's understanding of how the soul becomes disposed for union is that it is now malleable like wax and ready to receive union, but that there is no sense in which it can anticipate the form of union. Teresa says that we should not think we can change God; we can only change ourselves.[47] But we genuinely prepare for union by changing ourselves in the sense of removing the obstacles to union and acknowledging that the work of transforming our nature into supernature can only be done by God. The connection between this activity and union is that, once God is given to the soul in union, our human work continues, save that in union it is work done more deeply from "within" Christ and sourced more immediately within the divine dynamism of the Trinity.

The Beginning of Mystical Union

Union begins by introducing the division in the soul between the soul's natural activity and supernatural activity. When Teresa introduces the fourth dwelling place with the announcement, "supernatural things begin here," she means that these supernatural things occur to the exclusion of the soul's former activity.[48] The term "supernatural things" is equivalent to her terms "mystical theology" and "union," though as in previous works the "prayer of quiet" is the name given to the first union, which precedes full union or the "union of the whole soul with God."[49] "Supernatural" first of all means the opposite of "natural": she begins with the contrast between the supernatural things of union and the previous stages of "acquired" prayer. Very much as in the *Cuentas*, where she described the most distinctive feature of supernatural prayer as that it "cannot be acquired by effort or diligence, however much one tries,"[50] here she differentiates union from acquired prayer by saying that "however diligent our efforts we cannot acquire it."[51] Instead of stopping with that definition, however, she makes a more sophisticated distinction in the *Moradas* by adding that acquired prayers, which she calls "consolations" (*contentos*), have "their beginning in our own human nature and end in God," whereas supernatural prayers, which she calls the "prayer of quiet" or "spiritual delights" (*gustos*), "begin in God."[52] Effort (*trabajo*) or activity is no longer the sole criterion of acquired prayer as opposed to supernatural prayer but only a useful indicator.[53] The primary criterion is now the *source* of the prayer, which in the supernatural states is God and in the natural or acquired states is human nature.

Teresa draws attention to the discontinuity between these two sources of prayer with greater clarity than in previous works. "Let's consider, for a better understanding, that we see two founts with two water troughs," she says.[54] This image is no doubt based on the "four waters" in the *Vida*, but it is subtly different. Whereas in the *Vida* she held that in the prayer of quiet the soul started to draw the water from the "well" by means of "a water wheel and aqueducts,"[55] here her attention is to the distinction between the different *sources* of acquired and supernatural prayer, insisting that there are *two* founts. Further, she restricts the "aqueducts" to the acquired stage alone: the fount of our human nature is "far away" and so requires "aqueducts and the use of much ingenuity" in order to produce any water, she says, but in union we are placed "at the very source of the water" in God, without any intermediaries.[56]

This strong distinction between the mediated and unmediated sources of the two kinds of prayer is carried through to Teresa's distinction between "two troughs": not only are there two founts, but they flow into two distinct parts of the soul or troughs. She says that *contentos*, which come from our human nature, cause "noise" in the soul, which occurs in the "upper part of the head" or "superior part" of the soul; whereas *gustos*, where "the water comes from its own source which is God," cause "peace and quiet and sweetness in the very interior part of ourselves."[57] The distinction between the interior and exterior parts of the soul is nothing new, but here a new part is added: the "superior part" of the soul, which is the place where intermediaries between the soul and God have their effect, whether in acquired prayer or in supernatural prayer.[58] As we saw in the previous chapter, Teresa had formerly associated the superior part of the soul with suspension, and regarded it as central to union, but now she marginalizes the element of suspension by saying that the superior part is outside the interior of the soul. Union is only union inasmuch as it is received directly, without intermediaries, in the "very interior part" of the soul. *Contentos* have no part in union as they have their effect in the superior part of the soul. While the distinction of the superior part of the soul helps to downgrade the problematic element of suspension in Teresa's treatment of union, her intention is not to compromise her strong distinction between the interior and exterior parts of the soul. On the contrary, the superior is relegated to the side of the exterior to maintain the purity of the interior for union.

The Expansion of the Soul

Having set up this strong discontinuity between the two founts and the two troughs, Teresa introduces the idea of the expansion of the soul in order to look ahead to how unity will be attained in the soul in spite of this apparently unbridgeable division. This sets up her project for the remainder of the *Moradas*. Expansion is the means by which the soul is accommodated to the immediate relationship with God introduced in union. She says that in *gustos*, the water from the divine fount expands the interior of the soul and "overflows through all the dwelling places and faculties until reaching the body."[59] This overflowing activity of union ultimately rejoins the very interior part, which is opened up in *gustos*, to the superior and exterior parts of the soul from which it is divided. The crucial feature of this overflow is its *dynamism*, which is similar to the dynamism found in self-knowledge, though much greater: it is the dynamic power of the soul's *relationship* with God which is able to involve the whole soul in union, including the body and senses. This overflowing nature of union is the *inclusive* power of the relationship with God to bring every part of the soul into the interior activity of union. Teresa is looking ahead to the final union here: she says that *gustos* rise "from something deep," and adds, "I think this must be the center of the soul, as I later came to understand and will mention at the end."[60] The center of the soul is attained when the activity of the whole soul is conformed to the "deep" interior activity of union, which is a state clearly not yet reached. Union is divisive at the stage of *gustos*, but it also has within it a **deep** unifying power, in its overflowing or dynamic activity.

The obstacle to this inclusion of the whole soul in the activity of union is that the exterior parts of the soul remain merely natural in contrast to the supernatural activity of the interior. Another way of putting this is to say that the exterior parts of the soul have not yet been accommodated to the "uncreated" or unmediated grace of union in the interior and cannot therefore participate in union.[61] How can the overflow of union include the rest of the soul, if it is of a different nature from the rest of the soul? Teresa's answer is to introduce what she calls the idea of expansion (*ensanchamiento*) of the interior of the soul. Taking the term from the Psalm text, *Cum dilatasti cor meum* (Ps. 119:32), she says, "What I think is helpful in this verse for explaining this matter is the idea of expansion."[62] At the end of the fourth dwelling place, she makes the point that the soul must expand in order to *contain* the overflow of union within itself—it must "keep everything within itself."[63] Overflow in itself does not indicate that the final union has been attained. At the stage of *gustos*, overflow spreads "sweetness" and so on to the whole soul but does not *include* the outer parts of the soul within the activity of the interior. In spite of this overflow of sweetness, the exterior part of the soul remains paralyzed and unable to join in the activity of the interior, because it is stunned by the onset of union and by the contrast between the supernatural and its own merely natural state.[64] The "idea of expansion" expresses the fact that the whole soul must gradually *become* interior, that is, it must be *accommodated* to the uncreated grace of union, through the process of transformation. Teresa says that therefore, in a sense, the water from the fount in the interior of the soul "*doesn't* overflow into a stream because the fount itself is constructed of such a material that the more water there is flowing into it the larger the trough becomes."[65] The overflow is increasingly contained in the soul as the soul becomes accommodated or expanded to suit the overflow.

This apparently explains how the soul becomes accommodated to union; but it must still be asked: what is this "material" (*cosa*) that can expand to include the whole soul? Is there any "material" that could bridge the gap from the supernatural interior to the merely natural exterior of the soul? As we shall see, Teresa's answer is that this material is the human–divine nature of Christ, though she does not introduce Christ in this context until the fifth dwelling place. Thus, the idea of expansion is set up as the solution to the discontinuity introduced into the soul by union at the stage of *gustos*, but it is not yet fully explained. It is only when she returns to Christ that a continuity can be made to human nature in union.

The idea of expansion has a further important role in Teresa's argument in the *Moradas*, as the means by which the soul becomes capable of equality and mutuality with God in the spiritual marriage. Expansion is designed to increase the capacity of the soul to make it *like* God, and this goes back to her view in the *Camino* that God gives the soul the "capacity to drink" in accordance with how much water is given in union, like a glass-maker who makes a vessel's size in accordance with how much God intends to pour into it.[66] She did not intend this to refer to the inclusion of the exterior part of the soul in union, as in the *Moradas*, but rather to suggest the essential equality that must be attained in the interior between the soul and God for the state of union to be possible. If there is to be knowledge of God in union, the soul must have a capacity large enough not just to see God but to recognize *itself* as the "extremely rich palace" within which God dwells.[67] Knowledge of God in union is dependent on this reciprocal sense of the self as the place of God's dwelling, which in turn depends on the greatness of the soul's capacity in permitting a *mutual* reflection between itself and God. This argument is powerfully taken up in the *Moradas* in the later stages. In the seventh dwelling place, Teresa says that the soul no longer feels "the solitude it did before since it enjoys such company. . . . Perhaps the reason is that the Lord has now fortified, enlarged, and made the soul capable."[68] The company that the soul enjoys is the mutuality and equality of the relationship of spiritual marriage, through being "enlarged and made capable." Because of the enlargement of the soul, the vision of God in union is always combined with self-awareness.

The Beginning of Mystical Knowing

Even though the full possession of mystical knowing is not attained until the spiritual marriage, Teresa develops her distinction between the "two founts and two troughs" in the fourth dwelling place with a view to the type of *knowing* that is being developed in the soul. In a statement that closely resembles her introduction of mystical theology in the *Vida* but is clearer in its terminology, she describes the effect of *gustos* on the intellect:

> When His Majesty desires the intellect (*entendimiento*) to stop, he occupies it in another way and gives a light in its knowing (*conocimiento*) so far above what we can attain that it [the intellect] remains absorbed. Then, without knowing (*saber*) how, it is much better instructed (*enseñado*) than it was through all the soul's efforts.[69]

This knowing-without-knowing is like the state that Teresa had described in the *Vida*, where she said that "the intellect does not work, but stands as though amazed by all it understands," and then added, in some confusion, "because God desires that it understand . . . that it understands nothing."[70] Whereas she had used only one word for this kind of knowing in the *Vida—entendimiento/entender*—which gave rise to confusion over how the intellect could be both working and not working, here she uses no fewer than four words to clarify this complicated transition.[71]

First, there is a small element of continuity with ordinary knowing: it is the intellect (*entendimiento*) that is "occupied" in the knowing of union, the same faculty as in ordinary knowing, although it is "much better instructed (*enseñado*)" than it was before. There is continuity in that the same faculty is used but not in the content of what is known. Second, there is a strong element of discontinuity. The intellect is occupied "in another way" from ordinary knowing, and this new kind of knowing actually occurs in a distinct *part* of the intellect, called the *conocimiento*, which is so "far above" the ordinary operation of the intellect that the intellect "remains absorbed."[72] Further, in comparison with ordinary knowing, this kind occurs "without knowing (*saber*) how": it cannot be reflected upon, implying that the activity in the *conocimiento* occurs at a prereflective level. This combination of continuity and discontinuity is summed up in the view that the *conocimiento* is distinct from the intellect but also part of the intellect. The fact that both natural and supernatural kinds of operation occur in the same faculty shows that the same soul is the subject of both kinds of knowing, yet they remain distinct. The distinction is one of *depth*: union occurs "without knowing how" and "so far above what we can attain" because it occurs in the depth or very interior part of the soul, which is undeveloped and inaccessible under ordinary circumstances. The work of the remaining stages of union is therefore to develop this deep activity in the soul and to make it accessible to the whole soul. The main pieces of Teresa's final view of mystical knowing are now in place.

The Role of Christ

The centrality of the person of Christ in the remaining three stages of the *Moradas* cannot be overemphasized. All that Teresa has said up to this point about the division in the soul and the potential continuities with active work depends on the role of Christ to bridge the gap between the interior and exterior parts of the soul.

In the fifth dwelling place, Teresa confronts the fact that she is working with two apparently conflicting views of union. The "delightful union," on the one hand (*unión regalada*), is the union of *gustos* and favors, which are brief and cut the soul off from exterior activity, giving it a "painful desire to leave this world." Their advantage is that they put "charity in order" within the soul, and the awareness of this "greatly helps one to die."[73] The "true union" (*unión verdadera*), on the other hand, is attained without favors but only by working with "a great deal of effort" and being "resigned to God's will": that is, avoiding *gustos* and other favors and going straight from the detached activity of the preparatory stages to an active union. The soul attains Christ in its active work, like the silkworm which spins the cocoon "wherein it will die"; in dying it is transformed into Christ. To the little work of imitating Christ in his humanity, "which is nothing," God unites himself and gives himself as the divine reward.[74] Teresa avers that this "true union" is the "clearest and safest" kind of union, for four reasons.[75] First, it is not only for one's own benefit but "gives forth good seed" and is also for the benefit of others.[76] The soul is not only in union for itself but is active in the service of its neighbors out of "love of God as its root": this interior "root" is the source of its active life as well as of its own union.[77] Christ's "love for us cost him" his life, and so to be like him we must include the service of others as an essential part of our love of God.[78] Second, the command of obedience to God's law is the same for everyone: true union has this democratic imperative, as opposed to the "delightful union" which can only be enjoyed by contemplatives.[79] Third, the true union is not brief like the delightful union, which lasted no more than half an hour.[80] The aim is for the soul to "walk continually in an admirable way with Christ, our Lord, in whom the divine and the human are joined."[81] It is a continuous, permanent union of walking with Christ, unless the devil deceives the soul under the color of good.[82] Fourth, it is more peaceful than the delightful union: the disturbance and "disquieting passion" produced in human nature by suspensions no longer "reach the soul's depth," so that the soul is able to "live tranquilly in this life, and in the next as well."[83] In these four points Teresa clearly ranks the active "true union" ahead of the "delightful union" of *gustos* and other favors, and she suggests that it is only possible to follow Christ in the true union with its emphasis on active work and service of others.

This shift of emphasis from the divisive effects of *gustos* to the straightforward imitation of Christ in virtuous works removes the problem of the division in the soul, in that all the stress is on the exterior activity of the soul. But the cost is high—that of denying the value of *gustos* and other supernatural favors altogether. For Teresa, however, supernatural favors and the opening up of the interior relationship with God continue to play a central part in union. Teresa does not regard the delightful union and the true union as simple opposites, as is clear from the fact that she has not removed *gustos* from her treatment of union in the *Moradas* and goes on to consider the different kinds of supernatural favors at length in the sixth dwelling place. The purpose of the true union is to introduce a *corrective* to her old view, which left little room for the human activity of the soul in union. Teresa wishes to point out that while union introduces something "wholly other" into the soul, it need not for that reason remove the soul from its full creaturely humanity, *provided* that its humanity is joined to Christ. This reflects her statement in the *Vida* that one must continue to meditate on the humanity of Christ even in the highest unions, though here she is concerned with the earliest stages of union as well.[84] The key aspect of the true union is the emphasis on Christ as the cocoon within which the silkworm dies: the soul becomes Christ in its humanity by working to die with Christ, and to this God unites himself, just as God and humanity are united in Christ. The "little white butterfly" of favors then comes forth from the cocoon: favors have a wholly divine source and yet they come *only* through our solidarity with Christ in his humanity. But, against the true union, Teresa also argues that favors are needed to speed up the soul's progress to union. The delightful union "greatly helps one to die": favors *accelerate* the progress of the soul to becoming like Christ in order for it to advance to the true union. Teresa acknowledges that the delightful union is a departure from the correct order of things; the effect of these early unions is to cause great pain to the soul because they come before the soul is fully conformed to Christ. But she is also in no doubt that such favors are beneficial.[85] What she does not say, but implies, is that there would be very little chance of the soul ever reaching union in this life without these favors.[86] The true union is introduced to show that the ultimate purpose of union is solely to make us like Christ, but the delightful union remains the vital means by which we get there.

Thus, the role of Christ in this dwelling place is twofold. First, when Teresa says that the sufferings caused to human nature by favors "do not reach the soul's depth" in the true union, she is claiming the *same* benefit for the true union as was given by the delightful union in expanding or accommodating the soul to the divine. She is asserting an intrinsic connection between the two kinds of union, based on the fact that, in Christ, active work in the world and the interior relationship to God are united in the hypostatic union. In saying that we must enter by favors and works into Christ through "dying," Teresa is seeking to link our own active work to the interior union given by favors in an organic whole. Second, she is looking forward to her parallel assertion, developed more fully in the sixth and seventh dwelling places, that when the highest favors are received, Christ is attained in the interior not just in his divinity but in his humanity also. She made this point in passing in the *Vida*, where she said that Christ appeared to her in an intellectual vision in both his divinity and his humanity.[87] But the general implication in that work, as in all her writings before the *Moradas*, was that favors were to be associated with the divinity *as opposed to* the humanity of Christ—and indeed in the highest stages of union it was this that made her insist that the humanity of Christ must be brought in from the *outside*, by reflecting on a painting or image of Christ. Now, she is clear that Christ is to be found not just in active work or in pictures used to temper the divine force of union, but in a union of human and divine which is both exterior *and* interior to the soul. This union of human and divine in Christ is the material (*cosa*) by which the soul is expanded to have the capacity for God, that is, transformed by favors into the human-and-divine form of Christ. Without this mediation of Christ, both interiorly and exteriorly, we, as human, remain ontologically separate from God and opposed to the divine influx of union.

We see the intimate combination of divine and human, immediate and mediated, in this view of union: the favors received in the interior are already in the human–divine form of Christ, so that Christ *mediates* between divinity and our humanity, and yet we receive this union of natures *immediately* from God. From two angles, therefore, Teresa has justified the position of the supernatural grace of favors while also placing Christ at the center of her view of union: first, favors accelerate the process of actively conforming our humanity to Christ; and second, favors mediate with our humanity passively, "from above," in the deepest interior, by being given in the form of Christ. She differentiates these as two stages or deaths: first, the silkworm dies when we are conformed to Christ through active work in our humanity; and second, the butterfly dies when we become Christ-like in the very union of natures in our center, so that, in the final dwelling place, there is no further need for favors because our center is now permanently united to Christ.[88]

Visions and the Trinity

Teresa's treatment of visions and other supernatural apprehensions in the sixth dwelling place is an attempt to explain the effect of the soul's entry into Christ as entry also into the inner relations and structure of the Trinity. The sixth dwelling place occupies about one third of the *Moradas* and leads directly to the final point of arrival at the center of the soul in the seventh dwelling place. She links the two final dwelling places with the metaphor of betrothal and marriage: the favors of the sixth dwelling place are like the engagement or betrothal of a couple, when they have brief meetings, while the full union of the seventh dwelling place is the marriage when they are joined permanently and "consummate" their union.[89] Most importantly, the form in which the soul becomes divine in its depth is to take on an explicitly *trinitarian structure* through which it participates in God by sharing in the immediate relations of the persons in the Trinity, and this leads to the intellectual vision of the Trinity in the seventh dwelling place. This trinitarian participation is seen in the increasing ability of the soul to receive and distinguish the overflowing dynamism of favors within itself and in the growing mutuality and equality of its relationship with God. After the intellectual vision of the Trinity in the seventh dwelling place, no further visions or special favors are required because the trinitarian structure of the soul is fully formed, and Teresa's final view of mystical knowing emerges in terms of this inner trinitarian relationship with God.

In the *Vida*, Teresa had already established a connection between the highest level of visions and the inner relations of the Trinity, though she did not develop it. As in all her works, she based her treatment of visions on the Augustinian threefold distinction between bodily, imaginative, and intellectual visions.[90] She understands all three kinds of vision as supernatural, being unattainable through human nature, but intellectual apprehensions are the highest kind because they are wholly interior, that is, unmediated, while imaginative and bodily apprehensions involve exterior mediating elements. Bodily visions, at the lowest level, are seen with the bodily eyes and use created images; imaginative visions use only the spiritual eyes or "eyes of the soul" (*ojos del alma*), but still involve an image (*imagen*) of bodily things; while intellectual visions use no senses, either bodily or spiritual, and no images, but are "engraved" (*esculpido*) on the soul directly and known "very deeply . . . without an image or explicit words."[91] Teresa regards imaginative visions as having positive benefits in spite of their inferiority to intellectual visions, such as the fact that the images are "living" and convey the power of Jesus to the soul—the majesty and beauty of Jesus is "impressed" (*imprimida*) on the interior in an unforgettable way, and these visions are found afterward to have changed the soul for the better.[92] But intellectual visions achieve more. They have their effect in a more interior part of the soul.[93] She describes an intellectual vision of the Trinity in which the understanding that she receives is produced in a unique manner, like "two persons on earth who love each other deeply and understand each other well; even without signs, just by a glance (*mirarse*), it seems, they understand each other."[94] She relates this to the way the soul and Christ gaze at one another in union: "these two lovers gaze (*se miran*) at each other, as the Bridegroom says to the Bride in the Song of Songs."[95] This reference to the Trinity, though undeveloped in the *Vida*, is a crucial pointer to her later view in the *Moradas*. Building up through the different kinds of vision and found explicitly in the intellectual vision of the seventh dwelling place, the soul attains a new *relation* with God and a new kind of understanding, like the two partners in the marriage relationship described in the Song, who are united in the single activity of mutual gazing, and whose distinction from one another is found only *within* this unified activity. This view of unity and distinction in union, modeled on the inner relations of the Trinity and regarded as "within" the Trinity, was the basis for Teresa's later developments on the nature of mystical knowing.

The development of Teresa's view of the relationship between the soul and God in union, in the period between the *Vida* and the *Moradas*, is found most of all in her descriptions of the visions of the Trinity in the *Cuentas de conciencia*. The most fruitful period of development seems to have occurred in the month of May to June 1571, when Teresa had two visions in which she saw the three persons "very habitually present" in her soul: they were "fixed" (*imprimidas*) within her so that she was continually in the "divine company."[96] The visions were so clear that she could see the distinctions between the persons: "all three persons were represented distinctly."[97] In another later vision, she described a similar state, of having the three persons "imprinted" (*esculpidas*) in her soul.[98] The most important aspect of these visions was that she saw the mutual *activity* of the persons. In the first vision, each of the persons granted her a "favor"–charity; the ability to suffer gladly; and "feeling this charity with an enkindling of the soul"[99]–the latter showing that she was being drawn into the active processions of the persons in their shared love. In the second vision, she saw her soul as like a "sponge" saturated with water, which was "overflowing with that divinity and in a certain way rejoicing within itself and possessing the three persons." Far from being a static entity, the Trinity was overflowing in her soul. This overflow even included all creation: "it seemed to me that from within my soul . . . these persons were communicating themselves to all creation without fail, nor did they fail to be with me."[100] The fact that the persons could both communicate themselves to all creation and remain "with" her, that is, be both overflowing in the soul and fixed, was further explained by some words that she heard: "Don't try to hold Me within yourself, but try to hold yourself within Me."[101] The Trinity was not so much fixed in her as *she* was fixed in the Trinity: her deepest identity was found *within the activity* of the persons in their internal relations. In participating immediately in the overflowing activity of the Trinity, she saw how the dynamic relations and unity of the persons existed simultaneously with their inner distinctions, and so also how her own deepest identity was found in the same mutuality and distinctions between the persons.

This transformed her whole understanding of union with God. In the third vision, she said that her understanding of the Trinity was now "an *activity* very different from merely holding this truth by faith," and she contrasted this with the type of understanding that we commonly have through the "body" and our "lowliness."[102] Instead of working from distinct concepts based on bodily matter, as in ordinary knowing, she now saw that union worked in the reverse direction, beginning with the unity and distinctions of the Trinity, and working back to material creation, in the order of God's knowing. Her understanding was now within the Trinity rather than still on the outside: it was the same as the activity of the Trinity. Teresa says that she saw how the Trinity could be both three and one through this activity: that is, she could see the simultaneity of unity and distinction within the Trinity, and this was now a feature of her own understanding within union, showing her too how she was both one with God and distinct from God. In the *Cuentas*, Teresa therefore sets in place her trinitarian idea of distinction-within-unity, which she uses to explain the nature of mystical knowing in the *Moradas*.

The trinitarian elements in the visions and apprehensions of the sixth dwelling place are implicit, as opposed to the "very clear light" with which the Trinity is seen in the intellectual vision of the final dwelling place, but these favors are nevertheless important precursors which develop in two respects the trinitarian structure in the soul.[103] First, they expand the soul in its depth so that it can participate increasingly in the *dynamism* or overflowing nature of the Trinity. Second, they produce *clarity of understanding* through increasing the mutuality and equality of the soul with God, based on the internal unity and distinctions of the Trinity.

The first element, the dynamism of the Trinity, is found in Teresa's many references to the "force" and "power" with which the soul is drawn to God in its depth in the various apprehensions of the sixth dwelling place. Through these apprehensions the soul acquires an increased deep "movement" belonging to the Trinity. For instance, in an "impulse" which Teresa describes in terms similar to her transverberation in the *Vida*, the soul feels a "feeling of love" in its depths (*entrañas*) and in this love "God is drawing (*se lleva*) these very depths after him."[104] The soul feels a powerful movement within itself as it is drawn into God in its depths. Similarly, in another impulse, the "flight of the spirit," a swift movement is felt like a "huge wave," as the soul is swept up into God's infinitely greater power.[105] Gradually, the soul becomes better accommodated to these favors and finds that it can appropriate this dynamism in order to love God in return. Teresa says that in "a strange prayer it doesn't [yet] understand," the soul finds that "all its activity is directed" to the praise of God, so that it can scarcely "conceal this great impulse of happiness."[106] The soul begins to return to God the same deep movement that it first received, in a "great impulse of happiness" directed to God's praise, showing a pattern of activity which is clearly trinitarian, even though it is not yet explicitly recognized as such.

Second, the element of equality between the soul and God, and the corresponding clarity of the soul's understanding of its relationship to God, is found increasingly in the apprehensions of the sixth dwelling place. As we saw in the *Camino*, Teresa regards the reciprocal ability of the soul to see both God and itself simultaneously as a key part of the highest unions: there, she said that the soul was able to see itself as the "extremely rich palace" within which God dwells.[107] This theme appears first in the *Moradas* in the fifth dwelling place, where Teresa says that the death of the silkworm brings with it the ability to "see God, *as well as* ourselves placed inside his greatness."[108] In the sixth dwelling place, this reciprocity is focused on Christ, who in his humanity is the "companion" of the soul up to the highest levels.[109] Teresa describes an intellectual vision in which she receives "particular knowledge of God" through her companionship with Christ.[110] In this case, she is referring not to knowledge of Christ's humanity but to knowledge of God purely in God's divinity, which normally can only be general as opposed to particular knowledge, as we have no means of distinguishing objects at this level.[111] The fact that the soul receives particular knowledge is therefore significant, because it implies that the soul is able to distinguish the persons in the Trinity—there is no other distinction in God through which such particular knowledge would be possible. The soul is raised to this level through Christ, joining him in his divine relation to the Father within the Trinity. It is now capable of knowing God in union *in the same act* as distinguishing itself from God, and this is a trinitarian activity. In the *Meditaciones*, Teresa had made the same point, saying that in union the Holy Spirit was the only "mediator between the soul and God," by which the soul was able to enjoy the fruit of the "divine apple tree."[112] The soul's relation to the Father is that of the Son, in the bond of the Holy Spirit in the Trinity. This explains why the soul cannot now see God without also seeing itself: it is in a trinitarian relation to God in which the distinction between them cannot be seen without also seeing the unity of their relationship.

These elements of increasing conformity to the Trinity in the depth of the soul become fully explicit in the intellectual vision of the Trinity in the seventh dwelling place. In this vision, Teresa reiterates that the *activity* of the Trinity is seen and felt with "an enkindling of the spirit" in which understanding is given in a way very unlike "what we hold by faith," but is rather a matter of "sight." The soul participates immediately in this activity as "all three persons communicate themselves to it."[113] Through this activity, which is also "an admirable knowledge," the soul understands how the three persons are distinct and also "one substance and one power and one knowledge and one God alone."[114] The clarity of the soul's perception comes from the fact that it can see its own unity with and distinction from God in the "divine company" in its interior: "in the extreme interior, in some place very deep within itself, . . . it perceives this divine company."[115] It sees its own relation to God in the mutual relation between the Father and the Son. The great difference of the seventh dwelling place from the sixth is that this inner trinitarian company is no longer just momentary but is permanent in the soul "every time it takes notice."[116] The trinitarian structure of the soul in its extreme interior (*muy muy interior*) has now been fully formed. As Teresa says, whatever exterior activity she engaged in from then on, "the essential part of her soul never moved from that room": in the interior room of her soul, she was permanently in the Trinity.[117]

The Center of the Soul

The center of the soul is the goal of mystical transformation and the point at which Teresa's christological and trinitarian arguments come together. Her christological argument shows how the divine life of the center is mediated to the whole humanity of the soul, without removing the center from union, while the trinitarian argument shows the type of knowing that the soul has of God in this center.[118] The unity and distinction between the interior and exterior parts of the soul, between mystical knowing and activity in the world, are also contained in these two arguments. On the one hand, the center is distinct from the rest of the soul, in that it is the only part of the soul that is in an immediate union with God in the Trinity, while the rest of the soul remains "outside": in this respect, the soul has two distinct natures, like Christ. On the other hand, also like Christ, humanity is joined to divinity in this center, permitting the trinitarian activity of the center to overflow to the whole soul and body. Further, the presence of God is now fully differentiated in the trinitarian distinctions of the center of the soul, so that the soul knows God's will clearly and within this same understanding also knows itself. Teresa therefore uses the idea of the center of the soul as the final goal of union and also as the point to summarize her various arguments in the *Moradas*.

First, the center of the soul is the place where the spiritual marriage occurs, which is characterized by the loving mutuality between Christ and the soul, which Teresa first introduced in the idea of mutual gazing in the *Vida*. In an imaginative vision which follows the intellectual vision of the Trinity in the seventh dwelling place, she receives the spiritual marriage from Christ. He appears in his humanity in the same deep interior part of the soul where the intellectual vision took place, which is now revealed as the center of the soul, as he says to her "that now it was time that she consider as her own what belonged to him and that he would take care of what was hers."[119] In this loving mutuality, the spiritual marriage is "consummated," and the "loving expressions" (*palabras regaladas*) of this consummation overflow to the rest of the soul, so involving the whole soul in union and even the body.[120] Since the first mention of overflow in the *Moradas* in *gustos*, water from the supernatural fount flowed into the interior of the soul and then overflowed to the rest of the soul, allowing it to participate in the sweetness of the interior union; but the humanity of the soul was not accommodated to the divine nature of the overflow at that stage, and so the soul remained paralyzed in its exterior regions. Now, the soul has been expanded by favors in its interior to contain the overflow within itself. The soul has been conformed to Christ's human nature in two ways: first, through active effort, by "emptying ourselves of all that is creature and detaching ourselves from it for the love of God," and second, passively, through the expanding effect of favors, by being "fortified, enlarged, and made capable" in the interior of the soul.[121] As a result, the "loving expressions" between the soul and Christ in the center of the soul can extend to the whole soul. Teresa concludes that the soul's "life is now Christ."[122]

Second, the intellectual clarity that was first attained in the particular knowledge (*particular conocimiento*) of the intellectual vision in the sixth dwelling place, and then supremely in the admirable knowledge (*noticia admirable*) of the intellectual vision of the Trinity is now permanently maintained in the center of the soul. The "very clear light" of the intellectual vision passes, but the soul remains able to differentiate clearly the presence of God within it. Teresa likens this to the ability of a person who first sees the presence of others in a bright room, and then when the shutters are closed even though the room is in darkness continues to know quite clearly that the others are still present.[123] When the "loving expressions" occur after the intellectual vision, the soul remains able to "understand clearly" the nature of their source in God.[124] It is worth reiterating the background to this development, as it is a key theme running throughout the *Moradas*. In the first stage of self-knowledge, Teresa said that the "mirror for humility" enabled her to see that her fount was in God in her merely natural state. In the fifth dwelling place, the expansion of the soul in union led her to be able to see herself "placed in God's greatness," returning her to self-awareness after the suspensions of *gustos*. Now in the final dwelling place, she says that we see ourselves in God as in a mirror, "where our image is engraved."[125] This mutually reflective vision is both the inner dynamism of the Trinity and the ability by which we are able to know the will of God. That is, it is precisely in its shared and yet distinct character, at the level of equality with God, that the "particular knowledge of God" of mystical knowing is delivered. It is an understanding that Teresa describes as like receiving a letter from God "written with intense love and in such a way that he wants you alone to understand it and what he asks of you in it."[126] Not only is it an understanding of God's will, but it is immediately performative, producing the deed as soon as it is spoken.[127] In the last of her *Cuentas*, written after the *Moradas*, Teresa says that as a result of this understanding, "never, not even in its first stirrings, does the will turn from its desire that God's will be done in it."[128] Just as the soul receives the "letter" (*recaudo*) containing God's will, so in the same act it sends *recaudos* from "the interior center to the people at the top of the castle and to the dwelling places outside the center . . . [that is] the faculties, senses, and all the corporeal."[129] This does not imply that the soul has become an automaton with no free will of its own. On the contrary, the mutually reflective nature of this understanding permits the soul to see its actions as self-chosen even though they come immediately from God's will. In the act of understanding God's will, it also sees its own will distinctly from God's will, and acts out of the trinitarian mutuality between them, with an agency that is both human and divine.

Third, the understanding that is possessed in the center of the soul, because it is continually overflowing to the faculties and the rest of the soul, now gives the intellect permanent access to the deep level of the *conocimiento* which remained "far above" it at the stage of *gustos*. Except for an occasional lapse for a very short time (*poquísimo intrevalo*), the intellect retains a permanent view of union in the center: "the Lord who created it wishes to give it repose here and that through a small crevice it might observe what is taking place."[130] The intellect and the other faculties are the first part of the soul to receive the overflow from the center. There is a permanent knowledge of union in the intellect from this overflow, even though it is not quite as clear as in the intellectual vision of the Trinity; the will is in accordance with God's will even in its first stirrings; and Teresa regards the memory as retaining the imprint of union at all times.[131] Teresa suggests elsewhere that the center is located *in* the faculties—that the center *is* the deepest part of the faculties—as we saw in the case of the *conocimiento*, which is distinct from the intellect but also *part* of the intellect, "far above" the main part. To locate the center in the deepest part of the faculties is indeed the most logical position, as it retains the distinction between the center and the faculties, without setting the center apart entirely from the faculties and leaving the soul with a problematic division of powers. Teresa clearly intends to strike a balance in saying both that the faculties participate immediately *in* the center of the soul and that they are mediated *from* the center: they are on the dividing line, both uniting the center with the rest of the soul and keeping the center distinct.[132]

Finally, the fact that the soul is, anthropologically speaking, exactly like Jesus Christ in the final dwelling place begs the question of whether it has reached perfection and, particularly, whether it no longer has the ability to sin. Teresa says that the peace at the center of the soul now spreads from the center to the whole soul, so that it continues to do God's will whatever exterior pressures it faces.[133] It has great stability (*gran entereza*). But the Lord does not want the soul "to forget its being," and so sometimes the Lord removes it from union and allows it to fall back to its natural state.[134] The fact that Teresa calls this the natural state is a crucial reminder that the soul remains in union only by virtue of grace. This is the difference that it has from Christ: it is in a supernatural state in union, whereas Christ is perfect in his natural state. Thus, she says that the soul must remain fearful that it will fall back into sin, even mortal sin, and it continues to commit many imperfections and venial sins, though not advertently (*de advertencia*).[135] Nevertheless, to lose this union is very rare, and when lost it is only for "a short while, a day at most or a little more."[136]

A connected issue is whether the soul continues to suffer. Teresa repeats the point that she made in the fifth dwelling place, that the soul no longer suffers in its depth. The suffering of the faculties, senses, and passions does not affect the soul in its root (*raíz*), where it remains permanently in peace.[137] But the fact that the center of the soul is now permanently at peace does not mean that the whole soul has reached a state of beatific rest. On the contrary, "the calm that these souls have interiorly is for the sake of their having much less calm exteriorly": so "Mary and Martha must join together."[138] These souls must give their liberty to Christ, being branded with the cross and going out to work and suffer in the world in order to do good works.[139] There is still a war to be fought, which is no longer within the soul but outside.[140] Teresa's call to "determination" and the "cross" is little different from that in the early stages of the *Moradas*, only now the soul now fights *as* Christ, from within his divine being and in his strong humanity, rather than in its former weakness.[141]

At the heart of Teresa's anthropology lies a distinction between the interior, where the soul is in the immediate presence of God in the inner relations of the Trinity, and the exterior, where knowledge of God is mediated through the separate fount of created humanity. The process of transformation described in the *Moradas* only makes sense when the full strength of this distinction is kept firmly in mind. Teresa has to work hard to show how the "division in her soul" can be bridged, and her answer comes through considerable development of her anthropology and reflection on the role of Christology and the Trinity. She points to the dynamism of Christ's own union of natures and his access to the inner overflowing force of unity in the Trinity as the elements which are gradually developed in the soul in the process of transformation and found ultimately in the center of the soul. While it would be theoretically possible for the soul to reach this union merely by imitating Christ actively, Teresa's main interest is in the role of supernatural favors in accelerating the soul's progress, though she also seeks a synthesis between the two ways. Most important is the type of knowing attained in the center of the soul, which she shows to be trinitarian in nature—immediately participating in the activity of the Trinity— providing the ability to differentiate the particulars of God's will within the distinctions of the Trinity. The center of the soul is, in fact, a trinitarian act of self-understanding, which also includes the soul fully in a christological union of natures.

CHAPTER SEVEN

Conclusion: Mystical Knowing and the Mystical Self in John of the Cross and Teresa of Avila

JOHN OF THE CROSS and Teresa of Avila have been treated separately in the previous chapters, and it is now time to examine their accounts together. In this chapter, I shall conclude my study by rehearsing the main outline of the argument as it applies to both authors. In the epilogue which follows, I shall go on to consider the main differences between Teresa and John.

The main points of the argument that have been followed in both John and Teresa can be summarized as follows:

1. The soul is divided by the onset of mystical union between the interior part and the exterior part because of the special nature of union with God as a relationship "without intermediary,"[1] in contrast to the soul's ordinary exterior relations to creatures.

2. The relationship between the interior of the soul and God in union is a trinitarian relation, not merely in the created image of God in the soul, but immediately, as the soul enters the inner life of the Trinity and is formed habitually within the Father–Son relation.

3. The soul, while remaining human, becomes "divine" in this interior relation, raising the christological problem of how the separate ontological categories of divine and human are joined together within the soul. In the spiritual marriage, the soul finds that it has not only become divine, but that it has been *humanly* accommodated to union through the process of transformation, such that it participates in the inner-trinitarian relation in the center of the soul and attains the human–divine self-understanding of Christ.

4. The interior and the exterior parts of the soul retain their distinction, but the immediate relation to God in the center of the soul now overflows to include the whole soul and body in union, producing exterior works in perfect accordance with God's will.

5. The process of mystical transformation is seen in retrospect to possess a unity deeper than the division in the soul, so that mystical knowing and ordinary knowing are combined in a unified subject, culminating in the habitual possession of a mystical self.

Each of these points will be considered briefly in turn.

1. The Division in the Soul

We have seen that John and Teresa both hold that mystical theology is "mystical" on account of the special relation that is introduced between the soul and God in the state of "union with God." This relation is without intermediary, in contrast to the soul's ordinary relations to objects which require created images and forms as intermediaries. Neither John nor Teresa goes as far as to say that the soul merges with God without distinction, but they speak of the immediate contact between the soul's substance or center and the uncreated nature of God.[2] Using a modern term, I have called this an intersubjective relationship, as opposed to the ordinary subject–object type of relationship that we have with objects in the world. Importantly, for John and Teresa, it is not just intersubjective but also without created elements separating the soul from God—that is, it is an immediate participation in the Trinity: the soul is joined to God as the Son to the Father, in the bond of the Holy Spirit.[3] They describe the relation in terms of the spiritual marriage, in which the soul shares one "bed" or center with God. The unity of the relationship is prior to the distinction, though the distinction is also real.[4] The soul retains its human nature and its natural ability to relate to all things through created images and forms, and these two abilities and types of relation—the supernatural, innertrinitarian relation, and the continuing ability for natural, creaturely relations—present a fundamental conflict. The conflict is understood in terms of a *division in the soul* between two opposing parts.[5] The effect of union is to divide the soul between the deep interior part, which attains the immediate relation to God, and the remaining creaturely oriented exterior part. This division in the soul is based on the ordinary spirit–flesh distinction in Christian anthropology (first developed by Paul), but goes further: the distinction is not only between flesh and spirit, but between the natural and the wholly supernatural, the created and the uncreated.[6]

This division in the soul is especially intense for Teresa and John because it implies two kinds of *self*: a self formed, on the one hand, by mediated creaturely relations, and, on the other hand, by an immediate, inner-trinitarian relation with God. As we have seen, in the pre-Cartesian understanding of Teresa and John, the self is constituted "transobjectively," as Maritain puts it,[7] in relation to objects, so that when the soul is presented with two different ontological categories of object, in ordinary and mystical knowing respectively, it requires two correspondingly different capacities to know these objects and is divided in its very selfhood. This presents profound problems for the unity of the self in mystical union. Yet both Teresa and John argue that such unity is attained.

2. The Trinitarian Image and Center of the Soul

The most important route taken by Teresa and John to show the unity of the soul is to follow the development of the trinitarian image of God in the soul.[8] Following Augustine, they understand the image of God as a created *trinitarian dynamism* through which the soul participates in God, in spite of the "infinite difference," as John puts it, between the soul as creature and God as creator.[9] Both Carmelites begin with a low anthropology in which the image of God is obscured from sight and has lost much of its dynamism: the soul must turn to its creator and see its source in God in order to reestablish its own proper self-knowledge.[10] But in this inward turn, the soul finds the image of God in the dynamism of its own self-relation—"dealing in turn now with self and now with God," as Teresa puts it.[11] This dynamism increases as the soul sees its lack of God in relation to God and grows in desire for God. The growing awareness of self and of God is explored in terms of the activity of the three higher faculties of memory, intellect, and will. John investigates in more detail than Teresa the trinitarian image in the "threeness" of these faculties and their individual operations.[12] But for both writers, the important point is not the "static" analogy for the Trinity in the rational faculties but the *dynamic relations* between the faculties and their objects of knowledge, and beyond that, the raising of this dynamism to the level of the Trinity, as the faculties become spiritual and participate immediately in the inner relations of the Trinity in union.

The transition to union, for both Teresa and John, is from the natural trinitarian image of God in the soul to the wholly graced inner-trinitarian participation of the center of the soul. In union, the soul's own self-relation is raised to the level of the dynamism within the Trinity: the soul enters into the relations between the persons in the Trinity. The distant reflection of the Trinity in the created image becomes an immediate indwelling of the Trinity in the center of the soul. The soul "breathes" the dynamism of the bond that unites the Father and the Son, the spiration of the Holy Spirit, in its uncreated divine form.[13] At the same time, the soul remains other than God, first of all in its created nature, but more importantly, through entering spiritually into the actual relations between the persons: it is other than God in the very distinction between the Father and the Son—its self-relation is God's own self-relation. The soul attains its center at this point, in that it relates to itself and to all things *through* the inner relation of the Son to the Father in the Trinity. The image of God in the soul from creation is raised to the level of a shared center with God, as the soul now knows both God and itself, explicitly and clearly, in the inner-trinitarian self-relation, which underlies all its acts.

This would seem to suggest a smooth transition from the created state to the mystical state of union. But Teresa and John both stress the *divine* nature of union to such an extent that this is not the case. The problem of the division in the soul takes two forms. First, the humanity of the soul is threatened in the interior part or center, as this part has been raised into the uncreated inner life of the Trinity. Second, the exterior part, which remains merely human and engaged in bodily and sensory operations, is divorced from the purely spiritual, divine activity of the center.

3. The Christological Union of Human and Divine in the Center of the Soul

The genius of John and Teresa's Christology is that they place the hypostatic union within their dynamic view of the Trinity: the mutual relationship between the Father and the Son *includes* the humanity of Christ in its embrace, and this same Christ-within-the-Trinity is the soul's experience, in the center of the soul. The center of the soul is divine in that it is an inner-trinitarian relation with God, but in the act of seeing God in this union the soul also sees itself, and sees itself as *human*. John says that we receive the adoption of sons in union when we see ourselves in the beauty of Christ the Bridegroom through the mutual relation of the spiritual marriage, just as the Son shares everything with the Father. Our union "corresponds" to the "hypostatic union of the human nature with the divine Word," in that our divine self-understanding includes the "knowledge of the mysteries of the humanity of Christ."[14] Teresa makes the point even more clearly, when she links the moment that we attain the humanity of Christ, in the "death of the silkworm," with the moment that we no longer only see God in union, but also see "ourselves placed inside his greatness."[15] The soul can now see its own humanity united to the divine Word within its inner-trinitarian relationship.

The difficulty for the soul is that it does not become conscious of this involvement of its humanity in union until it reaches an advanced stage of union. To begin with, the soul feels only that its humanity is wholly opposed to the divine presence in its interior, as God is vastly in excess of its human capacity. The soul feels that it is ontologically divided between the interior part, which is in immediate contact with God, and its merely human, exterior part. As John says, the soul feels that it is divided into two parts which are "so distinct that one seemingly has no relation to the other," and Teresa asks how the interior part, which is in a "heavenly union with uncreated Spirit," can "keep company" with the exterior part, which is engaged in worldly occupations.[16] But the main difficulty here is one of self-understanding rather than of an ontological division in the soul. At least, the annihilation that the soul undergoes in being placed in immediate contact with God is the fully human experience of being transformed into Christ, who experienced annihilation in the same way: the soul is being accommodated to union, rather than excluded from its own humanity.[17] Teresa changed her view in the course of her writings, first seeing an unbridgeable divide between heaven and earth in the suspensions of union, but later realizing that the suffering of union was *part of* union, the christological element of the cross, by which the soul's full humanity was being accommodated to union.[18] For both John and Teresa, it is only once the soul begins to recognize itself as Christ-like in union that it sees the purpose of its suffering and the true nature of the division in the soul. This self-understanding is itself a feature of the spiritual marriage. The division in the soul is then revealed to be a genuine distinction between an inner-trinitarian relation with God in the interior part and mediated creaturely relations in the exterior part, but not an ontological division. The *distinction* between the two parts of the soul remains, but it is no longer a *division*, in that the christological center of the soul *includes* the human even at this most divine level.

4. The Overflowing Nature of Union, Which Includes the Exterior Part of the Soul and the Body in Union, Producing Virtuous Works

Only the three spiritual faculties are included in the center of the soul, while the rest of the soul remains bound to the body in performing the functions of natural sensation and so on. If the full humanity of the soul is to be included in union, it is not enough to show that a christological union of human and divine has been achieved in the center of the soul—we also need to know how this immediate level of contact between the soul and God can be *mediated* to the exterior part. The exterior part of the soul cannot join in union in the immediate relation to God of the interior part, as it must interact with the body and the world, which are not purely spiritual entities. The imperative for both John and Teresa is to show how the soul can produce exterior virtuous works in the world while remaining in union, in conformity with Christ.

John and Teresa argue that mediation from the interior union to the exterior part of the soul is produced by means of "overflow." Overflow is a mediating movement produced immediately out of the divine dynamism at the center of the soul. Teresa describes this overflow as messages (*recaudos*) which are sent from the interior to the exterior part of the soul, issuing directions to the soul that produce virtuous actions.[19] John describes it as the "sweetness of love," which produces the "actual practice of love . . . exteriorly in works directed to the service of the Beloved."[20] Overflow has two stages or levels. At the first level, it is an overflow of delight and sweetness, or an "impulse of love," which extends to the sensory part of the soul and the body, but does not produce exterior works. This occurs in the lower unions. In the *Moradas* Teresa identifies this stage with the first supernatural stage of *gustos*.[21] John says that these overflows, though delightful, are "not enough," because they do not "have sufficient quality for the attainment of my desire": that is, they produce a feeling of union in the exterior part of the soul but do not achieve any exterior action.[22] At the second level, however, overflow issues in exterior works in perfect accordance with God's will. Two changes have taken place. First, the soul is now "fortified" in its exterior part such that it is humanly capable of receiving the full force of the divine overflow from the interior, without being sent into ecstatic suspensions.[23] Second, the soul has attained the self-understanding associated with the spiritual marriage, by which it is able to know the divine will and direct it to the exterior part of the soul and the body in a single act.[24] Unlike the nonspecific sweet feelings of the first level of overflow, the soul sends explicit commands from the center to the exterior, resulting in directed, cooperative activity with God in the world.[25]

Overflow joins the two parts of the soul so that, as Teresa puts it, they "work together" out of the same "interior root."[26] They join in a unity of action. They remain distinct in the type of relation they have to God—one immediate and the other mediated—but the interior part is now found to be the root of the soul's activity, such that the entire operation of the soul is unified. John says that the soul now knows all things, including exterior objects in the world, *through* the interior union, and knows them "better in God's being than in themselves."[27] It is still the case that "l'homme est double," in André Bord's phrase,[28] in that there is a strong distinction between the two parts of the soul, but this doubleness is now an ordered hierarchy in which the soul's whole activity proceeds from the interior union. The key to this inclusion of the exterior part of the soul in union is, again, the Trinity. While the interior of the soul participates in the uncreated inner life of the Trinity, the exterior participates in the overflow of the Trinity into creation. The feature of the trinitarian life to which John and Teresa repeatedly draw our attention is this ability to include the other within its overflowing power, uniting the other within its internal relational distinctions.[29] The exterior part is united in the same trinitarian life as the interior part, only at a further level of mediation. Although the exterior part remains at the level of creaturely mediation, it is genuinely united to God in the overflow of the Trinity into creation.

We might still ask *how* the intersubjective relation in the interior union can be the root of sensory, subject–object relations in the exterior part of the soul. Here we must note John and Teresa's understanding of the self. Following Augustine, they assert that the self is fundamentally constituted by its relation to God, in the image of God. At this level, the soul is already, from creation, in an intersubjective, trinitarian relationship with God. The difference from union is that the trinitarian relation to God is possessed only *through* created things, in our relations to exterior objects and to ourselves. In union, the trinitarian activity of the image of God in the soul is greatly increased and becomes known first, a priori. The hierarchy in the soul is reversed: God is known before creatures. This is a vast change, but the *fact* of an intersubjective relationship with God in the soul underlying all our subject–object relations has not changed. Thus, no new problem arises in the self: as before, the self is rooted in an intersubjective relation with God, only now this relation has become dominant rather than hidden. Other problems have arisen, concerning the ontological relationship between the two parts of the soul, but these have now been resolved: the soul has attained a christological center and the exterior part has been included in union in the trinitarian overflow.

5. Mystical Knowing and the Mystical Self

For Teresa and John, mystical union is to be understood as the interiorization of the divine life of the Trinity into a Christ-like self. The impoverished and exterior self, which could relate to God only through creatures, is now a self like Christ, which can relate to God within God, without going outside through creatures. Has this removed the self from the world and from the need to relate to creatures? John and Teresa answer the question with an emphatic no, using their anthropology of division followed by unification in the overflowing center of the soul. The language of interiority stresses that union with God is in no way superficial to the self, nor does it remove the self from its authentic created existence, but rather deepens and transforms it. It remains to interpret further what kind of self this is.

I have examined John and Teresa's idea of the self from two perspectives: the structural (chaps. 2 and 5) and the dynamic (chaps. 3 and 6). These two aspects of selfhood cannot be separated in actuality but are a valuable way of distinguishing between the "fixed" parts and components of the self, on the one hand, and the operations of the self when in action, on the other hand. Structurally, the soul is divided into interior and exterior parts, a faculty psychology and so on, while dynamically, it is drawn into God, undergoes suspensions and other movements, and is transformed, taking on God's own dynamism. The problem of the division in the soul can be regarded as a conflict between the structural and the dynamic: the soul has a structure designed for relating to creatures, but in union it is drawn into a new dynamism in God, which bypasses creatures. This appears to destroy the structure of the soul, until the soul recognizes, at a high level of transformation, that a new structure has been formed within it, based on the pale image of God in the internal relations of memory, intellect, and will. This new structure is more fully trinitarian than the former image of God, entering immediately into the relations between the persons—first, in the memory, intellect, and will, when they relate to God as their immediate object, and second, in the distinction between the interior and exterior parts of the soul, which becomes a trinitarian relation through the act of overflow. Thus, the mystical self is a human trinitarian intentional structure possessing God's inner dynamism. The division in the soul does not disappear but becomes a trinitarian distinction in the unified, trinitarian self.

This mystical-trinitarian self has some remarkable capabilities. Principal among these is that in union, as John says, "the power to look at God is, for the soul, the power to do works in the grace of God."[30] The act of seeing God-within-God is the same dynamism that is the soul's whole activity, which also overflows into exterior activity in a single act. The inclusion of the self in the life of the Trinity has here reached its apogee, where *everything* that the soul does is itself an act of relation to God within the mutuality of the Trinity. This is what Teresa and John mean by saying that the soul has become divine. It also follows that every act performed by the soul is accompanied by an inner-trinitarian awareness. Thus, Teresa says that in the final union, the soul does not just see God but also sees itself placed within God's greatness.[31]

The nature of this self may be summarized in three points. First, like the natural self—but unlike the self of Descartes—the mystical self is constituted by relationality, only now by the immediate relation with God rather than relations with objects in the world. Second, just as the natural self can both know itself and what it knows outside itself at once, because of its fundamental constitution in relationality, so in union, the mystical self knows both God and itself at once, in the relationship of the spiritual marriage, yet without going through creatures as in natural knowing. Third, these two kinds of knowing are related in the self according to two distinct, symmetrical patterns of cognitive acts.[32] The fact that there is a symmetry between these two parts of the self is explained by the trinitarian pattern of all creation: the structure of ordinary knowing is the "first draft" of the much clearer representation of the Trinity that emerges in the structure of mystical knowing. But otherwise, the two sets of cognitive acts are wholly different from each other. Unity between the two kinds of knowing is possible only because the Trinity is also the source of the self and all its knowing. It is only when the self is brought to the source of creation in the Trinity, in union, that the two kinds of knowing can be reconciled: the subject–object structure of ordinary knowing is then *included within* the intersubjective structure of knowing in the Trinity. The self's constitution in relationality has not been violated, and yet ordinary knowing has been substantially changed into a knowing of the world-with-God in the Trinity.

For John and Teresa, union with God is not easy. The final union is reached by a radical process of "voiding" and "expanding" the interior of the soul, in order to give a new structure to the deep level of the soul which was not there before. They are adamant that mystical transformation is a real change of selfhood, moving the self outside the bounds of the present self and into God. As Teresa prays in one of her *Exclamaciones,* "May this 'I' die, and may another live in me greater than I and better for me than I, so that I may serve him."[33] Both she and John call this change "annihilation," and John even calls it "destruction" on one occasion.[34] The continuity of selfhood lies in the self–God relation rather than in the self as presently conceived. In mystical knowing, we do not become aware of the self–God relation in our own categories of selfhood and self-awareness, but only by being transformed into God's own self-relation: the difference, in John and Teresa's language, is between the *created* and the *uncreated.* We relate to ourselves now from within God.[35] Yet this entry into the Trinity does not mean that our knowing ceases to be human. The soul attains a human-trinitarian structure which is capable of mediating the uncreated self-knowing of God. It is truly *our* knowing, in that it is a human structure, built on the created image of God within the soul, but it is also God's knowing, formed perfectly within the structure and relations of the Trinity. Thus, ultimately, we are not annihilated or destroyed, but deepened and transformed, and the self is unified, but only after the painful process of division and transformation has done its work.

Finally, there is one restriction that Teresa and John place on union which must be noted in this concluding view of mystical knowing and selfhood. They both hold that the full clarity of an intellectual vision is not sustainable in the final union, even though this union is habitual and permanent. The final union is primarily active: the vision of God is mediated to exterior virtuous actions, rather than remaining as a clear intellectual vision. There are occasional exceptions to this, when the habitual union flares up into an actual union of explicit intellectual knowledge, as John says, and which Teresa likens to the shutters being opened in a dark room.[36] What is the distinction between these two levels of union? The main difference is not "clarity": while the intellectual vision is lost, the clarity of the soul's inner-trinitarian knowing is retained in the accuracy with which it continues to do God's will.[37] Rather, the difference is that the moment of "seeing" is bypassed. The soul does not rest in the vision of God, as it will be able to do in heaven, but having attained the permanent union of the spiritual marriage it goes out again into the world. Teresa stresses that the present need is for the soul to do the work of Christ in the world rather than to rest in the interior union. Peace has been attained within the soul so that it can go out to battle in the world in greater strength.[38] For John, the imperative to do works is less strong than for Teresa, but he too regards union as a vision which gives "the power to do works in the grace of God," as we have seen. Further, the fact that the soul remains sensory in part acts as a restriction on its ability for spiritual vision, even though the sensory part is now in full conformity with the spirit. John says that the soul has broken through the temporal and natural "veils," but the "sensitive veil," though rendered tenuous, remains a hindrance to union.[39] Thus, union is a knowing concomitant with action in the world, rather than primarily a beatific type of seeing as we will have in heaven, though moments of such vision occur occasionally.

Some Important Differences Between John of the Cross and Teresa of Avila

IN THIS BOOK, I have concentrated on the close parallels between John of the Cross and Teresa of Avila's accounts of mystical transformation, particularly in relation to the problem of the division in the soul. I end by noting some important differences.

The most prominent difference between John and Teresa's accounts of mystical knowing and transformation, to which all the other differences discussed here can be related, is that John's theology is more negative than Teresa's. Both Carmelites take the view that there are negative psychological effects caused by the entry into union, such as suspensions and the feeling of the division in the soul, but John alone makes this into a programmatic process of sensory and spiritual negation and suffering in the dark nights. John appeals to the works of Dionysius to explain his negativity—an influence lacking in the case of Teresa.[1] Having adopted the three-fold pattern of purgation, illumination, and union to describe the spiritual journey, John applies the Dionysian view that illumination is to see God not as light but rather as a "ray of darkness."[2] The light of God cannot be seen as light in the stage of illumination because it is so far in excess of the soul's natural capacity.[3] Purgation increases rather than decreases in the stage of illumination, as the light comes into immediate contact with the rational faculties, "voiding" and "darkening" them.[4] Teresa also regards the rational faculties as negated in regard to their ordinary operations when mystical theology begins, but at this point she thinks that the soul already has the ability, within these faculties, to recognize God's presence *as presence*, rather than feeling it only as absence.[5] In the first supernatural stage in the *Moradas*, the stage of *gustos*, for instance, she says that the soul is "aware (*se acuerde*) that it is in God's presence and who God is."[6] For John, God is felt as only as a *lack* in the soul at this stage. Even though this feeling of lack is a clear sign of God's presence—from a later perspective— the soul cannot yet recognize it as God's presence, such is the darkness in its rational faculties.

John, however, is not a thorough-going Dionysian. He thinks that God actually is light rather than darkness, and that in the later stages of union the rational faculties, now made spiritual, start to see God as light.[7] The "dark illumination" ceases to be so dark, as the light of "early dawn" arrives, and the soul "comes to *know* (*conoce*) the spiritual light it possesses."[8] Thus, John puts forward a kind of "temporary Dionysianism," applying the negativity of Dionysius to the rational faculties only in the middle, "midnight" stage of the mystical itinerary. Like Teresa, he thinks that the soul is expanded by illumination such that it becomes equal to the infinite greatness of God in its own infinite capacity, and at this point it starts to know God positively in union.[9] For this reason, I must differ from Denys Turner, who regards John's view of union more as an "absence of experience" than as anything that can be called "experience."[10] I have argued that experience, for John and Teresa, must be carefully interpreted as the dynamic structure of knowing as a whole rather than mere sensation or any single element in knowing, and this goes some way to distance my view from certain modern understandings of experience,[11] but this is not Turner's point. He argues that because John is a negative theologian, there is no analogy from ordinary experience by which we can call union "experience." But John and Teresa both furnish precisely this analogy in their view that a structure parallel to ordinary experience and knowing is formed in the interior of the soul in union. While the soul is unable to feel or know God in the midnight of the dark nights, it attains the ability to feel and know God positively when it enters into union proper—which John treats more fully in the *Cántico* and *Llama* than in the *Subida–Noche*—not in its ordinary feeling and knowing capacities but in a parallel mystical capacity.

The differences between John and Teresa are therefore to be seen in the approach to union and in the early stages of union, before the light of union starts to shine through for John and before God becomes distinguishable. John emphasizes the feeling of God's absence in the progress to union rather than presence and regards this as a cause of great suffering to the soul, while the element of suffering is less prominent in Teresa's account. For instance, in the first dwelling place of the *Moradas*, Teresa differentiates between "misery" (*miseria*) and "lowliness" (*bajeza*): misery is the state of mere introspection before the soul turns to God, whereas low-liness is the true self-knowledge that comes from reflecting on one's creation by God and God's "grandeur."[12] Misery is a feeling of stagnation and self-absorption, while lowliness is a sense of possibility, of the great capacity and beauty of the soul in its dynamic relationship with God. John makes no such distinction. The true self-knowledge, for John, is as much a state of misery as of lowliness, because until the soul reaches union the only authentic feeling it has is of the absence of God, and it feels this increasingly.[13] "Misery," he says, is a "more authentic" sign of the soul's progress than the gratification and sensory satisfaction enjoyed in spiritual exercises, as it proves that the soul is not under the illusion that of itself it can do anything to bring itself closer to God.[14] If we look carefully at what John is saying, we see that he is not far from Teresa in the respect that his misery is a feature of the soul's *relationship* with God rather than an autonomous self-absorbed state. But he sees the soul's rational ability as so seriously impaired that the soul cannot make the distinction between lowliness and misery. The soul may in fact be "beautiful" and have a "marvellous capacity" in relation to God, as Teresa says,[15] but it cannot *know* it until union, according to John.

The same difference is to be found in regard to John's and Teresa's treatments of *fear*. As one would expect, both recommend fear of God as part of a proper attitude of humility before God. But for John the fear is more intense, and Teresa makes a clear distinction between fear of God and other kinds of fear—fear of prayer, fear of deception, fear of the devil, fear of the Inquisition, fear of other people, fear resulting from natural weakness, fear of suffering in raptures, fear of hell and fear of death.[16] John would have to agree with Teresa that stagnation in prayer could not be a genuine part of the fear of God, but as in the case of misery and lowliness, he regards the soul as *unable* to distinguish between different kinds of fear prior to union.[17] All that the soul can see is its imperfection.[18] This difference between the two Carmelites takes on greater proportions in the early stage of union, when the soul first undergoes suspensions. John says that the soul's fear becomes more intense, as it feels "torment" and "terror" in its sense of God's absence, whereas for Teresa, the "fear" is accompanied by a secure feeling of God's presence and love.[19] For John, the soul still has further to go before it will know the presence of God, and meanwhile it feels only "its own intimate poverty and misery."[20]

Another difference between Teresa and John is to be found in regard to supernatural apprehensions, which cannot be known reliably for John before the final union, because of the darkness in the rational faculties, but which for Teresa are part of union as soon as they begin. This is the stage of crisis for John, where the soul must hold out for union in the darkness of faith, seeking no consolations of any kind. They both use the three-fold scheme of corporeal, imaginative, and intellectual apprehensions derived from Augustine, and the difference emerges most clearly in regard to imaginative apprehensions, which John says must be denied, but which Teresa thinks, in certain cases, are just as valuable as intellectual apprehensions. We have seen that there is a slight difference of terminology between John and Teresa: John divides intellectual apprehensions into two kinds, the "corporeal-intellectual" and the "spiritual-intellectual." The corporeal-intellectual kind are received in the intellect, but use created intelligible forms—these correspond to Teresa's "imaginative" apprehensions.[21] As they use created forms, John says that there is still the possibility of deception, so that they must be denied. He regards only the highest, spiritual-intellectual kind—which Teresa calls simply "intellectual" or "non-imaginative" apprehensions—as beyond deception and to be identified with union, as they have no created forms or images but are received through the immediate contact of our substance with God's substance.[22] Teresa agrees with this assessment of intellectual apprehensions, but regards certain imaginative apprehensions as positively valuable as well.

Teresa gives four reasons for accepting imaginative visions positively. First, though there is always the possibility that the devil will meddle, which is not the case in intellectual visions, they are "in greater conformity with our nature" and can be "more beneficial" than intellectual visions.[23] Other tests, which she sets out carefully, can be used to prove that they come from God and not the devil.[24] Teresa is prepared to accept the danger of deception because this kind of vision makes the *connection* between our human nature and the divine presence, through the intelligible forms used, which intellectual visions do not. Second, both John and Teresa agree that these visions leave an imprint on the memory which can be recalled with beneficial effects.[25] For John, it is even better to deny such visions, given their corporeal nature,[26] but he reaches a compromise position, saying that one should deny the outward form in favor of the inner benefit. One should "pay no attention to the letter and rind" of the images received, but only to the effect of love that is caused.[27] Conversely, Teresa says that one should value the "vessel" for what is contained within it.[28] She takes a more inclusive approach than John, regarding the outward form as valuable for its part in containing the inner benefit. Third, Teresa stresses that the images seen in these visions are "alive," like a living person rather than a painting, so that the vision "stirs all the faculties and senses."[29] Here she is pointing out how close these imaginative visions come to intellectual visions, in that they induce God's *activity* in the soul rather than merely showing it representations or concepts of God. The fact that concepts are given with this activity does not warrant the rejection of the vision for

Teresa, as it does for John. Fourth, Teresa's most important point is that in the case of imaginative visions of *Christ*, the image cannot be separated from the divine activity, in that we see and know Christ as "both man and God."[30] Unlike John, she regards the corporeal image as a direct mediation of Christ as "man," so that to deny the image would be to deny Christ's own humanity. The image joins us to God, just as the human and divine are joined in Christ. "Take care not to flee from corporeal things to the extent of thinking that even the most sacred humanity causes harm," she says.[31] Teresa is adamant that such visions should not be denied: even if a confessor says that they should be, "you should humbly tell him this reason and not accept his counsel."[32] This also explains her first point: the reason why imaginative visions can be "more beneficial" than intellectual visions is that their images can mediate between humanity and God, the connection being in the person of Christ.

Teresa widens considerably the terms of the debate here by suggesting that imaginative visions secure the place of the humanity of Christ in union in a way that intellectual visions cannot. Teresa raised the same issue in the *Vida* in relation to painted images of Christ.[33] There, she attacked those who said that one should rid oneself of painted images of the humanity of Christ in the higher levels of prayer, and commentators have noted that she was probably opposing the view of Osuna, which John shared. In John's view, no corporeal image, including images of Christ, can serve as a proximate means to union.[34] Yet to what extent did they differ over the humanity of Christ? Teresa clearly identifies the loss of *images* as "withdrawing completely from Christ," but John does not see such a simple connection between images and the humanity of Christ. They differ over the *means* of receiving the humanity of Christ, but not over the value of the humanity of Christ itself. John does not regard images of Christ as suitable mediators of Christ's humanity prior to union, but he has an alternative way. In the second book of the *Subida*, he says that the humanity of Christ is encountered in the soul's "annihilation" in the dark nights. Indeed, the sense of the absence of God and John's whole emphasis on the Dionysian negativity of the dark nights, including the torment and terror of suspensions in the early stages of union, are his way of showing how the soul is conformed to the humanity of Christ. "Christ is the way" for the entire "dark night," he says: our "annihilation" is a "death . . . patterned on Christ's," just as Christ in his humanity was "certainly annihilated in his soul, without any consolation or relief." We receive the humanity of Christ through the dark nights in our own "living, sensory and spiritual, exterior and interior death of the cross."[35] Certain difficulties of interpretation arise over precisely how far John thinks that we can identify with the humanity of Christ in our own dark night, given that

Christ's humanity was in some respects unique,[36] but it is clear that here he regards a genuine meeting as occurring between us and Christ, precisely in our humanity, and that it is sustained through to union. His emphasis on the suffering of the soul in the process of transformation is not an attempt to remove us from our humanity but to achieve the encounter with Christ and to conform us to Christ. Suffering, for John, continues for the whole mystical journey and into union because Christ's humanity is infinitely deep—there is always a "knowing from further within" for us to reach, and "suffering is the means of her [the soul] penetrating further, deep into the thicket of the delectable wisdom of God."[37] Such suffering is found most fully in Jesus' dereliction on the cross; to deny our participation in this suffering or to seek to escape from it would be to forego the entire purpose of the mystical journey. Just as Jesus achieved the "union of the human race with God . . . at the moment in which he was most annihilated in all things," so we must follow him into the depths of dereliction, in which we will feel the full torment of rejection by God, if we are to rise with him in union.[38]

Teresa's direct criticism in the *Vejamen* of John's view that we must be "dead to the world" before we can seek God properly is regarded by Carole Slade as further evidence that they disagreed over the humanity of Christ.[39] She casts John as a sort of gnostic, saying that he has "apparently divorced spiritual experience from the physical world."[40] But if this was John's opinion at the time of the *Vejamen*—and the evidence is insufficient to say that it was—we can confidently say that by the time he wrote his major works he had changed his mind, because the emphasis on identifying with the humanity of Christ, particularly in the midnight stage of annihilation, is very clear. John's descriptions of detachment, if anything, are to be criticized for being too enthusiastic in their portrayal of our shared sufferings with Christ in his death, rather than for separating us from the humanity of Christ.

In fact, it was Teresa, rather than John, who changed her opinion on the humanity of Christ most in her writing career. At the time of the *Vida*, her intention in stressing the importance of images of Christ was to maintain the incarnational link between the vision of God and our bodily human life. But later, like John, she came to regard the incarnational link as being more deeply maintained in the *sufferings* of the journey to union than in the use of images, and in the element of the cross in union itself. She never changed her view that images of Christ were not to "be counted in balance with other corporeal things"[41]—she thought that they were valuable at every stage of the journey—but she started to emphasize that the annihilation that the soul felt in suspensions was the more important aspect in conforming our humanity to Christ's humanity and not just an unfortunate side-effect of union.[42] She also read back this element into the active stages of preparation for union in the *Moradas*, insisting that the soul should strive for "nakedness" and being "abandoned" to God, in the third dwelling place.[43] Even after the initial suspensions of union had passed, she saw the suffering of the cross as continuing in union, with the difference that as transformation progressed, the interior of the soul increasingly attained a state of peace, and the battle shifted from the interior of the soul to the exterior, where the soul served Christ in active works in the world.[44] Her final position on how we attain the humanity of Christ is much closer to John's than to her own early position in the *Vida*.

Still, though Teresa shifted toward John's position, an important difference remains in their attitude to imaginative, or corporeal-intellectual, visions and painted images of Christ in the early stages of union. Why does Teresa insist that the humanity of Christ is mediated in corporeal images, when she also sees it as mediated in the soul's suffering, as John does? Why does she not restrict the place of the humanity of Christ in visions to the highest intellectual visions, where the soul's humanity is fully conformed to Christ, as John does?[45] John and Teresa's views of how Christ is encountered in mystical union reflect two distinct strands in the history of Christian thought.[46] John's is the more intellectualist, Origenist approach to spiritual sensation, which argues that the soul can "feel" Christ only by denying the bodily senses in favor of purely spiritual senses, whereas Teresa's is the more bodily approach found in Bernard of Clairvaux and various other late medieval mystics, which regards the *bodily* senses as capable of mediating spiritual benefits, in certain circumstances, through the union of spirit and flesh in the incarnation.[47] In epistemological terms, the difference is between receiving corporeal forms as the "first moment" of an apprehension, which is the case in the imaginative or corporeal-intellectual visions favored by Teresa, or receiving purely spiritual forms first, which is the case in spiritual-intellectual apprehensions and the only means allowed by John. For John, purely spiritual forms may overflow to the body, but they must be received first exclusively in the spirit rather than the corporeal senses. For Teresa, bodily forms may be received first, which then mediate spiritual forms, both in the case of painted images of Christ and in imaginative visions.

The difficulty with Teresa's position is that she includes elements of *both* approaches to the humanity of Christ. While the bodily approach, on which she differs from John, is a significant element in her account, it is less important to her overall understanding of mystical transformation than the intellectualist, or better, the interior approach that she shares with John. She agrees with John that the bodily senses, and our whole ordinary exterior means of knowing, must be completely transformed into an

interior means of knowing, as we have seen. This entails the painful experience of the "division in the soul" and the temporary loss of the use of
the bodily senses, which like John, she understands as a way in which we
are joined to Christ in his suffering on the cross.[48] The use of bodily
images of Christ is an *exception* to this general loss of the bodily senses, for
Teresa: she regards images of Christ as a unique kind of bodily form which
we continue to be able to feel in spite of the division in the soul. Teresa's
reason for allowing this exception is primarily practical. She thinks that
the loss of *all* bodily images carries a particular danger, which is that the
soul will become so withdrawn from the body that it will cease to make
progress, becoming trapped in a state of "absorption" (*embevecimiento*).[49]
Rather than conforming the soul to the humanity of Christ in his suffering, this state is a loss of direction, where the soul falls into self-indulgence
and ceases to advance in the way of the cross. Remembering Christ in his
humanity—including the images given in imaginative visions—and pon-
dering the example of the saints and the mysteries of faith are then essential to bring the soul back to the right path.[50]

For John, to allow this exception in the case of bodily images of Christ
is untidy and unnecessary. He suggests that we must welcome any suffering as beneficial at this stage, and that to return to the familiar images of
Christ that we know, in preference to the darkness that we do not know, is
to deny the full force of the suffering of the cross. John reveals this view
most clearly when, after giving some criteria by which to judge whether
imaginative visions are genuine, he argues that, even if they are true, it is
better to deny them, as then "the greater will be the infusion of faith."[51]
As Matthew has shown, a key aspect of John's understanding of the cross
is that Jesus lost his perception of the divine company at the moment of
his cry of dereliction and yet accepted his annihilation; this is why John
insists that we lose all our images, including those of Christ, in order to
conform to Christ's suffering, and this is behind his whole treatment of
negativity.[52] It is an aspect of Christology that is lacking in Teresa's
account: she regards the suffering of the cross as always combined with the
joy of God's presence. Teresa and John's difference over whether to allow
bodily images of Christ is in part caused by this difference in their understanding of the cross. Teresa is able to be more inclusive in her allowance
of images of Christ because she does not see them as detracting from the
suffering of the cross. John not only regards them as a detraction from the
cross but considers it unnecessary to include *two* ways to appropriate the
humanity of Christ, when suffering alone is both adequate and the most
effective way.

In summary, we must recognize that Teresa's use of bodily images of
Christ in the early stages of union is an exception to her overall episte-

mology of the "division in the soul" and a secondary strand to the primary way that Christ is appropriated through the interior of the soul. We must also take seriously her comment that bodily images of the humanity of Christ are "not to be counted in balance with other corporeal things." Though felt by the exterior bodily senses, they are felt in a way which *antici-pates* the flesh–spirit unity of the final union, rather than going back on the division in the soul. Finally, we must note that this way of appropriat-ing the humanity of Christ is a temporary stage which is superseded in the final union. Here Teresa joins John in saying that the soul no longer requires bodily images of Christ.[53] In the final union, the humanity of Christ is found within the soul in the same way for both Carmelites, in the soul's inner-trinitarian knowing which is mediated to every part of the soul. The soul is still able to find spiritual benefit in bodily images, but does not require them nor are they its main way of remaining in union.[54] The effect of the difference between Teresa and John in the earlier stages of union is that the division in the soul is rendered less systematically *painful*, for Teresa, because the pain is combined with the feeling of God's presence and the soul is able to fall back on images of Christ. But the fact of the division in the soul remains central to Teresa's mystical anthropol-ogy, and she does not think that it is *removed* by the use of bodily images of Christ. On the contrary, she thinks that the use of these images enables the soul to pursue the path to the fully interior knowing of union more effectively. Thus, the problem of the division in the soul and its resolution, which has been my concern in this book, is equally important for both Carmelites, in spite of Teresa's additional use of bodily images of Christ on the journey to union.

The Order of the Stages of Transformation According to John of the Cross: Reconciling the Main Accounts

THE PROCESS OF TRANSFORMATION according to John of the Cross is the description of a movement affecting the soul's relationality at the deep level, culminating in the dynamic union with the Trinity, which forms a chronological sequence or itinerary of stages and states of the soul. A major difficulty with John's description is that he does not follow the same order or the same stages in his four main accounts, the *Subida del Monte Carmelo* and *Noche oscura* (which together share a single structure), the *Cántico espiritual*, and the *Llama de amor viva*.[1] In this appendix, I shall outline John's basic stages at some length and attempt to reconcile them. My purpose is to provide additional background to my argument concerning John's view of transformation in chap. 3.

John has numerous different schemes for the stages of transformation, but there are two basic patterns: the twofold and the threefold. The twofold scheme is based on the division of the soul into its sensory and spiritual parts. The threefold scheme is based on the classical division of the mystical itinerary into purgation, illumination, and union, or the stages of beginners, proficients, and the perfect. Confusion is introduced by the fact that John is happy to work with both schemes at once. The *Subida del Monte Carmelo* and the *Noche oscura* were conceived as a single treatise and are primarily based on the twofold division, as is clear from his arrangement into two "nights":

138

> The first night or purgation . . . which will be under discussion in the first
> section of this book, concerns the sensory part of the soul. The second night
> . . . concerns the spiritual part. We shall deal with this second night, insofar
> as it is active, in the second and third sections of this book. In the fourth sec-
> tion we shall discuss the night insofar as it is passive.[2]

The basic division of the *Subida–Noche* is thus into two nights, corresponding to the purgation of sense and then of spirit, with a further division into active and passive stages, which subdivides each night into two.
These divisions correspond to the books of the *Subida* and the *Noche* taken
together. The *Subida* has three sections or books, the first of which concerns the active night of the senses, and the second and third the active
night of the spirit. The *Noche* represents the fourth book and concerns
both the active and passive nights of the spirit. (See table A.1.) The *Noche*
is divided into two books; but as Trueman Dicken points out, this is merely
editorial.[3] The division corresponds to the active/passive division, but
there was probably no such division of books within the *Noche* in John's
original scheme. The twofold/fourfold division is found most clearly
expressed in the tenth chapter of book II of the *Subida*. Here John divides
the supernatural and natural apprehensions of the intellect into four,
according to the organization of the soul and the order in which these
apprehensions are to be purged. As purgation moves through the soul,
starting from the lowest level of the exterior bodily senses and moving to
the interior bodily senses and then to the rational faculties, the soul is
purged of its natural and supernatural apprehensions on these levels. As
we saw in chap. 2, John divides the supernatural apprehensions in a threefold manner like Augustine, according to those which come through the
exterior senses, the imagination, and the intellect. He then divides the last
of these three stages, the intellectual apprehensions, into two: the first
kind are *gratiae gratis datae*, which use created images of corporeal substances, whereas the second kind have no form except the "touch" of an
incorporeal substance on the "substance of the soul"—these are the
"touches of union."[4] Thus, there are four stages in total, which correspond
to the fourfold division of books. This can be seen more clearly from table
A.1 on the following page.

  This fourfold division, based on the twofold division of the soul into
spirit and senses, is the main structure of the *Subida–Noche*. The fourth
stage, in which the soul enters union, is introduced in book III of the
Subida but is more fully dealt with in the *Noche*, in which the rational faculties are made spiritual so that they attain the "dark and general" knowledge of contemplation. At this stage, God "begins to communicate himself
through pure spirit by an act of simple contemplation in which there is no

**Table A.1. The Fourfold Scheme of the Process
of Transformation in the *Subida–Noche***

Book	Night	Part of Soul	Type of Apprehension and Level of Purgation
Subida I	active night of senses	exterior bodily senses	exterior bodily
Subida II	passive night of senses	interior bodily senses	imaginary/discursive
Subida III		rational faculties (oriented to creatures)	intellectual-corporeal (created; *gratia gratis data*)
Noche (I & II)	active and passive night of spirit	rational faculties made spiritual (oriented to God)	intellectual-incorporeal (uncreated; no corporeal corporeal element)

discursive succession of thought,"[5] that is, without any particular image or form in the mind.

John also uses a threefold division in the *Subida–Noche*, however, corresponding to the classical stages of purgation, illumination, and union. He introduces these as the three phases of one "night" which, confusingly, encompass the two or four nights already described.[6] (See table A.2.) The first phase is the point of departure and the stage of beginners, the night of the senses, in which John likens the level of purgation to "early evening" or "twilight"; the second phase is the means or road of traveling to union which is faith, the night of the spirit, "completely dark" to the intellect, "like midnight"—this is the stage of "proficients"; and the third phase is the point of arrival in God, "who is also a dark night to man in this life," although now, in union, a glimmer of light "like the very early dawn just before the break of day"[7] shines through, which is the "general knowledge" of contemplation attained by "the perfect" in union with God. The threefold pattern thus has no division into active and passive stages, and there is nothing in the fourfold pattern to correspond to the crossover from the second (illuminative) to the third (unitive) stages. The "illuminative way," according to the *Noche*, only begins in the final stage of the passive night of the spirit,[8] but it is also in the passive night of the spirit that union begins. John is left with no further division in the fourfold scheme by which to distinguish union from illumination. A smaller but significant difficulty is that the threefold division of purgation, illumination, and union does not exactly correspond with the stages of beginners, proficients, and the perfect. Purgation continues through the stage of proficients and only stops when union is reached, making illumination a second stage *within* the stage of purgation. Union is separated from illumination only as that part of illumination where purgation ceases, making union a second stage *within* the stage of illumination, beyond purgation. The attempt to match up the two schemes in the *Subida–Noche* is as follows:

**Table A.2. Comparison of the Threefold Scheme
with the Fourfold Scheme in the *Subida–Noche***

Night (single/threefold)	Nights (fourfold)	Stages (threefold)		
early evening	active night of senses	beginners	purgation	
	passive night of senses			
	active night of spirit			
midnight	passive night of spirit*	proficients	purgation	illumination
early dawn		perfect	union and illumination	

* The passive night of the spirit also completes the passive night of senses (2N 14:3); the nights are not as rigidly separated as the scheme suggests.

When we compare the fourfold scheme with the threefold, the fourfold scheme seems to weigh in heavily in the stage of purgation and to contribute relatively little to the stages of illumination and union, with only the last stage, the passive night of the senses, covering them both. But there are good reasons for this. First, the *Subida-Noche* is particularly concerned with the stage of purgation and its divisions; the *Cántico* and the *Llama* cover the later stages more fully. Second, the "illuminative way" appears relatively late in the *Noche* because John did not finish the treatise. He leaves off abruptly at the first line of the third stanza of the poem in his commentary. In the prologue he explained that the first two stanzas speak only of spiritual purgation, while spiritual illumination and union are mainly reserved for the remaining six stanzas, but he never reached these stanzas.[9] Third, in the *Subida* John does in fact trespass into the later stages while discussing the stage of purgation. He does not stick to the order he initially set out. As Trueman Dicken points out, the *Subida* is his only major treatise in which he abandons the poem-commentary format and follows instead a systematic division which deals with the stages in order of importance rather than in strictly chronological order.[10] The stage of "midnight," for instance, is reached early on, although it belongs to the passive night of the spirit, because it is the crisis stage, central to everything that John has to say. He introduces union at the same time, because "an understanding of the nature of union will shed more light on the subsequent doctrine."[11] He says in the prologue that "the latter parts [of the mystical itinerary] will explain the former."[12] The division according to the types of natural and supernatural apprehensions in chap. 10 of book II maintains a basically chronological scheme in the remainder of the work, but John continues to mix active, passive, sensory, and spiritual purgation in many of the stages. One reason for this is that as the soul progresses, it is harder to separate the purgative effects in the spirit from those in the senses, and vice versa, as both parts are jointly purified.[13] John goes into more detail on the passive night of the spirit in its "correct" position, in the *Noche*, but systematically he is forced to introduce it in the *Subida*. Also, experientially, he points out that the soul does not always keep "mathematically to this order," that is, to the order of apprehensions that he has set out, as "the process depends on what God judges expedient for the soul,"[14] not on a fixed itinerary.

Nevertheless, John has much more to say about union in the *Cántico espiritual* and *Llama de amor viva* than in the *Subida* and the *Noche*. The two former treatises have the bridal union of the Song of Songs at their heart, and the *Llama* in particular, written later than most of the *Cántico*,[15] contains John's fullest development of his teaching on union. The *Cántico* and the *Llama* cover the stage of purgation only in passing, and in the *Llama* John states his intention to move beyond purgation. The contrast to the *Subida–Noche* is noteworthy:

> In *The Dark Night* of *The Ascent of Mount Carmel* we dealt with the intensity of this purgation, how it is greater and how it is less, and when it is in the intellect and when it is in the will, and how it is in the memory, and when and how it is also in the soul's substance, also when it involves the whole soul; we discussed, too, the purgation of the sensory part, and how it can be discerned when this purgation is of the sensory part and when of the spiritual part, and the time or stage along the spiritual road in which it begins. Since we have already explained all of this, and such is not our aim here, I will not go into it again.[16]

John makes clear that the *Subida–Noche* was primarily concerned with purgation, while in the *Llama* he contrasts the way in which God is known in union with the former "night." The darkness of the night is said to have been surpassed:

> Now You [God] are no longer dark as You were before, but You are the divine light of my intellect by which I can look at You; and You not only have ceased making me faint in my weakness, but are rather the strength of my will, by which I can love and enjoy you, being wholly converted into divine love; and You are no longer heavy and constringent to the substance of my soul, but rather its glory and delight and amplitude.[17]

The state of union was described in the *Subida* and the *Noche*, but now the soul has entered into a fuller union. The majority of each of the *Cántico* and the *Llama* concerns union, and John provides new divisions *within* union. First, the distinction between "spiritual espousal" and "spiritual marriage" is new. In spiritual marriage, the soul does not merely have a capacity for God through having been purged of sin and opened to God but is able to return to God the love and knowledge that God has given to the soul in a two-way relationship. Although there is internal peace in espousal, the soul does not yet have the strength to love God actively within the partnership. In marriage there is not just love but communication: John says, "in the espousal there is only a mutual agreement and willingness between the two, and the bridegroom graciously gives jewels and ornaments to his espoused. But in marriage there is also a communication and union between the persons."[18] Spiritual marriage is also associated with greater permanence. John associates spiritual espousal with the stage of "spiritual flight" in the *Cántico*, which is a genuine touch of union, a "strong and overflowing communication and glimpse of what God is in himself," but very brief.[19] Spiritual marriage is more permanent, in that the soul does not wait for occasional touches of union but has been given the strength of will to love God of its own accord. The difference is also that between operative and cooperative grace. John says that spiritual marriage is cooperative: the "soul reflects the divine light in a more excellent way because of the active intervention of its will,"[20] not to the exclusion of grace, but by working in cooperation with grace. Works also follow from union. As we saw in chap. 2, the soul is now fortified in the corporeal part, so that the senses and body are not paralyzed by the overflow of union from the spirit, but energized.[21] Activity thus flows out of the divine communication to the soul in union. Spiritual marriage is best described as the "acquired equality" of the soul with God, enabling it to perform acts of love out of the permanent state of habitual union, of its own will.

A second distinction within union is that between "habitual" and "actual" union. We saw in chap. 1 that in the *Subida* the soul achieves "the habit of the perfect divine union," which is the interior capability for mystical knowing attained in union, as opposed to any particular experience.[22] Yet once the soul has been purged of all particular images and forms for God and entered into the "dark contemplation" of God in union, there is a further stage in which the knowledge and love of God is "made actual" in the soul. This is a further stage *beyond* the attainment of unity between the spirit and senses through the fortifying of the senses and overflows to the body. Habitual union is associated with the transformation of the soul into the "glowing embers" of love, but in "actual union" the embers "have become so hot that they shoot forth a living flame." "Hence," John says, "we can compare the soul in its ordinary condition (*hábito*) in this state of transformation of love [habitual union] to the log of wood that is ever immersed in fire, and the acts of this soul [actual union] to the flame that blazes up from the fire of love."[23] John is clear that this new "actualizing" of union does not add anything substantial: it is "accidental" in comparison with "the substantial good the bride already has within herself."[24] But it is a special favor and foretaste of eternal life,[25] which gives an added *awareness* and *clarity* to union. The state of habitual union is present in the soul like flower buds, which open out in actual union, so that there is a special awareness of what is happening in the soul.[26] It is as if God has awakened in the soul where normally God is "asleep," although it only happens rarely as "were He always awake within it, communicating knowledge and love, it would already be in glory."[27]

Most of the time, the soul in union does good works and acts spontaneously without awareness of this kind. John regards the change as mainly affecting the intellect: the will may "feel and enjoy" God in habitual union, but in the "awakenings" the intellect has knowledge also.[28] "Actual union" is thus primarily an intellectual vision that occurs in brief moments to the soul that has already achieved the stable state of habitual union. Anyone who has such an experience will be left in no doubt that they have reached union.[29] John describes something closely resembling Teresa of Avila's transverberation experience which he puts into this category.[30] Further, beyond actual union, additional physical manifestations which wound the body occur, such as Francis's reception of the stigmata, which John puts in an even more exalted category reserved "only to founders (*las cabezas*) . . . [having a] value commensurate with the greater or lesser following that they will have in their doctrine and spirituality."[31] "Actual union" is therefore something *between* habitual union and the extraordinary bodily effects given to founders, such as St. Francis. It delivers a special intellectual clarity over and above the habitual state of union. In chap. 3 I related this intellectual clarity to the type of knowing in union described as "distinct" by John because it is within the *relational distinctions* of the Trinity.[32]

There is then the question of how to reconcile the position of the *Subida–Noche* on union with the *Cántico* and *Llama* (see table A.3). First, the touch of union is to be equated with spiritual espousal, a genuine entry into the stage of union, but only the first brief intimation of what will follow. Second, habitual union is to be equated with spiritual marriage, in which the soul attains the "acquired equality" with God necessary to respond to God in the reciprocity of union and to act cooperatively with God's grace. But at the end of the *Noche*, the soul is left in a state of physical paralysis and division between the spirit and the senses, which keeps it from the full state of spiritual marriage. This is as far as the *Subida–Noche* goes.[33] In the *Cántico* and *Llama* the division is overcome when the senses are fortified and the impulses from the spirit overflow to the senses so that feelings of joy and, more importantly, good works are produced spontaneously out of union, which is the completion of spiritual marriage. Third, additional favors may be granted in union in its most exalted states. Actual union is an occasional awakening of God in the soul so that it is aware both of its own union with God and of the entire universe engulfed in a "sea of love."[34] In the highest state of all, there may also be a physical effect in the bodily flesh, such as St. Francis's stigmata. John is far from dismissive of these favors, but he stresses that they add nothing to the essential goal of union which is spiritual marriage, and the latter in particular is very rare. These stages of union are summarized in table A.3 on the following page.

There is therefore considerable agreement between John's main accounts of the stages in the process of transformation, but a rather different area is covered in the *Cántico* and the *Llama* in comparison with the *Subida–Noche*. The *Subida* is the nearest to a systematic account, but it only goes as far as the stage of the "touch of union" in detail and leaves out some of the significant developments of union in the *Cántico* and the *Llama*. The *Noche* goes further than the *Subida* in explaining the permanent nature of habitual union as an end to rapture and bodily torments and the beginning of the steady "divine inflow" of simple contemplation in the passive night, but the senses remain divorced from the spirit at the end.[35] While the *Subida* and the *Noche* detail the stages of purgation most fully, the *Cántico* and *Llama* assume this treatment and concentrate on the stages of union. We pass from "darkness" to "light." A fuller union is signaled by the fact that the spirit engages the senses in a positive overflow. There is also a new cooperative reciprocity between the soul and God, and the doing of good works. The final stage of the process is to receive favors which bring the soul very close to the beatific vision: actual union "greatly resembles the beatific state."[36]

**Table A.3. Reconciliation of the Stages of Union
in the *Subida–Noche*, the *Cántico,* and the *Llama***
(shaded area denotes stages not attained in these treatises)

Treatise		Stages of Union	
Subida del Monte Carmelo, Noche oscura	*Cántico espiritual, Llama de amor viva*	touch of union (*Subida-Noche*) = spiritual espousal (*Cántico & Llama*)	
		permanent habitual state of union (acquired equality with God) (*Subida–Noche*)	= spiritual marriage (*Cántico & Llama*)
		unity of senses and spirit (incl. "overflow" to senses/body)	
		favors (1): actual union (transient clarity/awareness)	
		favors (2): bodily wound in flesh (e.g., stigmata)	

Notes

Notes to Introduction

1. For the development of the idea of a mutual depth or "abyss" in which the soul merges with God's essence, which is most characteristic of the Beguine writers, especially Hadewijch of Antwerp, see Bernard McGinn, "Ocean and Desert as Symbols of Mystical Absorption in the Christian Tradition," *Journal of Religion* 74 (1994):155–81. The possibility of this Beguine literature or Eckhart being read by Teresa or John is slim, but it may have influenced them through John Tauler: this is the view advanced particularly by Jean Orcibal. See Jean Orcibal, *La Rencontre du Carmel Thérésian avec les Mystiques du Nord* (Paris: Presses Universitaires de France, 1959); "Le Rôle de l'intellect possible chez Jean de la Croix: ses sources scolastiques et nordiques," in *La Mystique Rhénane*, ed. Phillipe Dollinger et al. (Paris: Presses Universitaires de France, 1963), 235–79; *Saint Jean de la Croix et les mystiques rhénoflamands* (Bruges, Belgium: Desclée de Brouwer, 1966). Teresa and John, however, take great care *not* to use the "union of indistinction" formula of Eckhart, in which the distinction between the soul and God is entirely removed in the "ground," reflecting the suppression of this view between the time of Eckhart and the sixteenth century, and the presence of the Inquisition in Spain, which exercised a hawkish eye over all new spiritual writings.

2. This attention to "mystical epistemology" may be related to William of St. Thierry in the earlier mystical tradition. For a concise treatment of William of St. Thierry's theory of cognition, see Bernard McGinn, *The Presence of God. A History of Western Christian Mysticism*, vol. 2, *The Growth of Mysticism: Gregory the Great through the Twelfth Century* (New York: Crossroad, 1994), 225–74. John may have been influenced by reading William, but Teresa is unlikely to have been, as she was restricted by not being able to read Latin and the poor availability of spiritual works in Spanish for women religious.

3. The "interior" and "exterior" of the soul are called two "parts" (*partes*) by both Teresa and John. By "parts" they do not mean physical regions of the soul or cognitive powers but distinct *relations* between the soul and God. In mystical knowing, the soul relates to God in an interior way, as opposed to its ordinary exterior way through creatures.

4. "Le parecía havía división en su alma. . . . Se quejava de ella [parte interior del alma]—a manera de Marta cuando se quejó de María—y algunas veces la decía que se estava allí siempre gozando de aquella quietud a su placer, y la deja a ella en tantos trabajos y ocupaciones que no la puede tener compañía." 7M 1:10(11) (2:431–32/570).

5. "[El alma] conoce en sí dos partes tan distintas entre sí, que le parece no tiene que ver la una con la otra, pareciéndole que está muy remota y apartada de la una." 2N 23:14 (386/583).

6. Henri Sanson, *L'Esprit humain selon Saint Jean de la Croix* (Paris: Presses Universitaires de France, 1953), 49; Georges Morel, *Le sens de l'existence selon Saint Jean de la Croix* (Paris: Editions Montaigne, 1961), 64; André Bord, *Mémoire et espérance chez Jean de la Croix* (Paris: Beauchesne, 1971), 92. See also Eulogio Pacho, "El hombre, Aleación de Espíritu y materia," in *Antropología de San Juan de la Cruz*, ed. José Cepeda (Avila: Institución Gran Duque de Alba, 1988), 23–35.

7. Rowan Williams, *Teresa of Avila* (London: Geoffrey Chapman, 1991), 148, 161–62.

8. Iain Matthew, "The Knowledge and Consciousness of Christ in the Light of the Writings of St. John of the Cross" (D.Phil. diss., University of Oxford, 1991), 158–59.

9. "La unión hipostática de la naturaleza humana con el Verbo divino, y en la respondencia que hay a ésta de la unión de los hombres en Dios." C 37:3 (550/884). Teresa makes this analogy as well as John, for instance in her interpretation of the text from the Song, "Let the Lord kiss me with the kiss of his mouth," which she says refers to the "two natures" (*dos naturalezas*) in Christ, which the soul asks for itself, "asking for that union so great that God became man, for that friendship that he effected with the human race." MC 1:9(10)–10(11) (2:220–21/426–27).

10. The most important passages in which Teresa and John refer to the immediate participation of the soul in the inner relations of the Trinity in union are the following: for Teresa, V 27:10; CC 13(14); 14(15); 40(53); 42(40); MC 5:5(6–7); 7M 1:6(7)–10(11); 2:7(9); for John, C 39:3–5; L 1:2, 6, 15; 4:17. The means by which both Teresa and John relate this entry to the trinitarian life to their Christology is by speaking of the pain that mystical grace brings as the "annihilation" of the "cross": for Teresa, see V 16:5; 20:15; CV 18:5; MC 7:8; 7M 3:15; 4:8; for John (who emphasizes this element more rigorously), see esp. 2S 7. For a comparison of their different attitudes to bodily images of Christ, see the epilogue below, esp. pp. 132–37. I am influenced in my understanding of John and Teresa's *trinitarian* approach to mystical knowing by Mark A. McIntosh, *Mystical Theology. The Integrity of Spirituality and Theology* (Oxford: Blackwell, 1998).

11. In this distinction I follow Steven Payne, *John of the Cross and the Cognitive Value of Mysticism* (Dordrecht/Boston/London: Kluwer, 1990), chaps. 2 and 3; and Max Huot de Longchamp, *Lectures de Jean de la Croix: Essai d'Anthropologie Mystique* (Paris: Beauchesne, 1981), chaps. 1 and 2.

12. 1M 2:5, 8–10.

13. See esp. C 1:6 for John's Augustinian understanding of the image of the Trinity in "the innermost being of the soul" (*el íntimo ser del alma*). John's divergence from Augustine in his faculty psychology is discussed in chap. 2, pp. 24–26.

14. Jacques Maritain, *Distinguish to Unite, or The Degrees of Knowledge*, trans. Gerald B. Phelan (from 4th French ed.) (Notre Dame: University of Notre Dame Press, 1995), 100. Maritain's work was originally published in 1932 as *Distinguer pour unir, ou les degrés du savoir*. See the fuller treatment in chap. 3.

15. "[El alma] conoce [las criaturas] mejor en su ser [Dios] que en ellas mismas . . . que es conocer los efectos por su causa y no la causa por los efectos." L 4:5 (645/1030).

16. John makes clear that, for us, this is Christology attained "by adoption": we

may join Christ at his trinitarian point of origin, but we do so as followers of Christ, rather than as the first-born (C 36:5).

17. "Poder mirar el alma a Dios es hacer obras en gracia de Dios." C 32:8 (536/869).

18. C 31:4; 36:4; L 1:36; MC 7:3–10; 7M 2:6, 8–9; 4:6–12. In working out the issues of selfhood and knowing in this book I have been influenced by Bernard Lonergan's idea of mystical consciousness, particularly the interpretations of James R. Price and Mary Frohlich. See James R. Price, "The Reintegration of Theology and Mysticism: A Dialectical Analysis of Bernard Lonergan's Theological Method and the Mystical Experience of Symeon the New Theologian" (Ph.D., diss., University of Chicago, 1980), and idem, "Lonergan and the Foundation of a Contemporary Mystical Theology," *Lonergan Workshop*, vol. 5, ed. Fred Lawrence (Chico, Calif.: Scholars Press, 1985): 163ff.; Mary Frohlich, *The Intersubjectivity of the Mystic: A Study of Teresa of Avila's* The Interior Castle (Atlanta: Scholars Press, 1993). My own Ph.D. dissertation, which forms the basis of this book, includes a substantial engagement with this Lonerganian material. See my "Mystical Consciousness and the Mystical Self in John of the Cross and Teresa of Avila" (Ph.D. diss., University of Chicago, 1999), and also the works of Lonergan cited in the bibliography below. I have omitted, however, this element of comparison with Lonergan in the present study. Lonergan's "consciousness," as an interpretation of the Carmelites' "knowing," has the benefit that it indicates that there is much more to this knowing than in the conventional view of knowing today, but unfortunately there are two more pressing areas of difference. First, the dislocating impact that God has on the self for the Carmelites is to be contrasted with the much smoother, implicit role that the "transcendent ground" has in Lonergan's anthropology; and second, connected with this, the lack of trinitarian development in Lonergan's anthropology, in spite of his early movements in this direction in *Verbum: Word and Idea in Aquinas* (Toronto: University of Toronto Press, 1997), leaves inadequate room for the radical otherness, explicitly modeled on the Trinity, that is included in the mystical anthropology of the Carmelites. For these reasons, I have avoided the term "consciousness" here, preferring to retain the Carmelites' "knowing," though I hope indicating strongly that this knowing is not to be understood in modern terms but in the deeply theological terms in which it was conceived—as a knowing which can literally be shared with God, and which is accompanied by full awareness.

19. Alison Weber, *Teresa of Avila and the Rhetoric of Femininity* (Princeton: Princeton University Press, 1990).

20. The last detailed intellectual comparison between the thought of Teresa and Avila and John of the Cross was E. W. Trueman Dicken's *The Crucible of Love: A Study of the Mysticism of St. Teresa of Jesus and St. John of the Cross* (New York: Sheed and Ward, 1963).

21. Gillian Ahlgren, *Teresa of Avila and the Politics of Sanctity* (Ithaca: Cornell University Press, 1996).

22. I refer to works such as Réginald Garrigou-Lagrange's *Christian Perfection and Contemplation according to St. Thomas Aquinas and St. John of the Cross*, trans. Sr. M. Timothea Doyle (London: B. Herder Book Co., 1937), first published in 1932, and Jacques Maritain's *Degrees of Knowledge*, cited above, both of which draw close connections between John and Aquinas, while noting that John took a more "practical" approach. There are profound insights in these works into John's epistemology, but they pay little regard to the context in which he wrote, as a Discalced friar writing

on prayer, and his separation from the scholastic context in which he was trained at the University of Salamanca. A useful distinction is that made by Bernard McGinn between vernacular, scholastic, and monastic theology; these were different genres and approaches to theology which diverged to a large extent in the late medieval period: see Bernard McGinn, "The Changing Shape of Late Medieval Mysticism," *Church History* 65 (1996): 197–219. In addition, the distinction which we find prominently in Teresa's works between the "spirituals" (*espirituales*) and the "learned" (*letrados*) must affect the way we understand the context of both her and John's works. Teresa and John were clearly on the *espiritual* side of this dispute. (See the further discussion of this issue in chap. 4, pp. 62–63.) This division went back to the controversial reforms among the religious orders set in motion by Archbishop Cisneros at the beginning of the sixteenth century and was aggravated by further divisions over the nature of the reforms promulgated by the Council of Trent concerning clerical education, discipline, and authority in the church.

23. Ahlgren, *Teresa of Avila*, 28–29, 36–39, 78–79. See the further discussion of this work in chap. 4.

24. The hagiographical tradition regarding Teresa and John, which grew up soon after their deaths, has emphasized the unity of doctrine between them and papered over what appear to have been some disagreements. This anecdotal tradition remains a prominent part of the standard biographies but must be taken with a grain of salt—as found for instance in Marcelle Auclair, *St. Teresa of Avila,* trans. Kathleen Pond (New York: Pantheon Books, Inc.; London: Burns & Oates, 1952/1953), and in what remains the best biography of John: Crisógono de Jesús Sacramentado, *Vida de San Juan de la Cruz* (12th ed.; Madrid: Biblioteca de Autores Cristianos, 1991) (Eng. trans. Kathleen Pond, under the title *The Life of St. John of the Cross* [London: Longmans; New York: Harper, 1958]). Again, see the further discussion in chap. 4 below.

Notes to Chapter One

1. "Ni basta ciencia humana para lo saber entender ni experiencia para lo saber decir." S Prol. 1, 2 (69–70/255).

2. "No fiaré ni de experiencia ni de ciencia, porque lo uno y lo otro puede faltar y engañar; mas, no dejándome de ayudar en lo que pudiere destas dos cosas, aprovecharme he para todo lo que con el favor divino hubiere de decir . . . de la divina Escritura." S Prol. 2 (70/255).

3. Aquinas, *Summa Theologia* Ia q. 1; for John's relation to Aquinas and differences, see below, pp. 16–17, 24–26, 49, esp. chap. 2 n. 86, and chap. 3 n. 15.

4. E.g., Denys Turner, *The Darkness of God. Negativity in Christian Mysticism* (Cambridge: Cambridge University Press, 1995), 264. Turner avers that John of the Cross cannot be positive about experience because of his negative theology: what he intends is the "absence of experience." This is further discussed in the epilogue, p. 130.

5. "Por la experiencia": 2S 21:7 (175/362); "de experiencia": 1N 8:2 (312/501); C Prol. 4 (469/734); "hay experiencia ser experimentado": L 1:15 (584/924); L 3:30 (621/989).

6. L 3:30 (621/989).

7. To give a negative example of those directors who "do not understand what spirit is," see L 3:54 (631/1005).

8. "El hábito de la divina unión." 3S 2:13 (218/407).

9. "Consiste . . . en cierto toque que se hace del alma en la Divinidad, y así el mismo Dios es el que allí es sentido y gustado. . . . Y en éstas no digo que se haya negativamente como las demás aprehensiones, porque ellas son parte de unión." 2S 26:5, 10 (195–96/382–83).

10. The four kinds of purely spiritual apprehensions are first introduced in 2S 10, then treated fully in 2S 23–32. John says of them: "Llamamos puramente espirituales, porque no (como las corporales imaginarias) se comunican al entendimiento por vía de los sentidos." 2S 23:1 (187/374).

11. "Los que son de la sustancia del alma son altísimos y de gran bien y provecho." 2S 32:2 (212/400).

12. "Le parece que la colocan en una profundísima y anchísima soledad . . . tanto más deleitoso, sabroso y amoroso, cuanto más profundo, ancho y solo. . . . Y tanto levanta entonces y engrandece este abismo de sabiduría al alma, metiéndola en las venas de la ciencia de amor, que le hace conocer, . . . muy baja toda condición de criatura acerca deste supremo saber y sentir divino, . . . y cómo es imposible por vía y modo natural, poder conocer ni sentir de ellas [las cosas divinas] como ellas son, sin la iluminación de esta *mística teología*." 2N 17:6 (370/565–66).

13. Kavanaugh and Rodriguez (*The Collected Works of St. John of the Cross*, trans. and ed. Kieran Kavanaugh and Otilio Rodriguez [Washington D.C.: Institute of Carmelite Studies, 1979]) consistently translate *sentir* as "experience" when it is used in this sense; I have changed the translation to "feeling," "feel," etc., in my quotations.

14. Trueman Dicken, *The Crucible of Love*, 340.

15. There is a long process of transition from natural to spiritual feeling, in which spiritual feeling is strongly contrasted with that of the natural senses: e.g., "God, to achieve his work gently and to lift the soul to supreme knowledge, must begin by touching the low state and extreme of the [bodily] senses. And from there he must gradually bring the soul after its own manner to the other end, spiritual wisdom, *which is incomprehensible to the [bodily] senses*." 2S 17:3 (156/342), my emphasis.

16. "Si estriba en algún saber suyo o gustar o saber de Dios, como quiera que ello (aunque más sea) sea muy poco y disímil de lo que es Dios." 2S 4:3 (113/299).

17. E.g., 2S 18:9; 2S 22:13; 2S 29:10.

18. E.g., 2S 32:2 (212/400); L 2:21. John describes the parallel structures in the *Llama de amor viva*: spiritual feelings of God (savor, joy, delight, etc.) are felt in the soul in the "deep caverns of feeling," which administer to the "common sense of the soul" "just as the bodily senses go to assist the common sense of the fantasy with the forms of their objects." L 3:69 (637/1016–17). See chap. 2, pp. 29–31.

19. E.g., 2N 20:5 (377/573).

20. 2S 8:6 (128/314); 2N 12:2 (335/549); 2N 17:6 (370/566) as quoted above, n. 12; C 27:5 (518/849).

21. "Subidamente le da un vuelco en el cerebro . . . tan sensible, que le parece se desvanece toda la cabeza y que se pierde el juicio y el sentido." 3S 2:5 (215/404).

22. 2N 1:2.

Notes to Chapter Two

1. In making this distinction, John uses "spiritual" in same sense as "mystical," confining it to the state known as mystical theology, by which he means the same as union with God—and this is the sense of spiritual that I intend here. Lesser

states are referred to as natural or, in certain cases, as supernatural, as analyzed below.

2. "Teniendo el alma capacidad infinita," 2S 17:8 (159/345); "no se llenan con menos que infinito," L 3:18 (617/982).

3. For instance, by Réginald Garrigou-Lagrange, *Christian Perfection and Contemplation according to St. Thomas Aquinas and St. John of the Cross*; Jacques Maritain, *Degrees of Knowledge*—but see my comments on Maritain in the next chapter. Crisógono de Jesús Sacramentado was the first to reject this exclusively Thomist interpretation in *San Juan de la Cruz: su obra científica y su obra literaria* (Madrid: Mensajero de Santa Teresa y de San Juan de la Cruz, 1979), first published in 1929. Today, the battle lines remain drawn between Elizabeth Wilhelmsen in the Thomist camp, and André Bord in the anti-Thomist, more Augustinian camp (both of whom are discussed further below: see esp. n. 86). I take the side of Bord, for the reasons given below. Of course, there are points of contact between John's and Aquinas's writings, only they are not as significant as was previously thought: for a recent study, see Ross Collings, "Passivity in the Spiritual Life from the Writings of St. Thomas Aquinas and St. John of the Cross" (D.Phil. diss., Oxford, 1978).

4. John states that the soul in union knows God's effects through the cause (in God's being), not the cause through the effects: it is not knowledge a posteriori but essential knowledge. L 4:5 (see also C 12:5; C 14&15:5). Cf. Aquinas, *Summa Theologiae* Ia q. 2, a. 3.

5. For a recent treatment of John's university education, see Luis Enrique Rodríguez-San Pedro Bezares, *La formación universitaria de Juan de la Cruz* (Valladolid: Junta de Castilla y León, Consejería de Cultura y Turismo, 1992).

6. John quotes Aquinas occasionally, e.g., "the theologians say, *omnia movet secundum modum eorum*" (Aquinas, *De Veritate*, q. 12, a. 6). 2S 17:2 (155/342).

7. Crisógono de Jesús Sacramentado, *Vida de San Juan de la Cruz* (Eng. trans. Kathleen Pond under the title *The Life of St. John of the Cross* [which is the edition used here]): see pp. 35ff.

8. Bord, *Mémoire et espérance*, 75–80. See below, pp. 24–26.

9. Crisógono, *Life*, 33–34.

10. It must also be remembered that John prided himself on possessing no reference work other than the Bible (Crisógono, *Life*, 184ff.), so his works lack citations to his scholastic sources, even though these sources are an important influence. For further general information on John's life and works, see Federico Ruiz Salvador, *Introducción a San Juan de la Cruz: El hombre, los escritos, el sistema* (Madrid: Biblioteca de Autores Cristianos, 1968), and idem, *Místico y maestro: San Juan de la Cruz* (Madrid: Editorial de Espiritualidad, 1986).

11. E.g., J. Huijben, "Ruysbroec et saint Jean de la Croix," *Études Carmélitaines* (1932): 232ff., quoted in Sanson, *L'Esprit humain*, 10; Pierre Groult, *Les mystiques des Pays-Bas et la littérature espagnole du seizième siècle* (Louvain: Librairie universitaire, Uystpruyst, 1927).

12. Principally by Jean Orcibal, as noted in the introduction, n. 1. Alois Winklhöfer is quoted by Orcibal as having identified verbal links between John of the Cross and Surius's translation of Tauler, published in Spain in 1551: Alois Winklhöfer, "Johann van Kreuz und die Surius Übersetzung der Werke Taulers," in *Theologie in Geschichte und Gegenwart*, ed. J. Auer and H. Volk (Munich, 1957), 317–48, quoted in Orcibal, "Le Rôle de l'Intellect Possible chez Jean de la Croix," in *La Mystique Rhénane*, 264. See also Giovanna della Croce, "Johannes vom Kreuz und die deutsch-niederländische Mystik," *Jahrbuch für Mystiche Theologie* 1 (1960).

13. Bord, *Mémoire et espérance*, 74. (See my analysis of the distinction below, pp. 31–34.)

14. Jean Orcibal suggests that the Pseudo-Taulerian *Institutions*, also translated by Surius, were the source of John's view of the passive intellect and of the idea of the *fondo del alma*: see Orcibal, "Le Rôle de l'Intellect Possible," in *La Mystique Rhénane*, 263–64. See also Payne, *Cognitive Value*, 29. As shown in a recent publication of the stock of a bookseller in Spain at this time, Tauler was available in the 1560s, in the Latin translation of his sermons and some sermons attributed to John Ruusbroec, by Surius, published at Cologne in 1548 and Coïmbra (Portugal) in 1551. See William Pettas, *A Sixteenth-Century Spanish Bookstore: The Inventory of Juan de Junta* (Transactions of the American Philosophical Society, vol. 85, pt. 1; Philadelphia, 1995).

15. E.g., 2N 15:2; 2N 18:5.

16. E.g., 2S 29:1, 6; C 1:6; etc.

17. In the obvious respect of likening the mystical itinerary to climbing a mountain, as in the *Subida del Monte Carmelo* and *Noche oscura*.

18. L 3:82; L 4:17.

19. Sanson, *L'Esprit humain*, 41.

20. Colin P. Thompson, *The Poet and the Mystic: A Study of the Cántico Espiritual of San Juan de la Cruz* (Oxford: Oxford University Press, 1977).

21. There is a vast literature on the relationship between John's poetry and his prose, which there is not space to discuss here, other than the brief comments that I make below. In the main, I follow Colin Thompson's view (*The Poet and the Mystic*) that no strong distinction should be made between the two—they are closely related to one another in conception and expression.

22. Michel de Certeau (*The Mystic Fable: The Sixteenth and Seventeenth Centuries* [Chicago: Chicago University Press, 1992]) interprets John's distinction between poetry and prose in postmodern terms as a separation between the wandering "I" of personal experience, represented in the poems, and the fragmenting theological tradition, represented by the commentaries. My view is that there is no conflict here; on the contrary, we cannot speak of John's view of "experience" without reference to his theological context, in which he is firmly rooted.

23. Max Huot de Longchamp, "Les Mystiques Catholiques et la Bible," in *Bible de Tous les Temps*, vol. 5, *Le temps des Réformes et la Bible*, ed. Guy Bedouelle and Bernard Roussel (Paris: Beauchesne, 1989), 586–612.

24. It has become increasingly clear since Sanson's study that the scholastic approach existed apart from the mystical, as shown first in the contrast of monastic theology from scholastic theology made by Jean Leclercq, and more recently in the threefold division of theology in the late medieval period by Bernard McGinn, of scholastic, monastic, and vernacular. See Jean Leclercq, *The Love of Learning and the Desire for God* (New York: Fordham University Press, 1961); Bernard McGinn, "The Changing Shape of Late Medieval Mysticism," *Church History* 65 (1996): 197–219. For McGinn, there is a continuing conversation between these three categories of theology, but they diverge in the late medieval period. Mystical writings are increasingly written in the vernacular, and they have increasingly little connection with the scholastic life of the universities. There is also a divergence of ideas among the categories: in particular, mystical theology in the vernacular is increasingly concerned with the "immediacy" of the encounter with God in union (214–15), which is an important feature of John's thought, but not of scholastic thought.

25. 1S 3:3; as in the dictum quoted above: *nihil est in intellectu quod prius non fuerit in sensu.*

26. "La afición y asimiento que el alma tiene a la criatura iguala a la misma alma con la criatura," and "el amor hace semejanza entre lo que ama y es amado." 1S 4:3 (78/263).

27. "Dos contrarios no pueden caber en un sujeto." 1S 4:2 (78/263).

28. 1S 6:2.

29. 2S 12:5; C 5:1.

30. "Todos los medios han de ser proporcionados al fin." 2S 8:2, 3 (126/312).

31. 2S 5:3 (116/302).

32. 1S 4:4; C 6:2.

33. "Ni por vía del espíritu ni por la del sentido puede conocer a Dios la parte sensitiva." 3S 24:3 (254/444).

34. "Luego al primer movimiento se pone la noticia y afección de la voluntad en Dios dándole más gusto aquella noticia que el motivo sensual que se la causa"; "muy bueno es." 3S 24:5, 4 (255/444).

35. "De lo dicho infiero la siguiente doctrina, y es que hasta que el hombre venga a tener tan habituado el sentido en la purgación del gozo sensible, que de primer movimiento saque el provecho que he dicho de que le envíen las cosas luego a Dios, tiene necesidad de negar su gozo y gusto acerca de ellas para sacar de la vida sensitiva al alma, temiendo que, pues él no es espiritual, sacará, por ventura, del uso destas cosas más jugo y fuerza para el sentido que para el espíritu." 3S 26:7 (259/449).

36. "El ejercicio de su voluntad sólo trae en lo sensible . . . esotro que levanta a Dios la voluntad llama espiritual." 3S 26:4, quoting 1 Cor. 2:14 (258/448). For John's other comments on this scriptural text, see C 26:13; L 3:74; and on the *pneuma/sarx* distinction in Gal. 5:17, see 3S 22:2; C 3:10; C 16:5; and on *pneuma/sarx* in John 1:13, see 2S 5:5.

37. "No ocupan al alma las cosas de este mundo ni la dañan." 1S 3:4 (77/262).

38. For an exhaustive analysis of the Pauline dichotomy as it appears in John, see Miguel A. Diez Gonzalez, *Pablo en Juan de la Cruz: sabidura y ciencia de Dios* (Burgos: Editorial Monte Carmelo, 1990), esp. 137–80.

39. Following the Pauline formula of 1 Thess. 5:23, Origen distinguished three terms, *sōma, psychē,* and *pneuma,* of which the middle term, *psychē,* could be oriented to the body or to the spirit. See for instance Bernard McGinn, *A History of Western Christian Mysticism,* vol. 1, *The Foundations of Mysticism: Origins to the Fifth Century* (New York: Crossroad, 1991), 114.

40. 2S 10–32. Augustine's three categories of vision are corporeal, *spiritual,* and intellectual, and are treated in his *Literal Meaning of Genesis,* bk. 12.

41. Sanson, *L'Esprit humain,* 49; Bord, *Mémoire et espérance,* 92; Morel, *Le sens de l'existence,* 64. For examples of this kind of suffering, see 1S 4:2; 2S 1–4; L 1:22.

42. "Anihilado en el alma sin consuelo y alivio alguno." 2S 7:9, 11 (124/310).

43. 1S 6:4.

44. "Que Dios no destruye la naturaleza, antes la perfecciona . . . [a lo cual respondo que] necessariamente se sigue su destrucción." 3S 2:7 (216/405). See the fuller discussion of this passage and the question of the "destruction" of the soul in chap. 3, pp. 48–49.

45. Note John's description of the "three reasons for calling this journey a night": because (a) one is depriving the appetite of worldly possessions (night of the senses; "early evening"); (b) the means or the road to union is faith, which is a

dark night for the intellect ("midnight"); (c) the point of arrival is God, "who is a dark night to man in this life"—though here the light begins to be seen dimly and the night is over: it is "early dawn." 1S 2:1, 5; C 14&15:23.

46. 3S 24:5 (as quoted above, see n. 34); C 40:6; L 2:22; L 3:74.

47. In this state, the passions, one of which is joy in created goods, have effectively been removed, so that there is no "disturbance" to the spiritual part of the soul in union: C 20&21:9.

48. Bord, *Mémoire et espérance*, 90.

49. "El orden de conocer." 2S 17:3 (156/342); 1S 3:3; 2S 3:2.

50. C 18:7; 3S 23:3; 1S 3:3.

51. "Los sentidos corporales interiores; sentido común." 2S 10:3 (131/317); 2S 12:2–3; C 18:7; L 3:69 (637/1017).

52. "Imaginación, imaginitiva; fantasía." 2S 12:2–3 (137/323).

53. John does not always make this distinction between imagination and fantasy and sometimes seems to confuse their functions: I am following the analysis of André Bord for the sake of clarity. Bord, *Mémoire et espérance*, 81–86.

54. 2S 16:2.

55. See Bord, *Mémoire et espérance*, 84–85.

56. 2S 12:3, 4.

57. "La porción inferior o sensitiva de el alma, la sensualidad." C 18:7 (484/814).

58. "Que tiene capacidad para comunicar con Dios, cuyas operaciones son contrarias a las de la sensualidad." C 18:7 (484/814).

59. C 1:9.

60. 2S 11:2.

61. "Sacarla de lo interior a que quiera lo exterior que ellas quieren y apetecen." C 18:4 (484/813).

62. "Los afecciones." C 18:4 (484/813); 2S 4:4.

63. "Los apetitos," e.g., 1S 3:2 (76/261–62). This does not imply that the appetites cannot be spiritualized and participate in union, though they must first be "voided": John says that in union the "divine water" that flows into the soul from God "fills the voids of her appetites" (*llena los vacíos de sus apetitos*). C 14&15:9 (466/793).

64. 1S 11:6 (96/285).

65. "Pasiones": "gozo,esperanza, dolor y temor." 3S 16:2 (237/426); C 20&21:4, 9.

66. 2S 6:1. The distinction works better in French, as used by Bord: "*l'espoir*" is hope for created goods, "*l'espérance*" is hope for God. (In Spanish they are both "*esperanza.*") The usual designation for this passion is desire, not hope. Bord references Aquinas, *Summa Theologiae* Ia IIae q. 25, a. 4, where Aquinas says that the passion of desire culminates in hoping: Bord, *Mémoire et espérance*, 200. This may be John's source for naming nontheological desire "hope." In any case, John intends a strong contrast between this kind of hope and the theological virtue of hope.

67. 3S 17:1.

68. 3S 24:5.

69. 2N 24:2, 3; C 26:14.

70. 1N 4:2; 2N 3:1; L 3:7. Even in the severest stage of purgation, "a man is not required to cease recalling what he must do and know, for, since he is not attached to the possession of these thoughts, he will not be harmed." 3S 15:1 (236/424).

Also, acquired knowledge of the sciences is not lost in this state, nor the habits of such knowledge: C 26:16.

71. "La inteligencia natural." 2S 8:4 (127/313).

72. 1S 8:2.

73. E.g., C 18:4.

74. E.g., 2N 13:3.

75. 2S 8:4.

76. "El entendimiento que llaman los filósofos activo." C 39:12 (561/895). "El entendimiento pasivo." C 14&15:15 (469/796).

77. ". . . obra es en las formas y fantasias y aprehensiones de las potencias corporales." C 39:12 (561/895).

78. Following Steven Payne, *Cognitive Value*, 25. There are some notable differences from Aquinas in John's epistemology, of course; for instance, the interior senses number two (imagination and fantasy), not four, and memory is a spiritual faculty for John, but only a natural faculty for Aquinas, but they seem to agree on the active and passive intellect.

79. Bord, *Mémoire et espérance*, 76–80. (More references to John and to Augustine are to be found in Bord's text than are cited below.)

80. "Y no se ha de entender que, aunque el alma queda en este no saber, pierde allí los hábitos de las ciencias adquisitos que tenía." C 26:16 (515/846).

81. "De manera que luego, en poniéndose delante de Dios, se pone en acto de noticia confusa." 2S 14:2 (143/329).

82. "Receptáculo y archivo." L 3:69 (637/1017).

83. "La fantasía . . . por ser corporal . . . no tiene capacidad para formas espirituales—, sino que intelectual y espiritualmente [el alma] se acuerda de ella por la forma que en el alma de sí ['the soul itself'] dejó impresa." 3S 14:1 (235/423). For the memory working in tandem with the fantasy, see 2S 16:2; 3S 13:6; for the memory working with the "soul itself," see 3S 13:7–14:2. For this separation of corporeal from "purely spiritual" apprehensions and faculties in the soul, see 2S 23–32. On John's use of the "soul itself" to designate memory working without sensible forms, see Bord, *Mémoire et espérance*, 80, 88–89.

84. E.g., "Imagen . . . o noticia impresa . . . en la memoria." 3S 7:1 (224/413).

85. Bord, *Mémoire et espérance*, 91–96.

86. For instance by Payne, *Cognitive Value*, 20, 38–41. Elizabeth Wilhelmsen takes the opposite view here. Her disagreement is the traditional disagreement between Thomists and some followers of Augustine over whether memory is an autonomous faculty with a real distinction from the intellect and will. Bord argues that for John, memory is an autonomous faculty and must be really distinct from the intellect and will in order to form the trinitarian analogy that is central to John's theory of spiritual knowing, while Wilhelmsen argues that, like Aquinas, John subsumes memory under intellect and will, as memory has no object other than the objects of intellect and will. She finds a number of passages in John to back this up and does not think that Bord's rejection of them as "imprecision of expression" is adequate. She argues that the trinitarian analogy for John is between the intellect and will on the one hand, and the *two* inner-trinitarian *processions* on the other hand, rather than between the *three* spiritual faculties and the *three* persons of the Trinity. My own view is that Bord is correct: though it is the inner dynamism of the spiritual faculties that John is relating to the Trinity, as Wilhelmsen says, he is also impressed by the analogy of the "threeness" of the spiritual faculties to the three persons. Further, memory certainly has the status of an

autonomous faculty in such passages as "the memory does not recall these [uncreated things] through any form, image, or figure that may have been impressed on the soul, for these touches and feelings of union do not have any" (3S 14:2)—John is describing a relation between memory and "uncreated things" which is specific to the memory rather than subsumed under his treatment of intellect and will; this is also true of his whole organization of the second and third books of the *Subida*, where he considers the spiritual apprehensions of each of the three spiritual faculties in turn. See Elizabeth Wilhelmsen, "La memoria en Juan de la Cruz," *Carmelus* 37 (1980): 88–145; also her main work, *Knowledge and Symbolization in Saint John of the Cross* (Frankfurt am Main/New York: Peter Lang, 1993). For a concise statement, predating Bord, of the view that memory is really distinct from intellect and will in John, see Alberto de la Virgen del Carmen, "Naturaleza de la memoria espiritual según san Juan de la Cruz," *Revista de espiritualidad* 11 (1952): 291–99 and 12 (1953): 431–50.

87. Bord, *Mémoire et espérance*, 97.

88. L 4:5; C 12:5; C 14&15:5.

89. "Estas noticias divinas que son acera de Dios nunca son de cosas particulares, por cuanto son acera del Sumo Principio . . . porque consiste en tenerlas en cierto toque que se hace del alma en la Divinidad, y así el mismo Dios es el que allí es sentido y gustado." 2S 26:5 (194–95/382). Cf. also 2S 14:2; 2S 26:12; 2N 8:2 (etc.).

90. 2S 14:2.

91. "Comienza Dios a comunicársele . . . por el espíritu puro, en que no cae discurso sucesivamente, comunicándosele con acto de sencilla contemplacíon." 1N 9:8 (315/505).

92. "No cae en sentido," 2S 17:5 (157/344); "no se llenan con menos que infinito." L 3:18 (617/982).

93. "Las cuales son tan profundas cuanto de grandes bienes son capaces," ibid.; "teniendo el alma capacidad infinita," 2S 17:8 (159/345).

94. "No los puedan recibir hasta de todo punto vaciarse."

95. C 16:10. The process of purgation described by John is briefly passed over here; see chap. 3 for a fuller account.

96. 2S 6:1, 2 (119/305); C 2:7; C 12:7.

97. "La bajeza e impureza." 2N 5:2 (335/527).

98. "La parte sensitiva se purifica en sequedad, y las potencias en su vacío de sus aprehensiones, y el espíritu en tiniebla oscura." 2N 6:4 (339/531).

99. 2N 8:4.

100. 3S 33:4.

101. 2S 22:19; 3S 30:2.

102. See n. 40.

103. 2S 10:1–4.

104. "Todas aquellas cosas corporales no tienen . . . proporción alguna con las espirituales." 2S 11:3 (132/318).

105. 2S 12:6.

106. 2S 18:9; 2S 26:14.

107. 2S 12:3. This is also the case in Augustine. Of course, this supernatural source may not be God but the devil, and, John is keen to point out, it may be so mixed with natural sources as to be entirely unreliable.

108. 3S 30:2 (see n. 112). John appears to have thought of this distinction in the course of writing: spiritual visions are a subset of supernatural visions, which

he only comes to distinguish as the entirely noncorporeal kind in dealing with intellectual visions; before then he calls them all supernatural visions (e.g., in 2S 23:3).

109. 2S 24:5. See 2S 23–32 on the division of spiritual apprehensions into two kinds, those of "corporeal substances" and those of "separate or incorporeal substances" (2S 24:1); see also n. 83 above.

110. "No se pueden desnudar y claramente ver en esta vida con el entendimiento, puédense, empero, sentir en la sustancia del alma con suavísimos toques y juntas." 2S 24:4 (190/377). Rowan Williams notes that, for John, "*sustancial* should be taken to mean 'devoid of accidents': a 'substantial' contact is one which carries with it no contingent or perceptible features. It is entirely God's act": Rowan Williams,"Butler's *Western Mysticism*: Towards an Assessment," *Downside Review* 102 (1984): 205.

111. "Digo que dos maneras de visiones pueden caer en el entendimiento: unas son de sustancias corpóreas, otras de sustancias separadas o incorpóreas." 2S 24:1 (289/376); 2S 32:1.

112. "Y así hay diferencia en el objeto, pues que de los espirituales sólo es el Creador y el alma, mas de los sobrenaturales es la criatura; y también difieren en la sustancia y, por consiguiente, en la operación, y así también necesariamente en la doctrina." 3S 30:2 (267/456).

113. Ibid.

114. Ibid. and 2S 32:1.

115. "[Los aprehensiones espirituales son] en dos maneras: unas increadas y otras de criaturas." 3S 14:2 (235/423).

116. 2S 24:4 (190/377), q.v. n. 110.

117. "La divina junta y unión del alma." Ibid.; "Es toque de sustancia, es a saber, de sustancia de Dios en sustancia de el alma." L 2:21 (602/955); 2N 23:11, 12. Sometimes the "substance of the soul" is referred to simply as the "soul" or the "soul itself"—in these cases, the meaning is clear from the context. See Bord, *Mémoire et espérance*, 88–89, 93.

118. L 4:5, C 14&15:12.

119. E.g., L 2:34.

120. "Por el *sentido de el alma* . . . entiende aquí la virtud y fuerza que tiene la sustancia de el alma para sentir y gozar los objetos de las potencias espirituales . . . memoria, entendimiento y voluntad. . . . [El alma] conoce que tiene tanta capacidad y senos cuantas cosas distintas recibe de inteligencias, de sabores, de gozos, de deleites, etc., de Dios. Todas las cuales cosas se reciben y asientan en este sentido de el alma, que, como digo, es la virtud y capacidad que tiene el alma para sentirlo, poseerlo y gustarlo todo, administrándoselo las cavernas de las potencias, así como al sentido común de la fantasía acuden con las formas de sus objetos los sentidos corporales, y él es receptáculo y archivo de ellas; por lo cual este sentido común del alma, que está hecho receptáculo y archivo de las grandezas de Dios, está tan ilustrado y tan rico, cuanto alcanza de esta alta y esclarecida posesión." L 3:69 (637/1016). On the "*cosas distintas*" that the soul receives through this "feeling of the soul," see chap. 3, pp. 52–53.

121. From here on I use the term "spiritual knowing" as a shorthand for the knowing attained through spiritual apprehensions of incorporeal substances, that is, the knowing of union proper, which could equally be called "mystical knowing."

122. Thus, the "feeling of the soul" corresponds to what John elsewhere calls the "soul itself"—the *spiritual* equivalent of the storage faculty of the fantasy, also

known as the "common sense" (*sentido común*), now considered in its incorporeal function—as seen in Bord's analysis of memory above.

123. "Y *al silbo* de estos aires llama una subidísima y sabrosísima inteligencia de Dios y sus virtudes, la cual redunda en el entendimiento del toque que hacen estas virtudes de Dios en la sustancia de la alma. . . . Se sienten otras dos cosas, que son sentimiento de deleite e inteligencia; y así como el toque del aire se gusta en el sentido del tacto y el silbo del mismo aire con el oído, así también el toque de las virtudes de el Amado se sienten y gozan con el tacto de esta alma, que es en la sustancia della, y la inteligencia de las tales virtudes de Dios se sienten en el oído del alma, que es el entendimiento." C 14&15:12, 13 (467/795).

124. "Porque es en el entendimiento en que consiste la fruición (como dicen los teólogos) que es ver a Dios." C 14&15:14 (468/796).

125. John considers the intellect to be passive in spiritual knowing—using the passive rather than the active intellect: C 14&15:15; C 38:5; C 39:12.

126. 2S 32:2, 3 (212/400); C 14&15:13 (as in quotation above, n. 123).

127. 2N 13:3; again, identified with the passive intellect.

128. L 3:3.

129. 2N 12:7, L 3:49.

130. "Mas de las increadas digo que . . . desto [destas] no se acuerda la memoria por alguna forma, imagen o figura que imprimiesen en el alma, porque no la tienen aquellos toques y sentimientos de unión del Criador, sino por el efecto que en ella hicieron de luz, amor, deleite y renovación espiritual, etc., de las cuales, cada vez que se acuerda se renueva algo desto." 3S 14:2 (235/424).

131. Trueman Dicken, *Crucible of Love*, 33, 368–74; Payne, *Cognitive Value*, 43, 49 (n. 35); Bord, *Mémoire et espérance*, 74.

132. E.g., 2S 24:4; L 2:8; "Toque de sustancia,"L 2:21 (602/955).

133. "Un abismo llama a obro abismo (Ps. 41:8)." L 3:71 (638/1018).

134. "La íntima sustancia del fondo del alma." L 3:68 (637/1016).

135. For a history of this theme, see Endre von Ivánka, *Plato christianus: Übernahme und Umgestaltung des Platonismus durch die Väter* (Einsiedeln: Johannes Verlag, 1964), 315–51. John also speaks of it in terms of transverberation, as "a sharp point in the substance of the spirit, in the heart of the pierced soul" (*una viva punta en las sustancia del espíritu, como en el corazón del alma traspasado*) when the soul is "pierced" by a "seraphim." L 2:9 (598/949).

136. "Es una aspiración que hace al alma Dios, en que, por aquel recuerdo del alto conocimiento de la Deidad, la aspira el Espíritu Santo con la misma proporción que fue la inteligencia y noticia de Dios, en que la absorbe profundísimamente en el Espíritu Santo." L 4:17 (649/1039).

137. The fact that John does not mention memory here, but only "knowledge, understanding and love," makes this a key proof text for Wilhelmsen against the autonomous status of memory and against Bord's analysis (see n. 86 above). In Bord's view, with which I agree, memory is implied, even though it is not mentioned in this particular case, as other passages show and for the reasons given above.

138. "Total transformación . . . el alma en las tres Personas de la Santísima Trinidad." C 39:3 (558/891).

139. Bord, *Mémoire et espérance*, 90–91; see also Sanson, *L'Esprit humain*, 58–61.

140. "Sosegada." 1S 15:2 (106/292); "Adormidos." 1N 14:1 (327/518).

141. "En [los perfectos] . . . cesan ya estos arrobamientos y tormentos de cuerpos, gozando ellos de la libertad del espíritu, sin que se añuble ni transponga el sentido." 2N 1:2 (330–31/522); 1N 9:6; 3S 6:1.

142. "Como . . . estas dos partes son un supuesto, ordinariamente participan entrambas de lo que la una recibe." 1N 4:2 (304/493). "Cada uno en su manera de un mismo manjar espiritual en un mismo plato de un solo supuesto y sujeto." 2N 3:1 (333/524).

143. "Quietud." 2N 24:3 (387/583).

144. 2S 29:1–3.

145. "Ordenadas." 2N 24:2 (387/583).

146. 3S 26:7 (as quoted above, n. 35).

147. "Porque según la operación, que entonces es toda espiritual, no comunica en la parte sensitiva." 2N 23:14 (386/583). "Poniéndolos en sueño y silencio acerca de todas las cosas de arriba y de abajo." 2N 24:3 (387/584).

148. L 1:25.

149. "Amparando al natural"; "sabor y gólosina," L 1:27 (590/934); L 1:36; "Participar," C 40:5 (564/899).

150. "Y deste bien de el alma a veces redunda en el cuerpo la unción del Espíritu Santo y goza toda la sustancia sensitiva, todos los miembros y huesos y médulas, no tan remisamente como comúnmente suele acaecer, sino con sentimiento de grande deleite y gloria, que se siente hasta los últimos artejos de pies y manos. . . . Por eso baste decir, así de lo corporal como de lo espiritual, que a *vida eterna sabe*." L 2:22 (603/956). Note that the quotation "that tastes eternal life" is the line of the *Llama* poem being commented on. See also L 3:7; 3:16; 3:74; C 17:7.

151. "Los pasados ímpetus de amor no eran bastantes, porque no eran de tanta calidad para alcanzarlo, ahora que estoy tan fortalecida en amor, que no sólo no desfallece mi sentido y espíritu en ti, mas antes, fortalecidos de ti, *mi corazón y mi carne se gozan en Dios vivo* (Ps. 83:3) con grande conformidad de las partes, donde lo que tú quieres pida pido, y lo que [tú] no quieres no quiero, ni aun puedo ni me pasa por pensamiento querer; y . . . pues salen de ti y tú me mueves a ellas, y con sabor y gozo en el Espíritu Santo te lo pido, *saliendo ya mi juicio de tu rostro* (Ps. 16:2)." L 1:36 (595/942).

152. "Una sola pieza de perfección del alma, la cual . . . contiene en sí muchas perfecciones y virtudes fuertes." C 16:9 (477/806); L 2:34.

153. "Mi alma se ha empleado/y todo mi caudal en su servicio . . . todo lo que pertenece a la parte sensitiva del alma . . . el cuerpo con todos sus sentidos y potencias así interiores como exteriores, y toda la habilidad natural, conviene a saber, las cuatro pasiones, los apetitos naturales y el demás caudal del alma. . . . Porque el cuerpo ya le trata según Dios, los sentidos interiores e exteriores [rige y gobierna] enderezando a El las operaciones de ellos." C 28:4 (521/852).

154. "Esta parte sensitiva con sus potencias no tienen capacidad para gustar esencial y propiamente de los bienes espirituales . . . bajan de sus operaciones naturales, cesando de ellas." C 40:6 (565/899).

155. "Esta parte sensitiva con sus potencias . . . por cierta redundancia del espíritu reciben sensitivamente recreación y deleite de ellos; por el cual deleite estos sentidos y potencias corporales son atraídos al recogimiento interior, donde está bebiendo el alma las aguas de los bienes espirituales; lo cual más es descender *a la vista* de ellas que a beberlas y gustarlas como ellas son." Ibid. (565/899).

156. "Empleando el entendimiento en las cosas que son más de su servicio para hacerlas, y su voluntad en amar todo lo que a Dios agrada, y en todas las cosas aficionar la voluntad a Dios, y la memoria y el cuidado de lo que es de su servicio y lo que más le ha de agradar." C 28:3 (521/852).

157. "Aunque estotro es en más subida manera, por intervenir en ello el ejercicio de la voluntad." L 3:77 (640/1022); L 1:9.

158. L 3:78.

159. "Porque las virtudes no las puede obrar el alma ni alcanzarlas a solas sin ayuda de Dios, ni tampoco las obra Dios a solas en el alma sin ella." C 30:6 (529/861). Unlike the grace which was given in the purgative stages, as described in the *Subida* and *Noche*, here the soul receives cooperative and not operative grace (C 30:6). Even in the state of union, John asserted in the *Subida* that souls are "moved by God and not by themselves" (3S 2:16). The fact that he allows cooperative grace here emphasizes the free agency of the soul to do as it wills in union and to put its own actions into effect. This makes the union more complete rather than less, as the soul does God's will perfectly out of its own free will. On the mutuality and freedom of the spiritual marriage, see the appendix, p. 143.

Notes to Chapter Three

1. Morel, *Le sens de l'existence*, 2:26ff.; Max Huot de Longchamp, *Lectures de Jean de la Croix*, 36–39, 86–87.

2. "[El alma] nunca permanece en un estado, sino todo es subir y bajar." 2N 18:3–4 (372/568).

3. "Gran fuerza de deseo abisal por la unión con Dios." C 17:1 (479/807).

4. "Levántanse en el alma a esta sazón contrarios contra contrarios; los de el alma contra los de Dios." L 1:22 (587/929).

5. That is, the "B" redaction of the *Cántico*, as the "A" redaction was not one of his later works. See the appendix, n. 1.

6. Louis Dupré, *Transcendent Selfhood: The Loss and Recovery of the Inner Life* (New York: Crossroad, 1976), 93.

7. "El alma más vive donde ama que en el cuerpo donde anima . . . y ella vive por amor en lo que ama." C 8:3 (441/768). This view is derived in the Western tradition particularly from Augustine and Bernard of Clairvaux.

8. Jacques Maritain's *Distinguer pour unir, ou les degrés du savoir* (*Distinguish to Unite, or The Degrees of Knowledge*), first published in 1932, remains the most important attempt to relate John of the Cross's view of mystical knowing to the levels of knowing in the human subject. Maritain's approach is somewhat flawed by his reading of John of the Cross through Thomas Aquinas which, as we saw in the previous chapter, puts too exclusive an emphasis on Aquinas against the other important influences on John's thought. Nevertheless, his attempt is crucial for this study as he offers a view of both the connection and distinction between ordinary knowing and mystical knowing.

9. Ibid., 80–82. The contrast with the Cartesian view is also well set out by Pedro Cerezo Galán, "La Antropología del Espíritu en Juan de la Cruz," in *Actas del Congreso Internacional Sanjuanista (Avila 23–28 Sept. 1991)*, vol. 3, *Pensamiento* (Madrid: Junta de Castilla y León, Consejería de Cultura y Turismo, 1993), 126–53. For wider treatments of the Cartesian shift in the understanding of the self, see Louis Dupré, *Passage to Modernity* (New Haven: Yale University Press, 1993); and Stephen Toulmin, *Cosmopolis* (Chicago: University of Chicago Press, 1992).

10. Ibid., 100.

11. Ibid., 99. On this element in John's understanding of the self, see also David Centner, "Christian Freedom and The Nights of St. John of the Cross," *Carmelite Studies* 2 (1982): 3–80.

12. Ibid., 393, n. 49.

13. Ibid., 394.

14. Ibid., 263.

15. The difference between Aquinas and John is much greater than Maritain wants to acknowledge. He says that mystical experience, specifically as understood by John of the Cross, is the apex of the Christian life and that it is strictly speaking not understandable, but that it is also fully compatible with Aquinas's speculative theology as a kind of "superanalogy." He reconciles the two realms by saying that John and Aquinas use different words to speak of the same thing: the differences between them are superficial, a matter of terminology, while they agree in their basic doctrine (Maritain, *Degrees of Knowledge*, 297, 336, 347). But his attempt to reconcile the two thinkers reaches a level of absurdity at times. For instance, in response to the difference that, for Aquinas, it is not possible to know God a priori, without created intermediaries, before the beatific vision in heaven (*Summa Theologiae* Ia q. 2, a. 1), while for John we can know God in union as uncreated, without any created images or forms, by immediate contact with God's "substance," in this life, Maritain proposes something called "silent" concepts which "play the formal part" under the "connaturality of charity" in mystical knowing (281). In other words, he introduces the notion of "silent concepts" to maintain his conceptual account of knowing, in spite of John's unequivocal rejection of all created intermediaries. This is no help in interpreting John; but it says something interesting about Maritain's interpretation of Aquinas. Maritain is a conceptualist: he regards human knowing as inalienably requiring created concepts. This may be contrasted with Bernard Lonergan, for instance, who in *Verbum: Word and Idea in Aquinas* interprets Aquinas's understanding of human *intellectus* as first of all a participation in the processions of the Trinity and only *then* a matter of concepts: Lonergan emphasizes the dynamics of knowing ahead of the need for concepts. This Lonerganian interpretation of Aquinas would, clearly, be more applicable to John than Maritain's conceptualism, particularly in the interesting relationship that Lonergan highlights between human knowing and the processions of the Trinity. Unfortunately, Lonergan did not develop this Augustinian idea of a trinitarian basis for knowing in relation to mystical thought. But neither Maritain nor Lonergan, nor Aquinas, to my mind, really brings out the full trinitarian relationality, the *otherness* of relationship with God, and the inclusion of this otherness within the soul, that we find in John. It is better to treat John (and later Teresa) alone rather than to be saddled with the difficulties, first, of showing precisely where there is agreement with Aquinas, and second, of interpreting Aquinas in an appropriate way.

16. Ibid. C 7:2–5.

17. S Prol. 9.

18. "¡Oh si esas verdades que informe y oscuramente me enseñas encubiertas en tus artículos de fe acabases ya de dármelas clara y formalmente descubiertas en ellos, como lo pide mi deseo!" C 12:5 (455/782).

19. "Por grandes comunicaciones y presencias y altas subidas noticias de Dios que un alma en esta vida tenga, no es aquello esencialmente Dios ni tiene que ver con El." C 1:3 (417/742).

20. Ibid.; "Oscurecidas sus primeras luces, tiene más de veras éstas en esta tan excelente y necesaria virtud del conocimiento propio." 1N 12:2 (321/511).

21. "Las cuales tres virtudes [las tres virtudes teologales, fe, esperanza y caridad] todas hacen . . . vacío en las potencias." 2S 6:2 (119/305).

22. "Nunca te quieras satisfacer en lo que entendieres de Dios, sino en lo que no entendieres dél." C 1:12 (420/745–46); cf. 2S 4:2–3.

23. "Herida de amor." C 1:14, 17 (422/748).

24. "La hace salir fuera de sí y renovar toda y pasar a nueva manera de ser." C 1:17 (422/748).

25. C 2:6.

26. "Estas cavernas son las potencias de el alma: memoria, entendimiento y voluntad; las cuales son tan profundas cuanto de grandes bienes son capaces, pues no se llenan con menos que infinito. . . . Es, pues, profunda la capacidad de estas cavernas, porque lo que en ellas puede caber, que es Dios, es profundo e infinito; y así será en cierta manera su capacidad infinita, y así su sed es infinita, su hambre también es profunda e infinita, su deshacimiento y pena es muerte infinita." L 3:18, 22 (617–18/982–84).

27. "Que no quiera de hoy más entretenerla con otras cualesquier noticias y comunicaciones suyas y rastros de su excelencia." C 6:2 (436/762); C 7:6; C 22:7; C 35:6; L 4:11.

28. "Por tanto, que sea El servido de entregarse a ella ya de veras en acabado y perfecto amor." C 6:2 (436/762).

29. "De veras comunicándote por ti mismo . . . dándote todo al todo de mi alma, porque toda ella [te] tenga a ti todo." C 6:6 (437/763).

30. "Para lo cual es de notar que el Verbo Hijo de Dios, juntamente con el Padre y el Espíritu Santo, esencial y presencialmente está escondido en el íntimo ser del alma." C 1:6 (418/743).

31. "Nunca pares en amar y deleitarte en eso que entendieres o sintieres de Dios, sino ama y deléitate en lo que no puedes entender y sentir de El, que eso es, como habemos dicho, buscarle en fe." C 1:12 (420/746).

32. On the distinction in John between conceptual, propositional knowledge of the articles of faith and nonconceptual inner faith, see James Denis Edwards, "The Dynamism in Faith: The Interaction between Experience of God and Explicit Faith: a Comparative Study of the Mystical Theology of John of the Cross and the Transcendent Theology of Karl Rahner" (S.T.D. diss., Catholic University of America, 1979). Edwards draws out this contrast well in John, though I regard his Rahnerian reading of the distinction as somewhat overblown.

33. C 12:1 (453/780).

34. In this chapter I am not distinguishing "supernatural" from "spiritual," as this introduces unnecessary complexity; John makes this distinction at one point in the *Subida*, as we saw in chap. 2, but does not do so elsewhere; thus, supernatural here is used synonymously with spiritual, i.e., referring to "mystical theology" and "union with God."

35. C 11:12. "Cuando estén en clara visión estarán en el alma como perfecta y acabada pintura." C 12:6 (455/782).

36. C 9:6.

37. 2S 13. "Un olvido grande . . . porque solamente sabe a Dios sin saber cómo." 2S 14:10, 11 (145, 146/332).

38. 3S 15:2; C 26:16.

39. C 1:17 (as quoted above, n. 24).

40. 2S 13:6. See Denys Turner, "John of the Cross: The Dark Nights and Depression," in *The Darkness of God*, 226–51, for a rather different treatment.

41. "Viendo cómo anihilamos [las potencias acerca de sus operaciones, quizá le

parecerá que antes destruimos] el camino del ejercicio espiritual que le edifi-camos. . . . Cuando Dios hace estos toques de unión en la memoria, súbitamente le da un vuelco en el cerebro (que es donde ella tiene su asiento) tan sensible, que le parece se desvanece toda la cabeza y que se pierde el juicio y el sentido. . . . (Por estar la memoria unida con Dios) . . . se pasa mucho tiempo sin sentirlo ni saber qué se hizo aquel tiempo. . . . Estas suspenciones es de notar que ya en los perfec-tos no las hay así, por cuanto hay ya perfecta unión (que son de principio de unión). . . . Dirá alguno . . . que Dios no destruye la naturaleza, antes la perfec-ciona; y de aquí necesariamente se sigue su destrucción. . . . A lo cual respondo que es así." 3S 2:1, 5–8 (214–16/403–5).

42. Ibid.; see also 2S 7:11 (124/310): it is an annihilation modeled on Christ, who was "annihilated (*anihilado*) in all things," that is, signifying perfect *detachment* from all things.

43. For Aquinas, nature shades into grace much more smoothly than for John: see *Summa Theologiae* IaIIae q. 109, aa. 2, 3; q. 113, aa. 3, 10.

44. "Por la alteza de la Sabiduría divina, que excede al talento del alma." 2N 5:2, 3 (335/527).

45. "Siente en sí más el vacío de Dios . . . porque la luz sobrenatural oscurece la natural con su exceso con gran temor y pavor. . . ." C 13:1 (457/784).

46. See n. 15 above.

47. 3S 15:2; C 26:16.

48. "Se le acaban al alma sus ansias vehementes y querellas de amor . . . comién-zale un estado de paz y deleite y de suavidad de amor." C 14&15:2 (463/790).

49. "Según los grandes fervores y ansias de amor que han precedido en el alma, suelen ser también las mercedes y visitas que Dios le hace grandes." C 13:2 (458/785).

50. "*Un abismo llama a otro abismo* (Ps. 41:8), conviene saber: un abismo de luz llama a otro abismo de luz, y un abismo de tinieblas a otro abismo de tinieblas, lla-mando cada semejante a su semejante y comunicándosele." L 3:71 (638/1018). The origin of this interpretation of Ps. 41:8 in the Western mystical tradition appears to be Hadewijch. For Hadewijch's double abyss theory, see *Letter* 18, *Hadewijch: The Complete Works*, trans. Mother Columba Hart (New York: Paulist Press, 1980), 86. A history of the exegesis of this text quoted by John and behind Hadewijch's theory can be found in Bernard McGinn, "Ocean and Desert as Sym-bols of Mystical Absorption in the Christian Mystical Tradition," *Journal of Religion* 74 (1994): 155–81.

51. "En los enamorados la herida de uno es de entrambos, y un mismo sen-timiento tienen los dos. Y así, es como si dijera: Vuélvete, esposa mía, a mí, que, si llagada vas de amor de mí, yo también (como el ciervo) vengo en esta tu llaga lla-gado a ti." C 13:9 (460–61/788).

52. Joseph Patron points out that this is the turning-point in the *Cántico*, where the soul starts to live the Christ-life "from within," no longer seeing Christ as an external figure, but by participating in his inner-trinitarian life. See Joseph Patron, "Christ in the Teaching and Life of St. John of the Cross," *Mount Carmel* 30 (1982): 94–110.

53. C 13:11.

54. "Como unas muy desviadas asomadas." C 13:10 (461/788).

55. "La sustancia del alma," C 14&15:12 (467/795); "sustancia de Dios en sus-tancia de el alma," L 2:21 (602/955).

56. "I do not affirm that a person should be negative about this knowledge as

he should be with the other apprehensions, because this knowledge is an aspect of the union toward which we are directing the soul." 2S 26:10 (196/383), q.v. chap. 1, n. 9 for full citation.

57. "And, insofar as is possible in this life, He perfects the three faculties (memory, intellect, and will) in regard to their objects (*objetos*)." C 20&21:4 (489/819). These objects are God's simple being. For *objeto* in this sense see also L 3:19; L 3:69.

58. L 1:15; L 3:19–21.

59. C 14&15:9. Note that the will leads the intellect at the beginning of union–there is "knowledge through love": C 13:11; 2N 13:2–3. In the next stage, knowledge and love are given together, with the intellect receiving knowledge directly from God, as described below.

60. L 1:36; 2:22; see chap. 2, pp. 35–37.

61. "Llama bien propiamente aquí a esta luz divina *levantes de la aurora*. . . . Se ve el entendimiento levantado con extraña novedad sobre todo natural entender a la divina luz, bien así como el que, después de un largo sueño, abre los ojos a la luz que no esperaba." C 14&15:23, 24 (471–72/799); cf. 1S 2:5.

62. "Redunda en el entendimiento del toque que hacen estas virtudes de Dios en la sustancia del alma." C 14&15:12 (467/795).

63. C 13:11; see n. 59 above.

64. "Porque es en el entendimiento en que consiste la fruición (como dicen los teólogos) que es ver a Dios." C 14&15:14 (468/796).

65. L 1:25, 26 (589/933), q.v. the appendix, nn. 16 and 17.

66. "Aunque es desnuda de accidentes, no es por esto clara, sino oscura, porque es contemplación, la cual en esta vida, como dice san Dionisio, es *rayo de tiniebla*." C 14&15:16 (469/797).

67. "Cosas distintas." L 3:69 (637/1016), q.v. chap. 2, n. 120.

68. "¡Oh *lámparas de fuego*! . . . Por medio de la cual [esta unión] dice aquí que recibe muchas y grandes noticias de sí mismo; todas amorosas, con las cuales alumbradas y enamoradas las potencias y sentido de su alma, que antes de esta unión estaba oscuro y ciego. . . . [Dios] es omnipotente, es sabio, es bueno, es misericordioso, es justo, es fuerte, es amoroso, etc., y otros infinitos atributos y virtudes que no conocemos; y, siendo El todas estas cosas en su simple ser, estando El unido con el alma, cuando El tiene por bien de abrirle la noticia, echa de *ver distintamente* en El todas estas virtudes y grandezas, conviene saber, omnipotencia, sabiduría, bondad, misericordia, etc. . . . cada una de estas cosas sea el mismo ser de Dios [en un solo supuesto suyo] que es el Padre o el Hijo o el Espíritu Santo. . . . Y por cuanto en un solo acto de esta unión recibe el alma las noticias de estos atributos . . . pues de cada una tiene *distinta noticia*." L 3:1–3 (610–11/969–70), my emphasis.

69. L 3:69 (637/1016–17): q.v. chap. 2, n. 120.

70. "Dentro del alma en que siente ella estar el Amado como en su propio lecho." C 16:1 (475/802).

71. "El hondo escondrijo de su interior." C 16:6 (477/805).

72. "Por tanto, amar Dios al alma es meterla en cierta manera en sí mismo, igualándola consigo, y así ama a el alma en sí consigo con el mismo amor que El se ama." C 32:6 (536/868).

73. That is, according to an Aristotelian cosmology. L 1:11.

74. "Cuantos más grados de amor tuviere, tanto más profundamente entra en Dios y se concentra con El. De donde podemos decir que cuantos grados de amor de Dios el alma puede tener, tantos centros puede tener en Dios, uno más adentro

que otro, porque el amor más fuerte es más unitivo. Y de esta manera podemos entender *las muchas mansiones* que dijo el Hijo de Dios *haber en la casa de su Padre* (Io. 14:2)." L 1:13 (583/923).

75. "Como ella está con aquella gran fuerza de deseo abisal por la unión con Dios . . . bien así como a la piedra, cuando con gran ímpetu y velocidad va llegando hacia su centro." C 17:1 (479/807).

76. "Entendimiento, noticia y amor . . . en la Trinidad juntamente con ella." C 39:4 (558/892); L 4:17.

77. "Será transformarla y esclarecerla según todo el ser y potencia y virtud de ella, según es capaz de recibir, hasta ponerla que parezca Dios." L 1:13 (583/924).

78. "Es de saber que el alma en cuanto espíritu no tiene alto ni bajo, más profundo y menos profundo, en su ser, como tienen los cuerpos cuantitativos, que, pues en ella no hay partes, no tiene más diferencia dentro que fuera, que toda ella es de una manera y no tiene centro de hondo y menos hondo cuantitativo, porque no puede estar en una parte más ilustrada que en otra, como los cuerpos fisicos, sino toda en una manera en más o en menos, como el aire, que todo está de una manera ilustrado y no ilustrado en más o en menos." L 1:10 (583/922).

79. "Los hábitos de la ciencias adquisitos . . . que antes se le perfeccionan con el más perfecto hábito, que es el de la ciencia sobrenatural que se le ha infundido; aunque ya estos hábitos no reinan en el alma de manera que tenga necesidad de saber por ellos (aunque no impide que algunas veces sea), porque en esta unión de sabiduría divina se juntan estos hábitos con la sabiduría superior de las otras ciencias, así como, juntándose una luz pequeña con otra grande la grande es la que priva y luce y la pequeña no se pierde, antes se perfecciona, aunque no es la que principalmente luce." C 26:16 (515/846).

80. "[El alma] las [las criaturas] conoce mejor en su ser que en ellas mismas . . . conocer por Dios las criaturas, y no por las criaturas a Dios." L 4:5 (644/1030).

81. "El centro de el alma es Dios." L 1:12 (583/923).

82. "Solo . . . moras, no sólo como en tu casa, ni sólo como en tu mismo lecho, sino también como en mi propio seno, íntima y estrechamente unido." L 4:3 (644/1028).

83. L 3:77 (640/1022), q.v. chap. 2, n. 157; see also L 3:79.

84. "Su ser naturalmente tan distinto se le tiene del de Dios como antes." 2S 5:7 (117/304). There is no question of the soul merging with God, as in the Eckhartian view, but rather the soul becomes like God by "participation" rather than "essentially" (*por participación de unión, aunque no esencialmente*): 2S 5:5 (117/303). Even where John speaks of there being "no intermediary" between the soul and God (*sin otro algun medio*) (C 22:7(8) (499/829); C 35:6; L 4:11), he maintains that there is "contact" rather than merging between God and the soul (e.g., L 2:21). The strong contrast that he is drawing is between two kinds of mediation: the sensory and created, on the one hand, and the spiritual and uncreated, on the other hand. Through transformation, the soul is made "spiritual" so that there is no longer any need for knowledge of God to be accommodated to our sensory means of knowing through sensible and intelligible "forms." But though we have been made spiritual, we remain creatures with a human nature; we only become spiritual by participation.

85. "Por unidad y transformación de amor . . . como el Padre y el Hijo están en unidad de amor." C 39:5 (559/892); C 36:5.

86. "Una de las cosas más principales por que desea el alma ser *destada y verse con Cristo* (Phil. 1:23) es por verle allá cara a cara . . . sobre la unión hipostática

human con el Verbo divino, y en la respondencia que hay a ésta de la unión de los hombres en Dios." C 37:1-3 (549–50/883–84).

87. "*Y vámonos a ver en tu hermosura.* Que quiere decir: hagamos de manera que, por medio de este ejercicio de amor ya dicho, lleguemos hasta vernos en *tu hermosura* en la vida eterna. Esto es, que de tal manera esté yo transformada en *tu hermosura*, que, siendo semejante en *hermosura*, nos veamos entrambos en tu *hermosura*, teniendo ya tu misma *hermosura*; de manera que, mirando el uno al otro, vea cada uno en el otro su *hermosura*, siendo la una y la del otro *tu hermosura* sola, absorta yo en *tu hermosura*. . . . Esta es la adopción de los hijos de Dios, que de veras dirán a Dios lo que el mismo Hijo dijo por san Juan al Eterno Padre, diciendo: *Todas mis cosas son tuyas y tus cosas son mías* (Jn 17:10)." C 36:5 (547/880).

88. "La comunicación de dulzura de amor, no sólo en la que ya tenemos en la ordinaria junta y unión de los dos, mas en la que redunda en el ejercicio de amar efectiva y actualmente, [ahora interiormente] con la voluntad en acto de afición, ahora exteriormente haciendo obras pertenecientes al servicio de el Amado." C 36:4 (547/879–80).

89. L 1:36; C 31:4; cf. C 13:11; 36:4.

90. "Poder mirar el alma a Dios es hacer obras en gracia de Dios." C 32:8 (536/869) (my emphasis).

91. Matthew, *Knowledge and Consciousness of Christ*, 165–66.

92. "No . . . tan esencial y acabadamente como en la otra vida." C 26:4 (512/843). Also on the relation of union to the beatific vision, see C 39:6; L 1:6, 14; 4:15. "No queda por romper más que la tercera [tela] de la vida sensitiva." L 1:29 (591/936). This last passage is followed by the exhortation to good works, both before and within union (L 1:34–36).

93. As discussed in the appendix, John regards St. Francis's attainment of the stigmata as one of the greatest examples of this (L 2:13). "In this elevation of all things through the incarnation of his Son and through the glory of his resurrection according to the flesh, the Father did not merely beautify creatures partially, but rather we can say, clothed them wholly in beauty and dignity" (*En este levantimiento de la encarnación de su Hijo y de la gloria de su resurrección según la carne, no solamente hermoseó el Padre las criaturas en parte, mas podremos decir que del todo las dejó vestidas de hermosura y dignidad*). C 5:4 (435/761).

Notes to Chapter Four

1. Little has been written in recent years which directly compares the thought of Teresa and John or considers their work together on the Reform in detail. Trueman Dicken, *The Crucible of Love* (1963), remains the most recent thorough treatment and is rare in being an intellectual rather than a biographical or institutional-historical study. Among recent scholarship, there are some briefer and less substantial studies: e.g., Manuel Fernández Alvarez et al., *Teresa de Jesús y Juan de la Cruz: Convergencias, Divergencias, Influencias* (Burgos: Monte Carmelo, 1989); Ana Maria Lopez Diaz-Otazu, *Aproximación a San Juan de la Cruz de la mano de Santa Teresa* (Madrid: Narcea, 1990); Thomas Dubay, *Fire Within: St. Teresa of Avila, St. John of the Cross, and the Gospel—On Prayer* (San Francisco: Ignatius, 1989). Trueman Dicken is frank enough to say that very little is known of the relationship between John and Teresa and states only, without entirely resisting the traditional hyperbole, that "history has wrapped in complete obscurity one of the most fecund of all Christian relationships since the time of the apostles" (19). Trueman

Dicken's treatment on the gender differences between Teresa and John in relation to their education and writing style (28–30) is clearly out of date and has been overturned by the recent gender studies of Teresa cited below, and some of his assessments of Teresa's anthropology read too much of John's scholastic treatment into her thought. In other respects, however, much of his analysis remains valuable.

2. For recent works that have demonstrated the importance of gender in understanding Teresa, see especially Gillian Ahlgren, *Teresa of Avila and the Politics of Sanctity*, and Alison Weber, *Teresa of Avila and the Rhetoric of Femininity*. Also important are Carole Slade, *St. Teresa of Avila: Author of a Heroic Life* (Berkeley and Los Angeles: University of California Press, 1995); and Jodi Bilinkoff, *The Avila of St. Teresa: Religious Reform in a Sixteenth-Century City* (New York: Cornell University Press, 1989). Rossi, Weber, and Slade fall into the category of rhetorical/literary studies, while Bilinkoff's work is an institutional study of Teresa in the context of her Reform. Ahlgren is alone in drawing these strands together *and* giving primary attention to the intellectual context of Teresa's thought in relation to the theological tradition that she inherited. See also Mary Frohlich, *The Intersubjectivity of the Mystic: A Study of Teresa of Avila's* The Interior Castle (Atlanta: Scholars Press, 1993). The latter is not so much a gender study as a study of mystical consciousness as exemplified by Teresa, in relation to the thought of Bernard Lonergan, though it makes the important move of treating Teresa as a fully fledged theologian—a position not restricted to men—in line with these gender studies. The list could be extended considerably if all the recent articles on Teresa from a gender perspective were added.

3. Ahlgren's book is based on her Ph.D. dissertation, although it has some important additions: "Teresa de Jesús: A Case Study in Mystical Creativity and Inquisitional Censure" (Ph.D. diss., University of Chicago, 1991).

4. Ahlgren places Teresa's writing in the genre of "spiritual writing" in the vernacular, and in the intellectual-historical tradition of the "mystical tradition" (28–32, 38–39, 112, 133–40). The term "spiritual" refers to the contemporary sixteenth century sense of the word, as used for instance in the division among religious at this time between the *espirituales* and the *letrados* (see below). Ahlgren also uses the word "mystical" of this tradition, according to a categorization similar to Bernard McGinn's (see chap. 2, n. 24): first, Teresa and John's mystical writings were part of the larger category of vernacular theology in the late medieval period, which was distinct from—though in conversation with—scholastic and monastic theology; second, mystical refers to the interest in the higher stages of prayer, described as "union with God" in these writers, as found in Francisco de Osuna and other sixteenth-century popular writers in the Spanish spiritual tradition.

5. Ahlgren, *Teresa of Avila*, 68–69.

6. Ibid., 29, 39.

7. Ibid., 20, n. 41.

8. By a difference of genre I refer to precisely those rhetorical devices just mentioned which distinguish Teresa's writing from John's. Part of Teresa's rhetorical skill was to mix a number of recognized genres, such as spiritual autobiography, penitential confession, picaresque novel, and so on, in order to keep herself from being easily categorized. For a list of the various genres that scholars have identified in Teresa's writing, see Slade, *St. Teresa of Avila*, 11–12. The issue of genre commands a vast literature which cannot be considered here.

9. Teresa says that her first idea of reform was given her by a friend, María de

Campo, who wanted the Carmelites to be "nuns like the discalced"—a reference to the Franciscan *Descalzas Reales. V* 32:9.

10. Teresa came across the *Third Spiritual Alphabet* of Osuna at a young age, twenty-three, while recovering from an illness at the house of her uncle. She says how happy it made her to learn the method of recollection. V 4:7. See also chap. 5, p. 71.

11. The *reconquista* was finally completed in 1492 with the fall of the last Moorish stronghold in Granada.

12. Shortly after Teresa's death a still larger Index was produced, known as the Quiroga Index (1583–1584).

13. "When they forbade the reading of many books in the vernacular . . . the Lord said to me: 'Don't be sad, for I shall give you a living book.'" V 26:5(6) (1:226/142). Teresa begins all four of her major works by saying that her confessor has commanded her to write and that her purpose is to communicate this "living book" for the education of her nuns. In the *Camino,* she refers to the need to write to provide teaching on prayer for her nuns (Prol. 1); similarly in the *Meditaciones sobre los Cantares* she says that her "understanding of the meaning of certain words" will bring consolation to her sisters (Prol. 2)—bearing in mind that none of them, including Teresa, could read the original Song in Latin, and there was no vernacular Bible available to them. The *Moradas* begins with her explanation of the need for a book on prayer in the "language used between women" (Prol. 4), implying that there were no such books available for women at this time. Thus, she wrote all her major works for the same purpose, to provide otherwise unavailable teaching for women religious on prayer. Jodi Bilinkoff notes that the Inquisitor Valdés told Luís de Granada that the reason that his *Treatise on Prayer* (1554) and *Guide of Sinners* (1556–1557) had been placed on the Index was not for doctrinal reasons but simply because he had encouraged the "wives of carpenters" in the ways of contemplation: the explicit purpose of banning works in the vernacular was to remove them from women. See Jodi Bilinkoff, "St. Teresa of Avila and the Avila of St. Teresa," *Carmelite Studies* 3 (1982): 53–86.

14. All the books that Teresa cites in the *Vida,* for instance, would have been read by her at a date before the Valdés Index in 1559. Ahlgren points out that this conscious decision to write for her nuns runs counter to the often-quoted tradition that Teresa wrote in some kind of mystical trance, as her hagiographers started to say soon after her death, and as has been maintained by some scholars, such as Ramón Menéndez Pidal, up to this day. Rather, there is evidence that though she wrote fast she was painstaking in finding the right words. The view that she wrote while in ecstasy was perhaps an attempt to emphasize her divine inspiration, at the same time as to build on Teresa's own apologetic for her authority to write, rather than a genuine historical observation of her method of writing. Ahlgren, *Teresa of Avila,* 78–83.

15. Teresa always balances her praise for the *espirituales* with compliments directed at the *letrados,* but Teófanes Egido points out that there was no question that she took the side of the *espirituales* in this dispute: see "The Historical Setting of St. Teresa's Life," trans. M. Dodd and S. Payne, *Carmelite Studies* 1 (1980): 131. The Spanish original of this article, containing some extra information, is to be found in Alberto Barrientos, ed., *Introducción a la lectura de Santa Teresa,* 43–104. It should be remembered that the *espirituales* and *letrados* were not separate parties in the Spanish church but rather tendencies or movements among certain groups,

often within the same religious orders. The two tendencies could exist amicably side by side, for instance, in the person of the great reformer in Avila during Teresa's lifetime, Gaspar Daza, who founded several educational establishments in Avila, two of them for clergy, showing typically *letrado* values as promulgated by Trent, but who was also Teresa's great supporter and presided over the ceremony establishing her convent of St. Joseph's on August 24, 1562—a symbol of the *espiritual* movement—amid widespread controversy in the town. See Jodi Bilinkoff, "St. Teresa of Avila and the Avila of St. Teresa," *Carmelite Studies* 3 (1982): 53–68; and idem, *The Avila of St. Teresa*, 120, 145–47.

16. Ahlgren, *Teresa of Avila*, 45–65.

17. Ibid., 114–44.

18. V 3:7; 4:7; 5:9; 9:8; 12:2; 22:7; 23:12; 38:9; CV 19:13; CV 28:2.

19. For Augustine's threefold division, though it is not explicitly attributed to Augustine, see V 28:4; and for a rather different version, as applied to locutions, see 6M 3:1; for "mystical theology," see V 10:1; V 18:2; for Osuna, see V 4:7; Osuna's terms, "prayer of quiet," "suspension," etc., are found in profusion throughout, though with some developments of meaning. In fact, after the *Vida*, Teresa found that her works fared better with the censor if she left out the explicit references to her authorities, with the result that very few of these references are to be found in her other works; nor does she use the phrase "mystical theology" elsewhere: these were things women were not expected to know.

20. S Prol. 9.

21. C 13:7. See n. 43 below.

22. The most thorough studies of John's and Teresa's work together on the Reform remain the sections on this subject in the standard biographies: on John: Crisógono, *The Life of St. John of the Cross* (1958); Bruno de Jesus-Marie, *Saint John of the Cross*, ed. and trans. Benedict Zimmerman (New York: Sheed and Ward, 1932); and more recently, Efrén de la Madre de Dios y Otger Steggink, *Tiempo y Vida de San Juan de la Cruz* (Madrid: BAC, 1992); on Teresa: Marcelle Auclair, *St. Teresa of Avila*; Efrén de la Madre de Dios and Otger Steggink, *Tiempo y vida de Santa Teresa* (Madrid: BAC, 1968, 1977). The sources used in these biographies are mainly well noted but vary considerably in reliability—many are hagiographical stories that appeared in the proceedings for canonization of the two saints and that exaggerate the closeness of the relationship between them.

23. There are eighty letters to Gracián extant, and Teresa wrote to him virtually every day during the years of persecution, so that the total number was probably several hundred, according to Sonya Quitsland, "Elements of a Feminist Spirituality in St. Teresa," *Carmelite Studies* 3 (1982): 31–32. None of Teresa's letters to John of the Cross are extant. There is a traditional story that John burnt them near the end of his life on the grounds that they were the "one thing to which he was still attached": see Marcelle Auclair, *St. Teresa of Avila*, 387. Teresa makes only two references to letters she sent to John of the Cross in her extant letters (Cta. 319(326):6; 421(433):19), and the likelihood is that there were simply few of them—a few dozen, at a rough estimate.

24. F 3:17.

25. Teresa speaks of the rule adopted by the Discalced Carmelites as being the "unmitigated" or "primitive" rule of the Carmelite order, called the Rule of St. Albert, but in fact it was the mitigated version of 1247 that she adopted. This version was considerably more strict than the later, further mitigated rule of 1432 used by the rest of the order, which Teresa was not alone in regarding as a kind of

betrayal of the contemplative ideal. She called her reformed order "discalced" following a similar reform among certain Franciscans, who were known as the "Descalzas Reales" (see above, n. 9). The word literally means "without shoes," though the nuns soon began to wear poor rope sandals called *alpargatas*, and the friars ceased to go barefoot not long after. See *Collected Works of St. Teresa*, ed. and trans. Kavanaugh and Rodriguez, 3: 17–18, 30; also V 32:9–10; F 14:8.

26. F 10:4.

27. "Como estuvimos algunos días con oficiales para recoger la casa, sin clausura, havía lugar para informar al padre fray Juan de la Cruz de toda nuestra manera de proceder, para que llevase bien entendidas todas las cosas." F 13:5 (3:162–63/719).

28. "Espantada de ver el espíritu que el Señor havía puesto allí"; "hicieron poco caso de mis palabras." F 14:6, 12 (3:165–66, 168/721, 723).

29. E.g., Cta. 10 (13):2, 8 (52, 53/880); and see Teresa's comments to Madre Ana de Jesús, quoted below.

30. F 3:17; and see Crisógono, *Life*, 67. On Teresa's ambivalent attitude to harsh penances, see Ahlgren, *Teresa of Avila*, 154–56.

31. F 23:9; see *Collected Works of St. Teresa*, ed. and trans. Kavanaugh and Rodriguez, 3:31.

32. During this time Teresa used John to help make her foundations, for instance, taking him to make the foundation in Segovia in March 1574 ("a discalced friar," F 21:5). She also would send him on urgent business to the foundations she had already made, for instance, to assess a sister's illness in Medina and cast out a devil if necessary, "for God has been pleased to grant him grace to cast out devils from persons possessed." Cta. 43(50):2 (115/915).

33. "En lo interior." Cta. 160(173):2 (400/1072).

34. Cta. 210(216):10.

35. "Después que se fue allá, no he hallado en toda Castilla otro como él, ni que tanto fervore en el camino del cielo. . . . Miren que . . . todas las de esa casa traten y comuniquen con él sus almas, y verán qué aprovechadas están y se hallarán muy adelante en todo lo que es espíritu y perfección; porque le ha dado nuestro Señor para esto particular gracia. . . . Mi padre fray Juan de la Cruz, que de veras lo es de mi alma, y uno de los que más provecho le hacía el comunicarle. . . . Es muy espiritual y de grandes esperiencias y letras." Cta. 261(267 and 265) (624–25/1195–96). Peers's translation joins what were probably two separate letters (267 and 265 in the BAC edition) into one. John later worked with Madre Ana de Jesús on the last foundation of Teresa's lifetime—from which Teresa was absent—in Granada.

36. CC 31(29).

37. "Caro costaría si no pudiésemos buscar a Dios sino cuando estuviésemos muertos al mundo. . . . Dios me libre de gente tan espiritual que todo lo quieren hacer contemplación perfecta." Vej 6, 7 (3:361/1432).

38. See Slade, *St. Teresa of Avila*, 58. Slade reads too much into Teresa's criticism of John on this occasion, saying that John had "apparently divorced spiritual experience from the physical world," and by implication, that he had divorced spiritual experience from the encounter with Christ and from his Christology. This is a serious misreading of John of the Cross, as chaps. 2 and 3 above have made clear (and see esp. the treatment of John's Christology by Matthew, *Knowledge and Consciousness of Christ*), and Teresa would have distanced herself from John much more forcefully if she had really thought that this was his teaching. The differences between John and Teresa, as others have pointed out, lie in the role they give the

humanity of Christ in prayer; their attitude to certain kinds of vision/supernatural apprehension; and in their different aesthetic concerning nature and the beauty of God. See, e.g., Ana Maria Lopez Diaz-Otazu, *Aproximación a San Juan de la Cruz de la mano de Santa Teresa* (Madrid: Narcea, 1990), 107–17. These differences will be considered in more detail below (in the epilogue), but they do not suggest a basic difference on the status of the physical in relation to the spiritual.

39. See, e.g., John, 1N 12:2; Teresa, V 13:15; CV 39:5; 1M 2:8–11. John's approach to mortification seems very different from Teresa because of his ordering of *Subida* and *Noche*, which begins with active self-mortification apparently before the soul has any graced awareness of its divine goal. But the ordering of the *Cántico* and *Llama* is different, as we have seen, and closer to Teresa's ordering, with the first mystical apprehension of God preceding the stages of detachment and "annihilation." This is in fact what is happening in the *Subida* and *Noche*, also, as John says that the darkness encountered at the beginning of the process of purgation is found at the end of the journey to have been the light of faith, infused by God (2S 2:1, 2). That is to say, the active-passive division of purgation is somewhat artificial. Where John does differ from Teresa is in his attitude to certain kinds of vision, which he judges more harshly than Teresa. While Teresa admired his ability for diagnosing and treating demon-possession among her nuns, Ahlgren has pointed out that his attitude to visionaries was harsher than Teresa's: see Ahlgren, *Teresa of Avila*, 98; and the epilogue below.

40. Cta. 204(211), to King Philip; 207(214):8–10; 208(215):2; 210(216):1, 12; 224(228):8, 21; 232(236):6; 242(246):5; 243(248):8; 245(244):6; 246(250); 247(256).

41. Teresa refers to correspondence with John in a letter to Ana de Jesús, shortly after Ana had become prioress of the new foundation in Granada: Cta. 421(433):19. Teresa's earlier recommendation of John to Ana, quoted above, concerned the same foundation (Cta. 261[267 and 265]).

42. Cta. 358(368):6 (830/1321).

43. John describes something closely resembling Teresa's transverberation experience in *Llama* 2:9–10, probably with Teresa in mind, as noted in the appendix, p. 144. More significantly, in *Cántico* 13:7 (460/787) he says that he will not go into a full discussion of the "different kinds of raptures, ecstasies and other elevations and flights of the soul," as there is "someone who knows how to treat the matter better than I"—this is "Teresa of Jesus, our Mother, [who] left writings about these spiritual matters, which are admirably done and which I hope will soon be printed and brought to light." The printed edition of Teresa's works was prepared by Luis de León between 1586 and 1588, and John was one of those who voted for their publication at the discalced meeting of definitors in Madrid on 1 September 1586 (see Crisógono, *Life*, 247). Gracián and Ana de Jesús had worked avidly to achieve this end. It is unlikely that John had seen the manuscript of Teresa's *Vida* at this stage, as it was kept by the Inquisition until Luis de León acquired it, so here he must be referring to Teresa's treatment of these matters in the sixth "dwelling places" of the *Moradas*. He could have read this in the original manuscript, as Teresa had passed it to Gracián in 1580 for safe keeping, and Gracián had given it to the discalced nuns in Seville, where it stayed for the next two years (to return in 1618, where it has remained since). On Teresa and John's differences over visions, see the epilogue.

44. For a chronology of John's major works, see the appendix, n. 1.

45. Commentators have speculated that the "learned man" who told her of the distinction between the "intellect" (*entendimiento*) and the "mind" (*pensamiento*) was John of the Cross, as this permitted her to make the move that John makes in

separating the "voiding of the intellect" from the mind's knowledge and natural reasoning: the intellect is drawn into union, while the mind remains "outside." 4M 1:8–9, q.v. chap. 5, n. 32. See also below, pp. 77–78.

Notes to Chapter Five

1. The dates refer to the date of composition, which took place over a number of years in all but the *Moradas*, which Teresa did not revise. For information on the manuscripts and dates of composition, see the introductions to these works in *Collected Works of St. Teresa*, ed. and trans. Kieran Kavanaugh and Otilio Rodriguez. See also Alberto Barrientos, ed., *Introducción a la lectura de Santa Teresa* (Madrid: Editorial de Espiritualidad, 1978), esp. 210–18 (on V); 266–68 (on F); 270–78 (on CV/CE); 316–20 (on M); 375–78 (on CC); 383–86 (on MC).

2. These are also known as the *Relaciones*. Her other major work, the *Fundaciones*, a history of her seventeen foundations for discalced Carmelite nuns, is less useful for my purpose here. There are also preserved a number of her letters, her *Constitutions*, her poems, and various other minor works.

3. V 4:7.

4. In fact she was twenty-three. See *Collected Works of St. Teresa*, ed. and trans. Kavanaugh and Rodriguez, 1:469, n. 12.

5. "Por una parte me llamava Dios; por otra yo siguía a el mundo. Dávanme gran contento todas las cosas de Dios; teníanme atadas las de el mundo. Parece que quería concertar estos dos contrarios—tan enemigo uno de otro—como es vida espiritual, y contentos y gustos y pasatiempos sensuales. En la oración pasava gran travajo, porque no andava el espíritu señor, sino esclavo; y ansí no me podía encerrar dentro de mí (que era el modo de proceder que llevava en la oración) sin encerrar conmigo mil vanidades." V 7:17 (1:91/57–58).

6. The time between Teresa's reading of Osuna at her uncle's house, which was in 1537, and this "second conversion" is in fact seventeen years: by "twenty years" (V 8:1) she may be referring to the time since she entered the Encarnación two years earlier, which would make nineteen years; "twenty years" is intended only as a round figure.

7. "El corazón me parece se me partía . . . con grandísimo derramamiento de lágrimas." V 9:1 (1:101/63).

8. "Parecíame a mí que, estando solo y afligido, como persona necesitada me havía de admitir a mí." V 9:4 (1:101/64).

9. "No es otra cosa oración mental, a mi parecer, sino tratar de amistad." V 8:5 (1:96/61).

10. V 9:8.

11. "Dice san Agustín que le buscava en muchas partes y que le vino a hallar dentro de sí mesmo." CV 28:2 (2:141/349–50). This was from *Confessions* 10:27.

12. "[If] the Lord helped me . . . I found myself with greater delight and quiet than sometimes when I had the desire to pray." V 8:7 (1:98/62).

13. "En parte . . . se puede procurar." V 10:2 (1:105/66). "Sometimes it seems we draw forth the tears through our own effort, at other times it seems the Lord grants them to us, since we are unable to resist them." Ibid. (1:105/67).

14. "Acaecíame en esta representación que hacía de ponerme cabe Cristo . . . y aun algunas veces leyendo, venirme a deshora un sentimiento de la presencia de Dios que en ninguna manera podía dudar que estava dentro de mí u yo toda engolfada en El. Esto no era manera de visión; creo lo llaman 'mística teoloxía.' Sus-

pende el alma de suerte que toda parecía estar fuera de sí." V 10:1 (1:105/66).

15. In the next section. In adding the phrase "I believe they call it" (*creo lo lla-man*) to "mystical theology," Teresa is feigning a certain ignorance as part of her "rhetoric of femininity" rather than revealing a genuine lack of knowledge on the subject: see Ahlgren, *Teresa of Avila*, 79.

16. Teresa intends to exclude the "senses of the soul" associated with imaginative visions, also. See below, n. 27.

17. See below on the *Moradas*, p. 91; and in the next chapter, pp. 102–3.

18. "Lo que yo pretendo declarar es qué siente el alma cuando está en esta divina unión." V 18:3 (1:158/99).

19. "Ama la voluntad, la memoria me parece está casi perdida, el entendimiento . . . no obra, sino está como espantado de lo mucho que entiende." V 10 (1:105/66).

20. On Teresa's doctrine of the spiritual senses, see Maria Isabel Alvira, *Vision de l'homme selon Thérèse d'Avila: Une philosophie de l'heroïsme* (Paris: F.X. de Guibert, O.E.I.L., 1992), 320–34. Alvira avers that Teresa's teaching falls into the tradition of the spiritual senses from Origen but says that Teresa arrived at it mainly through experience (332). It seems more probable that Teresa first came to the doctrine through her reading of the spiritual classics and conversations with her confessors, rather than purely through experience, though we cannot know precisely what her sources were. Alvira provides lists of examples of Teresa's use of all five spiritual senses (323–32), and says that the spiritual senses are more than a metaphor for Teresa: they show "la possibilité réelle qu'a l'homme de saisir la réalité divine de différentes manières"—that is, her doctrine of the spiritual senses has the status of analogy and not just metaphor (333). Alvira's study is the only thorough treatment of Teresa's anthropology to have been published since Trueman Dicken's, though in places it is short on analysis, acting instead more as a concordance to her main anthropological terms. Most useful is part 3, "La structure de l'homme" (235–395). My view is that Teresa's theory of spiritual sensation is indeed like Origen's but also includes some more "bodily" elements than Origen would allow: see the epilogue, p. 135.

21. "Este dolor no es en el sentido, ni tampoco e llaga material, sino en el interior del alma sin que parezca dolor corporal." CC 59(58):17(14) (1:431/628).

22. V 29:13. See below, pp. 81–82.

23. "Parece ella tiene allá otros sentidos, como acá los esteriores, que ella en sí parece se quiere apartar de los bullicios esteriores." CC 59(58):3 (1:425–26/625).

24. "Es un recogimiento interior que se siente en el alma . . . que le da gana de cerrar los ojos y no oír ni ver ni entender sino aquello en que el alma entonces se ocupa, que es poder tratar con Dios a solas." Ibid.

25. "Lo que con mi industria ni deligencia no se puede adquirir, aunque mucho se procure." Ibid.

26. Teresa's main treatments of these categories of vision are in V 27–28 and 6M 8–9. The threefold categorization was a popular one derived from Augustine (see also in the next chapter, p. 110, and n. 90).

27. Teresa first mentions the "eyes of the soul" (*los ojos del alma*) in the context of one of her early visions of Christ before her second conversion. As in the later imaginative visions that she describes, the vision leaves her soul "imprinted" (*imprimado*) with the image. V 7:6 (1:85/54). Teresa's most thorough treatment of imaginative visions in the *Vida* comes in chap. 28, and there is little development between this and her final treatment in the *Moradas* (6M 9). In an imaginative

vision of Christ, Teresa says that "with the eyes of the soul" (*los ojos del alma*) we see the "excellence, beauty, and glory of the most holy humanity," through a "living image" (*imagen viva*): V 28:8–9 (1:240–42/151). In the case of imaginative locutions, Teresa says that the soul uses "other ears" (*otros oídos*) from its bodily ears, through which it hears what God says: these are the equivalent of the "eyes of the soul" in imaginative visions: V 27:8 (1:231/145). The fact that she calls them "*other* ears" causes confusion with the "other senses" of *Cuenta* 59(58), but she is not referring to the same senses (see below).

28. In the *Vida*, Teresa treats "nonimaginative" or intellectual visions in chap. 27. In contrast to imaginative visions, there is no "form" (*forma*) seen in the vision; rather, the Lord makes the vision or locution known in the soul "without an image or explicit words" (*sin imagen ni forma de palabras*). Thus, the soul does not "listen" for the words and does not use the "other ears" (*otros oídos*) that were required in imaginative locutions, but "there is nothing more to do than to enjoy." V 27:2, 6, 8 (1:228, 230, 231/143–45).

29. As we saw in chap. 2, John makes an additional distinction here in comparison with Teresa. He regards the fantasy and imagination as receiving the created images and forms of imaginative visions, but he then divides intellectual visions into two kinds, the "corporeal–intellectual" and the "spiritual–intellectual." The "corporeal–intellectual" are another kind of imaginative visions, having a supernatural source and using created images, but the "soul itself" senses the images rather than the imagination and fantasy, which is John's way of indicating that this is a genuinely supernatural kind of apprehension. The "soul itself" comes closer to Teresa's senses "of the soul" than the imagination and fantasy, in that it is *only* used in supernatural apprehensions and is not part of natural knowing. But spiritual–intellectual visions then go the further step, removing all created images and forms and bypassing both the imagination and fantasy and the "soul itself." They are received in what John calls the caverns of feeling, which then become fully known in the "substance of the soul," as we saw in chap. 2, pp. 29–31.

30. By the "faculties and senses," Teresa refers to the ordinary operation of the soul or exterior part. E.g., 1M 2:12; 4M 3:2; 5M 1:12; 6M 2:3, 5; 4:9, 13; 9:10; 7M 2:3, 10; 4:10.

31. V 14:2–3; 17:5; 18:1. See below for a fuller treatment of these stages in the *Vida*.

32. "El pensamiento . . . no es el entendimiento. . . . Yo vía—a mi parecer—las potencias del alma empleadas en Dios y estar recogidas con El, y por otra parte el pensamiento alborotado traíame tonta." 4M 1:8–9 (2:320/497). See chap. 4, n. 45.

33. Ibid; 5M 3:10; 6M 3:13–14.

34. 4M 3:6.

35. In the "suspensions" of the *Vida*, the exterior parts of the soul are paralyzed, but nevertheless they "share" in the "sweetness" of interior (see below on the transverberation, pp. 81–82). In the *Meditaciones sobre los Cantares* and the *Moradas*, Teresa shows that all the faculties and senses cease to be paralyzed but become active in union through this overflow from the center of the soul. V 29:12–13; cf. 4M 2:6; 7M 2:6; 7M 3:8. See below.

36. "Le parecía havía división en su alma. . . . Se quejava de ella—a manera de Marta cuando se quejó de María—y algunas veces la decía que se estava allí siempre gozando de aquella quietud a su placer, y la deja a ella en tantos trabajos y ocupaciones que no la puede tener compañía." 7M 1:10(11) (2:431–32/570). My emphasis.

37. The relationship between Teresa's experience and her theory is hard to uncover. Clearly both are involved, and one might speculate that her reception of the gift of spiritual marriage, which she dates to November 18, 1572, in *Cuenta* 31(29), was the moment that she changed her view of union, from one characterized by raptures and suspensions to the inclusion of virtuous activity that we see first in her *Meditaciones sobre los Cantares*; but though this change is evident from her writings, it is impossible to correlate it exactly with a moment or moments in her "experience," as her writings are our only source and include, inseparably, her later reflections on her experience.

38. In making this argument for the overcoming of the division in the soul in the process of transformation according to Teresa, I am opposing my former argument in "Mystical experience and the view of the self in Teresa of Avila and John of the Cross," *Studia Mystica* 18 (1997): 87–104, where I stated that even in the final union of the *Moradas*, Teresa retains the problematic division in her anthropology "between the center of the soul as the subject of mystical experience and the rest of the soul that remains divorced from this experience" (103–4). Further study has made clear to me that Teresa's understanding of the center of the soul is less reified than I had thought, being based on a trinitarian dynamism which is capable of including even the strongly distinct interior and exterior parts of the soul in a single and unified operation, rather than leaving the soul completely divided (as argued below).

39. Teresa regards all the supernatural stages of prayer as different kinds of union (see, e.g., V 17:5) and she equates union with mystical theology (V 18:1–2).

40. Teresa wrote the second draft after the foundation of St. Joseph's in 1562 and included these chapters in response to the suggestion of her confessor, García de Toledo.

41. V 11:9–12:6.

42. V 14:2.

43. V 17:5; "toda la fuerza esterior se pierde"; "suspención de todas las potencias": V 18:10, 12 (1:161–62/102).

44. For Teresa, union is a broad category containing many different types of union, of which rapture is one (and the highest, in the *Vida*). "Los efectos muy mayores hace y otras hartas operaciones." V 20:1 (1:172/108).

45. As Michel de Certeau describes, Teresa's transverberation was taken up increasingly in the early seventeenth century by the new mystics as the paradigm for their "extraordinary devotions": see *The Mystic Fable*, 254. Teresa's concern for the religious community and her subsequent development to include worldly activity in union were ignored in this emphasis on rapture; the same is true of Bernini's famous statue of the transverberation from this period.

46. "Víale en las manos un dardo de oro largo, y al fin de el hierro me parecía tener un poco de fuego; éste me parecía meter por el corazón algunas veces y que me llegava a las entrañas. Al sacarle, me parecía las llevava consigo. . . . La suavidad que me pone este grandísimo dolor. . . . No es dolor corporal, sino espiritual, aunque no deja de participar el cuerpo algo"; "Otra veces da tan recio . . . que corta todo el cuerpo; ni pies ni brazos no puede menear." V 29:13, 12 (1:252/157–58).

47. "Muy sobre sí y de todo lo criado." V 20:9 (1:176/110).

48. "El alma no en sí, sino en el tejado u techo de sí mesma y de todo lo criado; porque aun encima de lo muy superior del alma me parece que está." V 20:10 (1:176/111).

49. Teresa also says that frequently the body is made healthier and stronger by

raptures, after the event, perhaps referring to her improvement in health after she moved to St. Joseph's (cf. CV 34:6; CC 1:23), but there is no simultaneous participation of the body in raptures, as they exclude the body.

50. "Toda la ansia es morirme entonces." V 20:13 (1:178/112); also V 40:20.

51. V 19:3.

52. "Lo que ahora anda siempre mi alma." V 20:12 (1:177/111). "También una compañía santa no hace su conversación tanto provecho de un día como de muchos." V 22:16 (1:199/125).

53. "Vida tan mal concertada." V 21:6 (1:187/117).

54. "El cautiverio que traemos con los cuerpos." Ibid.

55. "El estremo de la solitud." V 20:10 (1:176/111).

56. "Ya no quiero que tengas conversación con hombres, sino con ángeles." V 24:5 (1:211/133).

57. "No ha de entrar en esta cuenta [de otras criaturas] la sacratísima Humanidad de Cristo." V 22:8 (1:195/122). See further on the implications of this approach to the humanity of Christ in the epilogue.

58. These books "give strong advice to rid oneself of all corporeal images" in the illuminative stage of prayer—and this "even when referring to the humanity of Christ." V 22:1 (1:191/120). Osuna may have been Teresa's opponent here. Williams notes that Osuna separates the "body's task" of following Christ in his humanity from the soul's task of "taking wing" to his divinity: *Teresa of Avila*, 70.

59. "Quisiera yo siempre traer delante de los ojos su retrato y imagen." V 22:4 (1:192/121).

60. "Es andar el alma en el aire. . . porque parece no trai arrimo [Peers: 'it has nothing to lean upon' (1:140)]. Es gran cosa, mientra vivimos y somos humanos, traerle humano. . . . Nosotros no somos ángeles, sino tenemos cuerpo." V 22:9–10 (1:195/123).

61. "Es un poco de falta de humilidad de . . . querer ser María antes que haya travajado con Marta." V 22:9 (1:195/123).

62. Teresa's awareness of the christological problem of the union of natures remains largely implicit in her Mary and Martha passages, until the *Moradas*. This will be considered mainly in chap. 6, but here we should note a number of references that signal her increasing awareness of the problem:

(1) She receives an understanding of Christ in an intellectual vision not just in his divinity but in his humanity also (V 27:4). Shortly afterward, she sees Christ in an imaginative vision in a "living image" as both man and God (V 28:8);

(2) She makes clear the Son's role in sharing his divine understanding of the Father with us, in her exposition of the "Our Father" (CV 24:2; 27:1; see below, p. 85);

(3) She sees Christ's union of natures in the kiss of the Song, when the soul asks for the union of God with man, and for the "friendship that he effected with the human race" (MC 1:10; see below, p. 86);

(4) By our active walking with Christ in his humanity as our "constant companion," we join him "in whom divine and human are joined" (6M 7:9). Christ in his humanity is attained interiorly by the soul in the final vision of the spiritual marriage in the seventh dwelling place (7M 2:1). (See the section on the *Moradas* at the end of this chapter, and further in chap. 6.)

63. "Gozando en aquel ocio santo de María . . . tambien ser Marta (ansí que está casi obrando juntamente en vida activa y contemplativa)." V 17:4 (1:153–54/97).

64. "No del todo están señores de sí, y entienden bien que está la mijor parte del alma en otro cabo." Ibid.

65. "En mucha quietud está sola la voluntad, y está por otra parte el entendimiento y memoria tan libres, que pueden tratar en negocios y entender en obras de caridad." Ibid.

66. "Le da tal guerra la memoria y imaginación que no la dejan valer." V 17:5–6 (1:155/98).

67. The *Vida* was written 1562–1565, while the *Camino* was begun, on the advice of Teresa's confessor, Domingo Bañez, in 1566 and finished certainly in its first draft in the same year, in order to replace the *Vida*, which had been forbidden from circulation among her nuns. See *Collected Works of St. Teresa*, ed. and trans. Kavanaugh and Rodriguez, 2:15.

68. "La voluntad estáse en su obra sin saber cómo obra y en su contemplación; las otras dos potencias sirven en lo que Marta: ansí que ella y María andan juntas." CV 31:5 (2:155/365). The only difference from the *Vida* is that this takes place in the "prayer of quiet," which appears to include the second and the third stages of prayer of the *Vida* in a single stage. There is evidence that Teresa is actually referring to the same occasion on which she experienced this prayer as in the *Vida*, as she mentions "someone" she spoke to about the experience who agreed that it was both possible and had happened to him. This was Francis Borgia, formerly Duke of Gandia, who had become a Jesuit and met Teresa when he was visiting Avila in about 1556, according to the *Vida*: Teresa says that he reassured her that her experience was from the Spirit of God; she mentions him again in the *Cuentas* in this same context of the Mary and Martha prayer (V 24:3; CC 59[58]:5). For this reason also, the account in the *Cuentas* of the Mary and Martha prayer, though dated 1576, must be a reference to Teresa's earlier position as in the *Vida* and the *Camino* and cannot be regarded as part of the subsequent development of her position.

69. "Todo este cimiento de la oración va fundado en humildad." V 21:11 (1:196/123); CV 4:4–7; CV 11:1–16:2. Humility not only produces the detachment from the world that is essential in adhering to God, but also, for instance, overcomes what Teresa regards as the most pernicious problem in communities, which is the concern for honor and dignity (CV 12:8): in this way it builds up both love of God and love of neighbor. Williams notes that Teresa's criticisms of the concern for honor in the community belong to her wider critique of honor as one of the most cherished and institutionalized values in Spanish society: *Teresa of Avila*, 18–26.

70. "This house is a heaven, if one can be had on earth." CV 13:7 (2:87/290).

71. CV 6:7–9; 10:5; 13:1. "Los contemplativos han de llevar levantada la bandera de la humilidad y . . . padecer como Cristo, llevar en alto la cruz . . . porque si él [el contemplativo] deja la bandera, perdese ha la batalla." CV 18:5(6) (2:103–4/308).

72. CV 28:4.

73. "No hace diferencia de El a nosotros." CV 33:4–5 (2:168/380). "Esto pasa ahora, y es entera verdad . . . pues está en nuestra casa." CV 34:8(9) (2:172/384).

74. CV 34:8. Most of Teresa's great experiences of union are described as occurring during the reception of the sacrament or shortly afterward: see particularly the *Cuentas*. She recommends this as the best time for prayer.

75. "No se la ocupe nada: esto es arrobamiento." CV 32:12 (2:164/375).

76. "Razón es le sirvamos con algo tan grandes mercedes." CV 32:1 (2:160/369).

77. "[El alma] no puede menos . . . de traer a el Todopoderoso a ser uno con nuestra bajeza y transformarnos en sí, y hacer una unión del Criador con la criatura." CV 32:11 (2:164/374).

78. Teresa had not yet attained spiritual marriage—which she dates to November 1572 in her *Cuentas* 31(29), as noted above, n. 37—but there is clear evidence here of her progress toward it. "Y comienza a tratar de tanta amistad, que no sólo la torna a dejar su voluntad, mas dale la suya con ella; porque se huelga el Señor—ya que trata de tanta amistad—que manden a veces." CV 32:12 (2:164/375).

79. The precise date is unclear. Teresa must have written it after the *Vida* and the *Camino*, as she refers to these works, i.e., in 1566 or later; and must have finished it by 1575, when her confessor Bañez approved it, on June 10, 1575. Kavanaugh and Rodriguez suggest that there were two drafts, the first in 1566–1567 and the second in 1572–1575 (*Collected Works of St. Teresa*, 2:213). The second draft may reflect the development in Teresa's position after her reception of spiritual marriage (CC 31[29]). The text is a meditation on a number of phrases from the Song of Songs, which Teresa says she heard read in the Latin and was given an understanding of by God (MC Prol.). She would also have read translations of these phrases in spiritual books; but a full translation of the Song was almost certainly not available to her. (Luis de León's was the first translation in Spanish and not available in Teresa's lifetime; it also caused him considerable trouble with the Inquisition.)

80. "Hay en Cristo dos naturalezas, una divina y otra humana. En esto no me detengo, porque mi intento es hablar en lo que me parece podemos aprovecharnos las que tratamos de oración. . . . 'Béseme con beso de su boca.' . . . Pedía aquel ayuntamiento tan grande, como fue hacerse Dios hombre, aquella amistad que hizo con el género humano." MC 1:9–10(10–11) (2:220–21/426–27).

81. "Aventurar al alma a ponerse a guerra con todas las del mundo, quedando ella con toda siguridad y pacífica." MC 3:1 (2:236/444–45).

82. "Si una labradorcilla se casase con el rey y tuviese hijos, ¿ya no quedan de sangre real? . . . qué hijos de obras heroicas podían nacer de allí." MC 3:9(8) (2:240/448).

83. "En lo activo, y que parece esterior, obra la interior . . . las obras activas salen de esta raíz." MC 7:3 (2:257/465).

84. "Se siente estar toda engolfada y amparada con una sombra y manera de nube de la Divinidad." MC 5:4 (2:249/455). "Querría no menearse ni hablar ni aun mirar, por que no se le fuese." MC 4:2 (2:243/450). She remains clear that this view of union is incompatible with simultaneous virtuous activity: see also MC 5:4; 6:3–5.

85. "Porque estando tan fuera de sí y tan absorta que ninguna cosa puede obrar con las potencias, ¿cómo havía de merecer?" MC 6:6 (2:253/460).

86. "Oro—que ya tiene aparejado . . . y tocado para ver de qué quilates es el amor que le tiene"; "ordenó en mi la caridad" (quotation from Song 2:4). MC 6:10–11 (2:254/461–62).

87. "Otro bien para salir de aquel tan grandísimo"; "tanta fuerza algunas veces, que se enseñorea de manera sobre todas las fuerzas del sujeto natural." MC 7:2–3(2) (2:256–57/464–65).

88. "Tiénele grande en padecer, mas no la consume y gasta la virtud—como lo deve hacer, si es muy ordinario esta suspensión de las potencias en la contemplación." MC 7:8(9) (2:259/467).

89. "[El alma] pide hacer grandes obras en servicio de nuestro Señor y del

prójimo, y por huelga de perder aquel deleite y contento"; "la ganancia de sus prójimos tienen presente, no más"; "un alma que está rodeada de cruces, de travajos y persecuciones." MC 7:3, 5(4), 8(9) (2:257–59/465–67).

90. "Criadas." MC 7:9(10) (2:260/468).

91. "Menester . . . con la leche"; "no sea para sí la ganancia." MC 7:9(10), 10(12) (2:260/468).

92. "El centro del alma": 1M 2:3; 4M 2:5; 5M 1:12; 7M 2:3; 7M 2:10; 7M 3:8; 7M 4:10.

93. "Palabras regaladas." 7M 2:6(7) (2:435/572). Twice Teresa deleted the word "consummated" from her description of spiritual marriage in this section of the work (7M 2:2, 3; see notes given in *Collected Works of St. Teresa*, ed. and trans. Kavanaugh and Rodriguez, 2:433–34), most probably because she knew that it might cause difficulties with the censor. It may be for the same reason that she removes "offspring" from her notion of spiritual marriage, but this is unlikely given that "loving expressions" refer to the same fruitful and passionate relationship in the soul; rather, here she aims to emphasize the *simultaneity* of works with the interior *activity* of the spiritual marriage, as opposed to speaking of "offspring" which only arrive at a later time after the consummation.

94. "Era tiempo de que sus cosas tomase ella por suyas y El ternía cuidado de las suyas." 7M 2:1 (2:433/570).

95. "Se entiende claro, por unas secretas aspiraciones, ser Dios el que da vida a nuestra alma . . . las siente muy bien el alma . . . producen unas palabras regaladas. . . . De aquellos pechos divinos . . . salen unos rayos de leche que toda la gente del castillo conhorta." 7M 2:6(7) (2:435/572).

96. The "light" from the interior of the soul is "sent to the faculties." Ibid.

97. "The words His Majesty spoke to her produced (*hicieron efecto*) the deed in her." 7M 3:2 (2:438/574). "Su gloria tienen puesta en si pudiesen ayudar en algo al Crucificado." 7M 3:6(4) (2:439/575).

98. "Marta y María han de andar juntas"; "recaudos que envía el alma de el centro interior a la gente de arriba del castillo y a las moradas que están fuera . . . potencias y sentidos y todo lo corporal"; "fuerzas para servir." 7M 4:10(11), 12(14) (2:447–48/580–81). Teresa reiterates the idea from the *Meditaciones* of exterior works proceeding from the interior root: she says that the desires which motivate the soul to serve come from its root (*raiz*) where it is planted in God: 7M 2:9(12) (2:437/573).

99. "De esto sirve este matrimonial espiritual, de que nazcan siempre obras, obras." 7M 4:6 (2:446/579).

100. "Su vida es ya Cristo." 7M 2:5(6) (2:435/572).

101. 1M 1:1, 3.

102. V 40:5.

103. CV 28:9.

104. "Vemos a Dios y nos vemos tan metidas en su grandeza." 5M 2:6 (2:343/513); cf. 5M 1:9–10. "Vemos en este espejo que contemplamos, adonde nuestra imagen está esculpida." 7M 2:8(10) (2:436/573).

105. Teresa says that in the suspensions of the old union the soul doesn't recognize itself or its image (*no parece ella ni su figura*), whereas in the new union it sees its image in God (5M 2:8 [2:344/514]; as above, 7M 2:8[10]). She speaks of this awareness in terms of a new clarity in the relationship: from the "secret aspirations" the soul "understands clearly" (*se entiende claro*) that it is God who gives life to the soul (7M 2:6[7]); God makes his presence very well known (*darse a conocer*

tan conocidamente su presencia), and even though the clarity of the vision may vary, the knowledge of his presence remains: 7M 1:8(9)–9(10) (2:431/569).

106. "La compañía que tiene le da fuerzas muy mayores que nunca. . . . Con los santos seremos santos"; "esforzado con el esfuerzo que tiene el alma beviendo del vino de esta bodega adonde la ha traído su Esposo." 7M 4:10(11)–11(12) (2:447–48/580).

107. 7M 1:6–9.

108. "Entrar en el centro del alma sin ninguna, como entró a sus discípulos, cuando dijo: 'Pax vobis.'" 5M1:12(13) (2:341/511); 7M 2:3.

109. Ibid.; also 5M 2:10; 3:4.

110. 7M 2:7.

111. "Unión regalada" vs. "la verdadera unión." 5M 3:3 (2:349/517). She adds, "This union with God's will is the union I have desired all my life; it is the union I ask the Lord for always and the one that is clearest and safest." 5M 3:5 (2:350/517).

112. "Ninguna cosa se os dé de estotro unión regalada . . . no poder llegar a lo que queda dicho, si no es muy cierta la unión de estar resignada nuestra voluntad en la de Dios." 5M 3:3 (2:349/517).

113. 5M 4:4–5 (2:355/521). "Ayuda mucho para morir." 5M 3:5 (2:350/517).

114. "[Este padecer] es purificar esta alma." 6M 11:6 (2:424/564).

115. V 20:10, as quoted above: see n. 48.

116. 7M 1:5.

117. See pp. 77–78. This distinction between *pensamiento* and *entendimiento* belongs to Teresa's wider distinction between the soul and the faculties in union (7M 1:11). Instead of seeing the faculties as divided among themselves when the mind is wandering or engaged in external affairs, as in the *Vida* and *Camino*, she now sees the faculties as capable of being in union while the lower rational faculties of mind and imagination attend to external affairs.

Notes to Chapter Six

1. Given the development in Teresa's thought, considered in chap. 5, I shall not make a full comparison between the various orders of transformation in her different works (as I have done for John of the Cross in the appendix). Here the *Moradas* will be taken as the primary text, with her previous works cited only where they shed light on the meaning of the *Moradas*.

2. "En casas de spíritu en poco tiempo tiene mucha espiriencia." V 34:11 (1:298/187).

3. V 13:14; 30:4. Teresa bases her own teaching authority on her experience in prayer (V 7:22; 10:9; 26:5 [the "living book"]; CV Prol. 3); and she says that she is speaking the "language of the spirit" (*lenguaje de espíritu*), which is only understandable to those who "have experience" (V 12:5; 15:4; CV 2:6; 6:3; 23:5; MC 6:13; 1M 1:9; 4M 1:5).

4. "He lástima a los que comienzan con solos libros, que es cosa estraña cuán diferentemente se entiende de lo que después de espiritmentado se ve." V 13:12 (128/81). Teresa frequently makes this contrast between "experience" and "learning" in the case of spiritual directors: experience is the most important qualification, though learning in Sacred Scripture is a help also (V 13:16–18; 34:11). The best is to have experience *and* learning (V 40:8; CV 5:7; 2M 1:10; 6M 1:8; 9:11).

5. Unfortunately, this distinction is not respected by the translators—as we saw was the case for John of the Cross also (see chap. 1, p. 11). As with John, the trans-

lators use "experience" to translate the "feeling" words used by Teresa. There is a good reason for this: in modern English, feelings suggest a merely *emotional* sense, whereas Teresa's emphasis is on the *sensory*, epistemological value of these feelings, which the translators judge is better rendered as "experience." The problem is that Teresa's distinction between feelings and experience is then lost.

6. 5M 1:5 (337/509).

7. There are inferior levels of experience before the mystical state of *gustos*, such as "consolations" (*contentos*), which she introduces with the phrase, "the experience that I have of this state" (*lo que tengo de espiriencia de este estado*) (4M 1:6); or her description of a state in which the devil can cause the soul to have "no memory of what it has experienced within itself" (*no hay memoria de lo que ha espirimentado en sí*) (V 30:12).

8. "Esta presencia tan sin poderse dudar de las tres Personas, que parece claro se esperimenta lo que dice san Juan, 'que haría morada con el alma.'" CC 65:9 (10) (438/633). This *Cuenta* was written after the *Moradas*, in 1581, and reflects the full development of Teresa's view of union, similar to her position in the *Moradas*.

9. 1M 1:1 (2:283/472). A reference to Gen. 1:26. Teresa may have gained her understanding of the "image" from her reading of Augustine's *Confessions* (e.g., bk. 10, chap. 18).

10. "En el centro y mitad . . . es adonde pasan las cosas de mucho secreto entre Dios y el alma." 1M 1:3 (2:284/473).

11. "Sol resplandeciente que está en el centro del alma. . . . Si sobre un cristal que está a el sol se pusiese un paño muy negro, claro está que, aunque el sol dé en él, no hará su claridad operación en el cristal." 1M 2:3 (2:289/476).

12. "La gran hermosura de un alma y la gran capacidad . . . apenas deven llegar nuestros entendimientos—por agudos que fuesen—a comprenderla. . . . Hay la diferencia de él a Dios que del Criador a la criatura." 1M 1:1 (2:283/472).

13. "No entendamos a nosotros mesmos ni sepamos quién somos." 1M 1:2 (2:284/472).

14. "El mesmo dice que nos crió a su imagen y semejanza." 1M 1:1 (2:283/472). My emphasis.

15. "Entiendo que algunas no las havía entendido como después acá." 1M 2:7 (2:290/477).

16. S Prol. 8 (72/257), q.v. appendix, n. 12 (see also n. 11).

17. 1M 2:8 (2:291/477).

18. "Porque está tan muerta la fe, que queremos más lo que vemos que lo que ella nos dice." 2M 1:5 (2:300/483). This theme of the activity of faith and love recurs throughout the *Moradas*: 4M 3:9; 5M 4:10; 6M 9:4; 7M 1:8.

19. "Son las almas que no tienen oración como un cuerpo con perlesía u tollido. . . . Y si estas almas no procuran entender y remediar su gran miseria, quedarse han hechas estatuas de sal." 1M 1:6, 8 (2:286/474).

20. "Muy atadas a nuestra tierra"; "considerar la grandeza y majestad de su Dios"; "tratando a vueltas de sí con Dios." 1M 2:8, 10 (2:291–92/477–78).

21. "Un espejo para la humilidad, mirando cómo cosa buena que hagamos no viene su principio de nosotros, sino de esta fuente adonde está plantado este árbol de nuestras almas. . . . Y entendía cómo sin esta ayuda no podíamos nada." 1M 2:5 (2:290/476).

22. "Bajeza," "grandeza." 1M 2:8 (2:291/477).

23. 1M 2:5, q.v. n. 21. When Teresa speaks of this stage in terms of the soul "entering within" itself (*entre dentro de sí*), and says that you must "turn your eyes

toward the center" (*poned los ojos en el centro*), she does not mean an isolated intro-spection, but to turn to God in order to see your *source* in God. 1M 1:5; 2:8 (2:286, 291/474, 477).

24. 1M 1:1 (2:283/472), q.v. n. 12. "In my opinion we shall never completely know ourselves if we don't strive to know God." 1M 2:9 (2:292/478).

25. "Las cosas del alma siempre se han de considerar con plenitud y anchura y grandeza, pues no le levantan nada, que capaz es de mucho más que podremos considerar." 1M 2:8 (2:291/477).

26. "Absorbed in the world" (*embevidas en el mundo*). 1M 2:12 (2:293/479).

27. "It is very important for any soul that practices prayer, whether little or much, not to hold itself back and stay in one corner. Let it walk through (*andar por*) these dwelling places." 1M 2:8 (2:291/477).

28. "Legiones de demonios para combatir que no pasen de unas a otras." 1M 2:12 (2:293/478–79).

29. Teresa makes many references to this "war," "battle," and "fight": e.g., 2M 1:9–10; 4M 1:3, 12; 7M 3:13; 7M 4:10; see also V 8:2–3; 17:5; 25:1; CC 1:22; MC 2:3–4, 12, 15; 3:2.

30. "Truly, in all states, it's necessary that strength come to us from God" (*A la verdad, en todos estados es menester que [fuerza] nos venga de Dios*). 1M 2:12 (2:293/479). This means that there is no stage at which Teresa considers souls before they receive any grace at all: she is writing for nuns and Christians, not addressing the modern theological debate over nature and grace, where "nature" is usually understood as a state separate from and prior to grace.

31. "Aquí . . . no tienen la fuerza los vasallos de alma—que son los sentidos y potencias que Dios les dio de su natural." Ibid. It is also the case, however, that when the soul enters the mystical stages, it is not yet fully restored to its prelapsar-ian state, and the process of perfecting its humanity continues; but the level of grace that it receives in union is markedly different from that in the preparatory stages, raising the soul above nature to the supernatural level.

32. "Aquí está el entendimiento más vivo y las potencias más hábiles." 2M 1:2, 3 (2:299/482, 483).

33. 2M 1:6.

34. "Let this war be ended," Teresa says; "what hope can we have of finding rest outside of ourselves if we cannot be at rest within?" (*Acábese ya esta guerra. . . . ¿Qué esperanza podemos tener de hallar sosiego en otras cosas, pues en las propias no podemos sosegar?*). 2M 1:9 (2:302/485). This is the state fully attained only in the last dwelling place: see 7M 4:11, n. 138, below.

35. 3M 1:5, 7.

36. 3M 1:8; 2:6 (2:308, 311/489, 491).

37. "Libertad de espíritu"; "rendir nuestra voluntad a la de Dios en todo." 3M 2:4(3); 6 (2:310, 311/491, 492).

38. "Since we are so circumspect, everything offends us because we fear every-thing; . . . let's abandon (*dejemos*) our reason and our fears into his hands; let's for-get our natural weakness." 3M 2:8 (2:312/492).

39. "Procurar quien esté con mucho desengaño de las cosas del mundo. . . . Parece que con su vuelo nos atrevemos a volar." 3M 2:12 (2:314/493).

40. "El alma allí no hace más que la cera cuando imprime otro el sello, que la cera no se le imprime a sí; sólo está dispuesta, digo blanda." 5M 2:12 (2:346/515); 5M 2:5.

41. 1M 2:5, 10 (2:292/476, 478). See nn. 20, 21.

42. 7M 2:8(10) (2:436/573), q.v. n. 125.

43. "Abrazos con la cruz que vuestro Esposo llevó sobre Sí y entended que ésta ha de ser vuestra empresa. . . . Toda la pretensión de quien comienza oración . . . ha de ser trabajar y determinarse y desponerse con cuantas diligencias pueda a hacer su voluntad comformar la de Dios; y, como diré después, estad muy cierta que en esto consiste toda la mayor perfeción que se puede alcanzar en el camino espiritual." 2M 1:7–8 (2:300–301/484–85). Teresa introduces this christocentric perspective once in the first dwelling place, where she says in the context of attaining self-knowledge that "we should set our eyes on Christ" (*pongamos los ojos en Cristo*): 1M 2:11 (2:293/478). But the theme is not developed until the second and third dwelling places. "Determination" (*determinación*) is probably the most frequently used term in Teresa's vocabulary for the attitude that the soul must take throughout the spiritual life, especially in the beginning stages, against all kinds of opposition: e.g., 2M 1:2, 6, 8; 3M 1:7; 4M 1:7; 5M 3:10; 4;4; 6M 2:6; 9:16; 7M 4:2, 8; also V 4:2; 6:9; 11:6, 10; 13:2, 3; 15:13; 19:11; 24:7; CC 1:9; 25(26):3; E 3:2; CV 3:5; 11:5; 12:2; 14:1; 16:9, 10; 18:8; 20:3; 21:2; 23:1; 26:10; 28:12; 32:8; 41:3, 4; 42:3; MC 3:5, 6, 12; 4:12; 6:1; F 2:7; 14:5; 28:19.

44. In the *Vida*, Teresa understood the cross as the suffering of the world in *contrast* to the sweetness of union: e.g., V 16:4–5. In the *Meditaciones*, Teresa interprets the apple tree as the cross in the phrase from the Song, "under the apple tree I raised you up": the soul is not removed from the cross in union but attains the cross more fully, continuing to suffer but no longer being consumed by suffering—this suffering "doesn't consume it and waste it." MC 7:8(9) (2:259/467), q.v. chap. 5, n. 88.

45. "No está aún el amor para sacar de razón; más querría yo que la tuviésemos para no nos contentar con esta manera de servir a Dios siempre a un paso paso. . . . ¿No valdría más pasarlo de una vez?" 3M 2:7 (2:312/492).

46. Rowan Williams, *Teresa of Avila*, 73.

47. 5M 2:5.

48. "Comienzan a ser cosas sobrenaturales." 4M 1:1 (2:316/495). Kavanaugh and Rodriguez's "supernatural *experiences* begin here" is a free translation of *cosas*: I prefer to leave *cosas* as "things," for the reasons outlined above, though this gives a bland tone in English. See below, n. 53, for the way that the natural activity of the soul is excluded at this stage of union.

49. As we saw, Teresa only used the term mystical theology in the *Vida* twice (10:1 and 18:2) and stopped using it presumably because as a woman she was drawing too much attention to this aspect of her teaching by doing so (following Ahlgren, q.v. chap. 5, n. 15). Teresa used the term in a sense equivalent to "union" and to the "supernatural" state. The "union of the whole soul with God" is described at 5M 1:11 and is the first explicit mention of "union" in the *Moradas*.

50. CC 59(58):3 (1:425/625), q.v. chap. 5, n. 25.

51. "Por diligencias que hagamos no lo podemos adquirir." 4M 2:6 (2:325/501).

52. "Estos contentos . . . comienzan de nuestro natural mesmo y acaban en Dios. . . . Los gustos comienzan de Dios." 4M 1:4(4–5) (2:318/496).

53. The soul is paralyzed and unable to act at this stage, as in Teresa's previous accounts, but the difference from previous accounts is that this is a transitory paralysis rather than part of the definition of union. In *gustos*, "the faculties are not united but absorbed (*embevidas*) and looking as though in wonder at what they see." 4M 2:6 (2:325/401). The faculties cannot direct the soul to exterior activity

at this stage, and so the soul is unable to engage in any action for the duration of the union.

54. "Hagamos cuenta, para entenderlo mejor, que vemos dos fuentes con dos pilas que se hinchen de agua." 4M 2:2 (2:323/499).

55. V 11–18, esp. 11:7.

56. "Estos dos pilones se hinchen de agua de diferentes maneras; el uno viene de más lejos por muchos arcaduces y artificio; el otro está hecho en el mesmo nacimiento del agua y vase hinchendo sin nengún ruido." 4M 2:3 (2:323/500).

57. "Gran ruido . . . no en los oídos, sino en lo superior de la cabeza, adonde dicen que está lo superior del alma. . . . Viene el agua de su mesmo nacimiento, que es Dios . . . produce con grandísima paz y quietud y suavidad de lo muy interior de nosotros mesmos." 4M 1:10; 2:3–4 (2:320, 323–24/498, 500).

58. Teresa uses this third category of the superior part of the soul to apply to such mediating elements whether they are found in supernatural *or* acquired prayer. This is new in the *Moradas*. She had already spoken of the superior part of the soul in the *Vida* in relation to suspension and rapture, but she did not distinguish it clearly from the interior part until the *Moradas*: suspension was intrinsic to union, but in the *Moradas* she relates suspension to the superior part of the soul in order to *reserve* the interior part for union proper. She continued to hold that many genuine unions, such as raptures, *included* suspension, but suspension was a secondary effect in the superior part of the soul—associated with intermediaries, as we see here—while union proper occurred only in the interior part.

59. "Vase revertiendo este agua por todas las moradas y potencias hasta llegar a el cuerpo." 4M 2:4 (2:324/500).

60. "Su nacimiento es de . . . una cosa profunda. Pienso que deve ser el centro del alma, como después he entendido y diré a la postre." 4M 2:5 (2:324/500).

61. The "uncreated" nature of the grace of union is something that Teresa mentions in the seventh dwelling place, where she describes the soul as being "in pure spirit . . . in heavenly union with uncreated Spirit" (*en puro espíritu . . . en esta unión celestial con el espíritu increado*). 7M 2:7 (2:435/572). This locates Teresa in the late medieval debate over whether grace must be created to be received by the soul, or whether the Holy Spirit enters the soul in uncreated form. The most important aspect of union, which makes it "mystical" for Teresa, is its unmediated or uncreated nature: she takes the view that the Holy Spirit enters the soul in uncreated form. But it is also the case that the soul is initially unable to receive this grace without being thrown into physical paralysis, raptures, and so on, which shows that human nature is not naturally able to receive it and must be accommodated to it.

62. "Tornando a el verso en lo que me puede aprovechar—a mi parecer—para aquí, es en aquel ensanchamiento." 4M 2:6 (2:324/ 500). The expansion of the soul is a repeated theme in the *Moradas*: see also 4M 1:5; 2:5; 3:9; 7M 2:12.

63. "Dios . . . la habilita y va dispuniendo para que quepa todo en ella." 4M 3:9 (331–32/505).

64. In *gustos* world-directed activity is excluded, as noted above, n. 53.

65. "Ansí como se entiende claro un dilatamiento u ensanchamiento en el alma, a manera de como si el agua que mana de una fuente no tuviese corriente, sino que la mesma fuente estuviese labrada de una cosa que mientras más agua manase más grande se hiciese el edificio." 4M 3:9 (2:331/505).

66. "Si [Dios] da mucho, hace, como he dicho, hábil el alma para que sea capaz

de bever mucho; como un vidriero que hace la vasija de el tamaño que ve es menester, para que quepa lo que quiera echar en ella." CV 19:9 (2:111/316).

67. "The Lord doesn't give it this knowledge [that he dwells within it] until he enlarges it little by little and it has the capacity to receive what he will place within it" (*no se da a conocer hasta que va ensanchándola poco a poco, conforme a lo que más ha menester para lo que ha de poner en ella*). CV 28:12(11) (2:144/354). See also CV 39:3.

68. "No se halla con aquella soledad que solía, pues goza de tal compañia. . . . Quizá es que la ha fortalecido el Señor y ensanchado y habilitado." 7M 3:12 (2:442/577).

69. "Cuando Su Majestad quiere que el entendimiento cese, ocúpale por otra manera y da una luz en el conocimiento tan sobre la que podemos alcanzar, que le hace quedar absorto; y entonces, sin saber cómo, queda muy mejor enseñado, que (no) con todas nuestras diligencias." 4M 3:6(8) (2:330/504).

70. "El entendimiento . . . no obra, sino está como espantado de lo mucho que entiende; porque quiere Dios entienda que . . . ninguna cosa entiende." V 10:1 (1:105/66).

71. There is a fifth term that she uses in the *Moradas*, "mind" (*pensamiento*), which is that aspect of the faculties which distracts the soul from union: the mind (*pensamiento*) and the imagination (*imaginación*) remain outside union while the intellect (*entendimiento*) enters into union (4M 1:8–9), as we saw in chap. 5, pp. 77–78.

72. There is evidence that Teresa carefully considered this distinction as she was writing, as the manuscript shows that she wrote the first five letters of *entendimiento*, crossed it out, and replaced it with *conocimiento*: see *Obras Completas* (Madrid: BAC, 1997), 504, note d.

73. "Del mesmo descontento que dan las cosas el mundo nace un deseo de salir dél, tan penoso"; "la metió Dios a la bodega del vino y ordenó en ella la caridad"; "ayuda mucho para morir." 5M 2:10, 12; 3:5 (2:345, 346, 350/514, 515, 517).

74. "Resignada nuestra voluntad en la de Dios. . . . Yo os confieso que será a mucho o más trabajo." 5M 3:3, 5 (2:349, 350/517). "Este gusano . . . comienza a labrar la seda y edificar la casa adonde ha de morir. . . . Este trabajillo—que es nada—junte Dios con su grandeza." 5M 2:4–5 (2:342–43/512–13).

75. "Esta es la unión que toda my vida he deseado, ésta es la que pido siempre a nuestro Señor y la que está más clara y sigura." 5M 3:5 (2:350/517); 5M 3:12.

76. "Echa la simiente . . . siempre hace provecho a otras almas." 5M 3:1 (2:348/516).

77. "Es naciendo de raíz del amor de Dios." 5M 3:9, 12 (2:351/518). See "interior root," MC 7:3 (2:257/465), q.v. chap. 5, n. 83.

78. "Mirad lo que costó a nuestro Esposo el amor que nos tuvo." 5M 3:12 (2:353/519); looking forward to the position where the soul's "life is now Christ" in the seventh dwelling place: see 7M 2:5; 3:2, and below, pp. 114–17.

79. 5M 3:2.

80. 5M 3:5; 5M 2:7.

81. "Es muy contino no se apartar de andar con Cristo nuestro Señor por una manera admirable, adonde divino y humano junto es siempre su compañía." 6M 7:9 (2:401/550). This quotation refers to a later state attained in the sixth dwelling place but it equally applies to the path that Teresa is advocating here.

82. The devil can still remove the soul from union at this stage, but in the seventh dwelling place only God can. 5M 4:6; and see below, p. 117.

83. "Vivirá [el alma] en esta vida con descanso y en la otra también"; "una

pasión inquieta, desasosegada. . . . Estas penas pasan de presto; . . . parece que no llegan a lo hondo del alma." 5M 3:3–4 (2:349/517).

84. V 22:1, 4, 9. See chap. 5, pp. 82–83. See also 6M 7:5–14.

85. Favors are highly beneficial, but the soul should not seek them, as they are "freely added on" (*acesoria*), that is, *gratis datae*: 2M 1:7 (2:301/484); also 6M 8:4, 6, 10; 9:15, 16; CV 38:4.

86. Favors accelerate the soul's progress to union. The controversial aspect of Teresa's teaching is contained in this view. Although she advocates active works as the superior path to union in the "true union," she continues to imply that those who receive favors are in the "fast stream" to union, and that in practice those who merely engage in active works will not reach union in this life. The fact that those who receive favors outstrip those on the ordinary path of active works is common enough in the mystical tradition, but it is what attracts the attention of Teresa's opponents at the time and continues to lay her open to the charge of esotericism today. John of the Cross is more negative on favors in general than Teresa but this does not make his position any different on the extraordinary nature of union and the fact that union is the highest favor of all.

87. V 27:4.

88. 5M 2:4; 7M 2:5.

89. 5M 4:3–5. The reason that they remain brief is that our human nature still requires some conforming to the divine nature, and for this reason they continue to cause deep pain: esp. 6M 11:1–12.

90. Teresa describes the distinction between the three kinds of vision (introduced in chap. 5 above, p. 76 and table 5.1): e.g., "Esta visión . . . es imaginaria. . . . Dicen los que lo saben mijor que yo, que es más perfecta la pasada [visión no imaginativa] que ésta, y ésta más mucho que las que se ven con los ojos corporales." V 28:4 (1:238/149). She avoids the term "intellectual vision" for the highest kind in the *Vida*, preferring the term "non-imaginative vision," even though her treatment in chap. 27 shows that she understands the nature of intellectual visions perfectly well. This is another case of her hiding her knowledge of mystical theology so as not to attract unwanted attention. The threefold division came originally from Augustine (*De Trinitate*, bk. 12), but it was a common way of distinguishing between visions which she could have found in a number of the authors that she read. This categorization includes not only visions but other supernatural apprehensions such as locutions.

91. Ibid.; V 28:8–9 (1:240, 242/150, 151); "pone el Señor lo que quiere que el alma entienda, en lo muy interior del alma, y allí lo representa sin imagen ni forma de palabras." V 27:5, 6 (1:230/144). In the case of intellectual locutions, the soul does not "listen" with the spiritual ears, as in lesser kinds of locution, but "there is nothing more to do than enjoy." V 27:8 (1:231/145).

92. V 28:8–9, 13 (1:240–41/151).

93. Teresa describes this part as "very interior" (*muy interior*). V 27:6 (1:230/144). In the *Moradas*, Teresa argues that some imaginative visions are "more beneficial" than intellectual visions, because they unite the soul with Christ bodily as well as spiritually (6M 9:1): this state *anticipates* the human–divine unity of the seventh dwelling place. See the epilogue, pp. 132–37.

94. "Si dos personas se quieren mucho y tienen buen entendimiento, aun sin señas parece que se entienden con sólo mirarse. Esto deve ser aquí, que sin ver nosotros, como de en hito se miran estos dos amantes, como lo dice el Esposo a la Esposa en los Cantares." V 27:10 (1:232/145).

95. Ibid.

96. "Las tres Personas . . . presentes en mi alma muy ordinario." CC 14(15) (1:392–93/600); "divina compañía," CC 13(14):3(4) (1:392/600).

97. "Todas tres Personas . . . se representavan dentro en mi alma distintamente." CC 13(14):1 (1:391/600).

98. CC 42(40) (1:410–11/612).

99. "Sentir esta caridad con encendimiento en el alma." CC 13(14):1 (391/600).

100. "Una esponja se encorpora y embeve el agua, ansí me parecía mi alma que se hinchía de aquella divinidad y por cierta manera gozava en sí y tenía las tres Personas. . . . Parecíame que dentro de mi alma . . . estas tres Personas se comunicavan a todo lo criado, no haciendo falta ni faltando de estar conmigo." CC 14(15) (1:392–93/600–601). See CC 40(53) for the same image of the soul as sponge.

101. "'No trabajes tú de tenerme a Mí encerrado en ti, sino de encerrarte tú en Mí.'" Ibid.

102. "Se me dio a entender . . . que ha hecho bien diferente operación que de sólo tenerlo por fe"; "este embarazo que hace el cuerpo para no gozar dellas [grandezas], que . . . parece no son para nuestra bajeza entender algo dellas." CC 42(40) (1:410–11/612). My emphasis.

103. "Tan clara luz." 7M 1:9(10) (431/569). See below on this vision.

104. "Parece le llega a las entrañas esta pena y que cuando de ellas saca la saeta el que la hiere, verdaderamente parece que se las lleva tras sí, según el sentimiento de amor siente." 6M 2:4 (2:368/529).

105. "Vuelo de espíritu": "muy de presto algunas veces se siente un movimiento tan acelerado del alma, que parece arrebatado el espíritu. . . . Con un ímpetu grande se levanta una ola tan poderosa que sube a lo alto esta navecica de nuestra alma. . . . Me voy espantando de cómo se muestra aquí el gran poder de este gran Rey y Emperador." 6M 5:1, 4 (2:386–87/540–41).

106. "Oración estraña que no sabe entender qué es[;] . . . alabar a nuestro Señor, que aquí va todo su movimiento. . . . Es harto, estando con este gran ímpetu de alegría, que calle y puede disimular, y no poco penoso." 6M 6:10–11 (2:395/546).

107. CV 28:9; and see above, p. 105.

108. "Vemos a Dios y nos vemos tan metidas en su grandeza." 5M 2:6 (2:343/513). My emphasis.

109. 6M 7:9. See quotation given above, n. 81.

110. "Ésta [merced] trai consigo un particular conocimiento de Dios, y de esta compañía tan contina nace un amor ternísimo con Su Majestad." 6M 8:4 (2:407/553).

111. Teresa refers to the general way of knowing God with disapproval in the *Vida* in relation to the books on prayer which advise ridding oneself of corporeal images of Christ (V 22:1): she regards all corporeal images and forms as excluded from intellectual visions, but *not* those of Christ in his humanity, as we have seen. Here she is not referring to the humanity of Christ, however, as the context is rather of Christ's own knowledge of God; so this "particular knowledge of God" must be that possessed by the Son in the Trinity.

112. "Paréceme a mí que el Espíritu Santo deve ser medianero entre el alma y Dios, y el que la mueve con tan ardientes deseos, que la hace encender en fuego soberano, que tan cerca está . . . que vea y goce del fruto que sacó Jesucristo Señor nuestro de su Pasión." MC 5:5(6–7) (2:249/456). Though the Holy Spirit is a mediator here, Teresa regards the Holy Spirit as given to the soul in union in uncreated form, as in the Trinity. See n. 61.

113. "Con una inflamación que primero viene a su espíritu a manera de una nube de grandísima claridad . . . de manera que lo que tenemos por fe, allí lo entiende el alma—podemos decir—por vista. . . . Aquí se comunican todas tres Personas." 7M 1:6(7) (2:430/569).

114. "Se le muestra . . . estas Personas distintas, y por una noticia admirable que se da a el alma, entiende con grandísima verdad ser todas tres Personas una sustancia y un poder y un saber y un solo Dios." Ibid.

115. "En lo muy muy interior; en una cosa muy honda . . . siente en sí esta divina compañía." 7M 1:7(8) (2:430/569).

116. "Siempre que advierte se halla con esta compañía." 7M 1:9(10) (2:431/569). As seen below, the clarity of the intellectual vision does not persist. It is brief, because otherwise "the soul would find it impossible to be engaged in anything else or even to live among people," but unlike previous visions, after this one is over the soul remains fully aware of its place within the Trinity and of the trinitarian distinctions.

117. "Lo esencial de su alma jamás se movia de aquel aposento." 7M 1:10(11) (2:431/570).

118. Teresa also sees her christological and trinitarian arguments as reflecting the two main biblical strands of the theory of union, which she quotes to the best of her memory: "He that is joined or united to the Lord becomes one spirit with him," 1 Cor. 6:17 (7M 2:5[6]); and "while Jesus our Lord was once praying for his apostles . . . he said that they were one with the Father and with him, just as [he] is in the Father and the Father is in him," Jn. 17:21 (7M 2:7[9]).

119. "El Señor . . . le dijo que ya era tiempo de que sus cosas tomase ella por suyas y El ternía cuidado de las suyas." 7M 2:1 (2:433/570).

120. Teresa introduces "consummation" (*consumarse*) at the beginning of the seventh dwelling place (7M 1:3), but she removed later uses of the word from her second draft, preferring this term "loving expressions." From these "loving expressions," "there flow (*salen*) streams of milk bringing comfort to all the people of the castle." 7M 2:6(7) (2:435/572). See chap. 5, p. 89, esp. n. 93. Even though the soul is permanently aware of the presence of God following the intellectual vision, "consummation" is still required to bring the interior and exterior parts of the soul together. Significantly, Teresa's clearest statement of the "division in her soul" comes immediately after the intellectual vision of the Trinity: "it seemed to her that there was, in a certain way, a division in her soul. . . . She complained of that part of the soul, as Martha complained of Mary." 7M 1:10(11) (see chap. 5, n. 36 for full citation). Thus, even the intellectual vision of the Trinity is not enough without the "consummation" in human nature also.

121. "En vaciando nosotros todo lo que es criatura y desasiéndonos de ella por amor de Dios." 7M 2:7 (2:435–36/572–73); 7M 3:12 (see citation above, n. 68).

122. "Su vida es ya Cristo." 7M 2:5(6) (2:435/572). Teresa quotes from Phil. 1:21, "For me to live is Christ, and to die is gain."

123. "Mas aunque no es con esta tan clara luz, siempre que advierte se halla con esta compañía, digamos ahora como una persona que estuviese en una muy clara pieza con otras y cerrasen las ventanas y se quedase ascuras, no porque se quitó la luz para verlas y que hasta tornar la luz no las ve, deja de entender que están allí." 7M 1:9(10) (2:431/569).

124. "*Se entiende claro*, por unas secretas aspiraciones, ser Dios el que da vida a nuestra alma. . . . Como he dicho, ansí *se entiende claro* que hay en lo interior quien arroje estas saetas y dé vida a esta vida." 7M 2:6(7–8) (2:435/572), my emphasis.

125. "Vemos en este espejo que contemplamos, adonde nuestra imagen está esculpida." 7M 2:8(10) (2:436/573).

126. "Cierto es suyo aquel recaudo u billete escrito con tanto amor, y de manera que sólo vos quiere entendáis aquella letra y lo que por ella os pide." 7M 3:9 (2:441/576).

127. 7M 3:2.

128. "Nunca, ni por primer movimiento, tuerce la voluntad de que se haga en ella la de Dios." CC 65(66):9(10) (1:438/633).

129. "Aquellos recaudos que envía el alma de el centro interior a la gente de arriba del castillo y a las moradas que están fuera de donde ella está . . . potencias y sentidos y todo lo corporal." 7M 4:10(11) (2:447/580).

130. "No hay para qué bullir ni buscar nada el entendimiento, que el Señor que le crió le quiere sosegar aquí, y que por una resquicia pequeña mire lo que pasa; porque aunque a tiempos se pierde esta vista y no le dejan mirar, es poquísimo intrevalo." 7M 3:11 (2:442/576).

131. In both intellectual visions and some imaginative visions, as we have seen, Teresa stresses the fact that they are "engraved" (*esculpidas*), "impressed/imprinted" (*imprimadas*) or "stamped" (*estampanse*) on the memory (or often she says simply on the soul): this gives the soul a "habitual remembrance of God" (*una ordinaria memoria de Dios*) in God's immediate presence. See 6M 3:7; 4:5; 5:11; 7:11; 8:3; 9:3; 10:2.

132. Teresa says less on this issue than John of the Cross, for the obvious reason that she knew less about the technicalities of faculty psychology, but she appears to arrive at very much the same position as John, in taking the view that the faculties are both *the same as* the center in their depth and *outside* the center in receiving mediated "letters" from the center.

133. 7M 2:10.

134. "Algunas veces las deja nuestro Señor en su natural. . . . Verdad es que dura poco—un día lo más, u poco más. . . . Quiere nuestro Señor que no pierda la memoria de su ser." 7M 4:1-2 (2:444/578).

135. 7M 4:3 (2:444/778).

136. See n. 134 for citation.

137. 7M 2:9–10(12–14) (2:437/573).

138. "El sosiego que tienen estas almas en lo interior, es para tenerle muy menos, ni querer tenerle, en lo esterior"; "Marta y María han de andar juntas." 7M 4:10(11), 12(14) (2:447–48/580–81).

139. "Poned los ojos en la Crucificado," etc. 7M 4:8(9) (2:446/580) (see also n. 170). "De esto es la oración, hijas mías; de esto sirve este matrimonio espiritual, de que nazcan siempre obras, obras." 7M 4:6 (2:446/579).

140. 7M 4:10.

141. "Señalados con su hierro, que es el de la cruz, porque ya ellos le han dado su libertad—los pueda vender por esclavos de todo el mundo, como El lo fue . . . y si a esto no se determinan, no hayan miedo que aprovechen mucho." 7M 4:8(9) (2:446–47/580); see 2M 1:7–8, as cited above, n. 43. Favors are given in the seventh dwelling place only when the soul suffers from weakness and needs to be returned to full strength (7M 4:4); for the most part, they are unnecessary, and even if they are given, they do not cause suffering but are easily accommodated by the soul, as it is now "enlarged" and "made capable," as we have seen (7M 3:12).

Notes to Chapter Seven

1. The phrase is used by John ("sin otro algún medio": C 22:7(8) [499/829]; also C 35:2, 6), and strongly implied by Teresa in her image of the "two founts with two water troughs": she says that in union the trough of our interior part is "made at the very source of the water" in God, so that it fills "without any noise," whereas in acquired prayer the fount is "far away" and the water reaches us only through "aqueducts and the use of much ingenuity": 4M 2:3 (2:323/500) (see chap. 6, and nn. 56–57).

2. Teresa and John speak of this immediate contact with God using *sentir* words, as in Teresa's "sentimiento de la presencia de Dios" in her first apprehension of mystical theology (V 10:1), and John's "touch of union" (*toque de unión*): "Dios es el que allí es sentido," he says (2S 26:5). For the uncreated nature of what is touched in union, see 3S 13:2 ("las increadas") and 7M 2:7(9) ("el espíritu increado").

3. John and Teresa refer to this inner-trinitarian participation in many passages, as we have seen, but most important are the following: for Teresa, V 27:10; CC 13(14); 14(15); 40 (53); 42(40); MC 5:5(6–7); 7M 1:6(7)–10(11); 2:7(9); for John, C 39:3–5; L 1:15; 4:17.

4. Esp. L 4:2, 3; 7M 4:10.

5. Teresa speaks of the "división en su alma" (7M 1:10), and John of a point at which the two parts of the soul seemingly have no relation to each other. See further below, n. 16.

6. No part of the soul is "uncreated" in union, for John or Teresa, but the interior part of the soul must be raised above even the perfect natural state in order to make immediate contact with the uncreated form of God, which is in no way accommodated to the soul's ordinary means of knowing through created images and forms.

7. Maritain, *Degrees of Knowledge,* 100. See chap. 3, pp. [42–43].

8. John treats the Augustinian "image of God" in the soul most fully in the *Cántico*. Initially, he uses the term "el íntimo ser del alma" instead of "imagen de Dios" (C 1:6), but when the soul becomes deiform and participates fully in the Trinity in union he says that it has achieved the goal of its creation in God's "image and likeness" (C 39:3). See also 1S 9:1: "[el alma] en sí es una hermosísima y acabada imagen de Dios." Teresa begins the *Moradas* with the Genesis text of our creation in God's "image and likeness" (1M 1:1) and proceeds with an Augustinian process of introspection. Later in the *Moradas,* she speaks of the soul seeing itself in union as an "image" reflected immediately in God: 7M 2:8; cf. 5M 2:8.

9. 2S 8:3; 1M 1:1.

10. C 12:1; 1M 2:3, 8.

11. 1M 2:10, q.v. chap. 6, n. 20.

12. John's examination of the faculties in turn is the organizing structure of books 2 and 3 of the *Subida*. This kind of detail is not provided by Teresa, and she does not explicitly relate the three faculties to the three persons, as John does (2N 13:11; L 1:15). But she provides in passing considerable reflection on the operation of the faculties and the trinitarian structure of knowledge and love that exists between the soul and God in union.

13. The "breathing" of the Holy Spirit by the soul in union is John's particular image for the immediate nature of the participation of the soul in the Trinity (C 39:3). "Uncreated" as n. 2 above.

14. C 36:5; "la unión hipostática de la naturaleza humana con el Verbo divino, y en la respondencia que hay a ésta de la unión de los hombres en Dios. . . . Fue darle conocimiento de los misterios de la humanidad de Cristo." C 37:3–4 (550–51/884–85). Similarly, Teresa relates the kiss between the bride and the Bridegroom in the spiritual marriage to the union of God with man in Christ (MC 1:10).

15. 5M 2:6, q.v. chap. 6, n. 108.

16. "[El alma] conoce en sí dos partes tan distintas entre sí, que le parece no tiene que ver la una con la otra, pareciéndole que está muy remota y apartada de la una." 2N 23:14 (386/583). "En esta unión celestial con el espíritu increado," 7M 2:7(9) (437/572); "lo esencial de su alma jamás se movía de aquel aposento, . . . no la puede tener compañía," 7M 1:10(11) (2:431–432/570). See full quotation in chap. 5, n. 36.

17. 2S 7:5–11; 2N 6:1.

18. For this important development in Teresa's thought, see chap. 5, p. 88, and chap. 6, pp. 99–100.

19. 7M 3:9; 4:10(11).

20. "La comunicación de dulzura de amor . . . que redunda en el ejercicio de amar efectiva y actualmente . . . exteriormente haciendo obras pertenecientes al servicio de el Amado." C 36:4 (546–47/879–80); C 31:4; L 1:36.

21. 4M 2:3–4, 6.

22. "Los pasados ímpetus de amor no eran bastantes, porque no eran de tanta calidad para alcanzarlo." L 1:36 (595/942).

23. Teresa is not alone in regarding suspensions as characteristic of the early stages of union—John does so also: e.g., 3S 2:8. But both Teresa (in her mature view) and John regard suspensions as absent in the later stages, because the soul has been fortified: C 28:4–5; L 1:27, 36; 4:12; MC 7:8; 7M 3:12; 4:11(12).

24. John: C 32:8, q.v. n. 30 below; Teresa: as in the *recaudos* noted above, n. 19.

25. Ibid. We also saw that John identifies a third level of overflow, which he associates particularly with St. Francis's stigmata, in which the body receives physical wounds from a still more forceful overflow of the interior union, producing a physical representation of Christ, bearing his wounds (L 2:13–14).

26. MC 7:3; 7M 4:10(11).

27. "Las [criaturas] conoce mejor en su ser [Dios] que en ellas mismas . . . que es conocer los efectos por su causa y no la causa por los efectos." L 4:5 (645/1031).

28. See chap. 2, p. 21.

29. As seen in Teresa's visions of the Trinity in the *Cuentas*: she sees the persons communicating themselves to *all creation* and is told, "Don't try to hold Me within yourself, but try to hold yourself within Me" (CC 14[15], q.v. chap. 6, n. 101). John speaks of being engulfed in a "sea of love" in this indwelling of the Trinity, from where he sees the whole universe, "reaching to the heights and depths of the earthly and heavenly spheres," all imbued with God's love. L 2:10 (599/949); see also L 4:5 as above, n. 27.

30. "Poder mirar el alma a Dios es hacer obras en gracia de Dios." C 32:8 (536/869).

31. 5M 2:6; 7M 2:8.

32. See especially table 1, referring to John. We have seen the same symmetry in Teresa, as she enumerates a distinct series of cognitive acts produced by the higher faculties in union, particularly the intellect, culminating in the act which she names the *conocimiento*.

33. "Muera ya este yo, y viva en mí otro que es más que yo, y para mí mejor que yo, para que yo le pueda servir." E 17:3 (1:462/648).

34. On "annihilation," see the epilogue, nn. 42–43, below. John uses the word "destruction" in 3S 2:7; see the discussion of this passage in chap. 3, pp. 48–49.

35. As Iain Matthew has said, this is to possess the consciousness of Christ: "the mystic is witness to Jesus' consciousness because Jesus himself forms him from within." Matthew, *Knowledge and Consciousness of Christ*, 284.

36. L 1:3–4, 16; 4:14–15; 7M 1:9.

37. As Teresa says, even after the intellectual vision of the Trinity passes, the soul remains clearly aware that it is in the divine company "every time it takes notice": this is a permanent clarity, not as bright as the intellectual vision, but nevertheless retained permanently in union (7M 1:9[10]). John also maintains that the soul sees things clearly and distinctly in God in the final union (L 3:1–3, 69) and that this clarity is still there—though, again, not as fully—in the inner-trinitarian communication in the soul, even when the soul is not "awake" to it (L 4:14).

38. 7M 4:4–10(11).

39. L 1:29.

Notes to Epilogue

1. In fact, John quotes only from *De Mystica Theologia* among Dionysius's works (as cited below, n. 2).

2. "Rayo de tiniebla": 2S 8:6; 2N 5:3; 17:2; C 14&15:16; L 3:49.

3. 2N 5:2. John uses the image of the cloud that appeared to the Israelites in the desert, hiding the brighter light of God's presence: "clouds and darkness are near God and surround him (Ps. 96:2), not because this is true in itself, but because it appears thus to our weak intellects, which in being unable to attain so bright a light are blinded and darkened." 2N 5:3 (336/528); see also 2S 3:4 (referring to Exod. 14:20).

4. "Vacían," "oscurecen."2S 6:1 (119/305). On the voiding/darkening of the rational faculties in John, see also: 2S 6:2; 9:4; 10:3, 4; 14:10, 13; 3S 3:6; 2N 2:5; 2N 5.

5. The intellect is "lost" at the start of union, while the will is "taken captive," but in this state of unknowing the intellect is already "amazed by all it understands" (V 10:1; MC 6:9). Does Teresa have any of the other elements of rational negativity that we find in John? She speaks of "darkening" in relation to the rational faculties in one case only: she says that the soul's "understanding is so darkened (*está entendimiento tan escuro*) that it becomes incapable of seeing the truth," immediately following the "wound of love," in the sixth dwelling place (6M 1:9 [2:363/527])—but here she regards the darkness as caused by God's genuine absence rather than God's presence, as God "draws out the arrow" after wounding the soul, so removing this presence (6M 2:4; V 29:10). She also speaks of "voiding" or "emptying" (*vaciando*) the soul, though rarely, and refers to detachment as a whole rather than in the rational sense used by John (7M 2:7; also CV 28:12, "*desembaracemos*"). Similarly, she uses "darkness" to refer to a state of sin (1M 2:2, 14), or to doubt from the devil (V 36:8), or to stress the contrast between two kinds of union (7M 1:3, 9; V 37:7), rather than for the state of the rational faculties, as John does.

6. "Se acuerde que está delante de Dios y quién es este Dios." 4M 3:7(8) (331/504).

7. 2N 5:3, q.v. n. 3. I am grateful to Alois Haas for pointing out to me John's divergence from Dionysius here. Von Balthasar is mistaken in describing John's negativity as "truly Dionysian": Hans Urs von Balthasar, "John of the Cross," in *The Glory of the Lord: A Theological Aesthetics*, vol. 3, *Studies in Theological Style: Lay Styles* (Edinburgh: T. & T. Clark, 1986), 116.

8. On the dawn after the night: see 1S 2:5; 2S 2:1; C 14&15:23–24; L 1:25; and see chap. 3, pp. 52–53. "Conoce la luz que tiene espiritual." 2N 8:4 (345/538). The soul still does not see the light directly, but in the way that light is seen when it lights up the dust particles in the air, that is, as dust revealing the presence of light. 2N 8:3; L 1:22.

9. 4M 1:5; 2:5–6; also CV 28:12. John says that the flame of love "enlarges, widens, and makes it [the will] capable (*la dilate y ensanche y haga capaz*) of receiving the flame itself." L 1:23 (588/931).

10. Turner, *The Darkness of God*, 264.

11. As for instance in Maritain's contrast of John's understanding of the self and experience from the Cartesian view.

12. 1M 1:6; 2:8, 10.

13. "La dificultad que halla el alma en las cosas buenas la hacen conocer de sí la bajeza y miseria." 1N 12:2 (321/511). John explains later in the *Noche*: the light given by God shows up the soul's impurity, like light illuminating the dust particles in the air. The soul cannot see the light but only the dust (2N 8:3). It therefore sees not the light but only the darkness of its own imperfection and impurity (2N 5:2). Later on, as the soul approaches union more closely, it begins to see the light also (2N 8:4).

14. "Y éste es el primero y principal provecho . . . que causa esta seca y oscura noche de contemplación [es] el conocimiento de sí y de su miseria. . . . Oscurecidas sus primeras luces, tiene más de veras éstas en esta tan excelente y necesaria virtud del conocimiento propio." 1N 12:2 (321/511).

15. John only affirms that this is the case in retrospect (1S 9:1).

16. For the various fears which Teresa contrasts with fear of God, see: V 6:4; 7:1; 20:7; 23:2; 25:22; 31:12; 33:7; CC 30; MC 6:3; 1M 2:10–11; 3M 2:8; 4M 3:9; 6M 9:10. Teresa says that the primary difference between fear of God and fear of the world is that fear of God is accompanied by love: 1M 2:11; MC 2:28; see also CV 40:1; 41:1, 4. Fear of God also produces *determinación*, unlike fear of the world: CV 20:3, 4; 23:5; MC 3:12; 6:1, 3. In the *Vida*, she gives an example of a pernicious fear which kept her from prayer: she thought that she had offended God by her sins so greatly that humility demanded that she refrain from prayer while in this state (V 6:4; 7:11).

17. John mentions various different kinds of fear: we have a fear that we are not serving God in the dark night (1N 11:2); the soul feels "terror" in the early stages of "suspensions" in union—as discussed further below—though this lessens as it progresses (C 13:4; 14 and 15:2, 21); fear as a natural passion is gradually better controlled by reason (C 20&21:4); and in the final union the soul no longer fears at all, since God is "his brother and equal" (L 4:14). But there is no means of distinguishing between these various fears until the "midnight" of the dark night passes.

18. 1N 11:2; 2N 8:1, 3; L 1:22. Here gender is certainly involved: Teresa is describing fears that particularly affected women, sometimes actively inculcated in them by their confessors, which she wants them to be able to distinguish from the true fear of God and to resist with great determination. Ahlgren says that John was

typical of many male confessors in inculcating unnecessary fears in nuns in order to control them. She quotes a letter he wrote concerning one nun: "[she] has too much confidence and too little caution about erring internally. . . . What I would suggest is that they [her confessor and the community] . . . belittle it [her visionary pretension] and put it down; and they should test her harshly in the exercise of virtues, primarily in self-contempt, humility and obedience . . . and the tests must be good ones, because there is no devil who will not suffer anything for the sake of his honor." Quoted in Ahlgren, *Teresa of Avila*, 98. Ahlgren suggests that Teresa would never have suggested shaming a nun in this way but would have applied objective tests that were carefully explained, if she believed that devil-deception was occurring. Certainly John's approach is less sensitive to the fears of many nuns, but I would argue that his theological negativity prior to union is the explanation for this difference rather than any pernicious desire for control over women.

19. Compare these quotations from John and Teresa: "El gran tormento que siente el alma al tiempo de este género de visita y el gran pavor que le hace verse tratar por vía sobrenatural le hacen decir: *¡Apártalos, Amado!*" C 13:4 (459/786); "Muéstrase una majestad de quien puede hacer aquello, que espeluza los cabellos, y queda un gran temor de ofender a tan gran Dios. Este envuelto en grandísimo amor." V 20:7 (1:175/110). John goes on to say that this "torment" occurs at the beginning of union but lessens thereafter, however (C 14&15:21).

20. "La . . . pena que el alma aquí padece es a causa de otros dos extremos, conviene a saber, divino y humano, que aquí se juntan; . . . hace sentir en el alma otro extremo que hay en ella de íntima pobreza y miseria." 2N 6:1, 4 (337–38/529, 531).

21. See chap. 5, p. 76 and table 5.1. On John's treatment of visions, see chap. 2, pp. 27–29.

22. 2S 24:3–4; 26:5.

23. "Las visiones imaginarias . . . me parecen más provechosas, porque son más conformes a nuestro natural [que en las dichas (visiones intelectuales)]." 6M 9:1 (2:410–11/556). The comparison that Teresa is making is with the intellectual visions that she has treated in the previous chapter. (It is noteworthy that she says that the intellectual vision of the Trinity in the seventh dwelling place is superior to all imaginative visions, yet even in the seventh dwelling place, an imaginative vision of Christ follows the intellectual vision, and she says that it occurs in the same place in the "interior of the soul" where she had the intellectual vision, as we saw in chap. 6.) In the *Vida*, she also recommended imaginative visions on the grounds that they "almost always come together" with intellectual visions (V 28:9).

24. V 28; 6M 9.

25. On Teresa's view, see chap. 6, n. 131. John regards the "inner," non-corporeal part of imaginative visions as imprinted or stamped on the soul (3S 13:6), but he differs from Teresa in denying that spiritual-intellectual visions have any form to imprint on the soul (3S 14:2). Teresa thinks that intellectual visions are also imprinted/engraved, and more deeply than imaginative visions: V 27:5; 40:5; CC 42(40); 5M 2:13; 6M 3:7; 4:5; 5:11; 7:11; 10:2; 7M 2:8.

26. 2S 24:8–9.

27. "Es no haciendo caso de la letra y corteza . . . sólo advertir en tener el amor de Dios que interiormente le causan al alma." 3S 13:6 (233/422); also 3S 13:7–14:2; L 3:41.

28. Teresa likens the outward form to a "golden vessel" (*pieza de oro*) which is like a "reliquary" containing the living image of Christ's humanity. Although she is clear that we prize the vessel only for its contents, we may also see in this image

the fact that she regards the vessel, like a reliquary, as the beautiful and valuable container of the contents. 6M 9:2–3 (2:411/556); also V 28:9.

29. "Aunque digo imagen, entiéndase que no es pintada al parecer de quien la ve, sino verdaderamente viva . . . y revuelve todas las potencias y sentidos." 6M 9:4, 10 (2:411, 413/556, 558).

30. "Si es imagen, es imagen viva; no hombre muerto, sino Cristo vivo; y da a entender que es hombre y Dios." V 28:8 (1:240/151).

31. "No huir tanto de cosas corpóreas, que les parezca aún hace daño la Humanidad sacratísima." 6M 7:14 (403–4/551). Teresa recalls her similar statement in the *Vida*, as discussed below.

32. "Si el confesor le da este consejo . . . le digáis esta razón con humildad y no le toméis." 6M 9:13 (2:415/559).

33. See chap. 5, pp. 82–83.

34. V 22:1–4; 2S 12:3–4. John apparently takes this view from Osuna: see Williams, *Teresa of Avila*, 69–70. Matthew also regards this as a genuine difference between John and Teresa (*Knowledge and Consciousness of Christ*, 196). John values the senses only when union has been reached and they are hierarchically included in the operation of the spirit. Then, he says, the soul can raise its sensory joy in corporeal images "at the first moment" to the purely spiritual love of God, and this is the purpose for which the senses were created. At this point, but not before, he fully endorses Teresa's high estimation of images of Christ. 3S 15:2; 24:4–5; 26:7.

35. "He dicho que Cristo es el camino, y que este camino es morir a nuestra naturaleza. . . . Cierto está que al punto de la muerte quedó también anihilado en el alma sin consuelo y alivio alguno. . . . No consiste, pues, en recreaciones y gustos y sentimientos espirituales, sino en una viva muerte de cruz sensitiva y espiritual, esto es, interior y exterior." 2S 7:9, 11 (124–25/310–11).

36. The difficulty arises over the sense in which Christ's *spiritual* suffering was like our own. Iain Matthew treats this question in detail (Matthew, *Knowledge and Consciousness of Christ*, 262–80). John seems to take the view of Aquinas, that while we suffer in the sensory and spiritual parts of our soul on the journey to union, Christ only suffered in the "sensory" part, because he enjoyed the permanent union with the Word in his "spiritual" part (2S 7:11). In this passage, however, John is also clear that Christ's suffering is the model for our suffering in *both* parts of the soul, suggesting that this differentiation between sensory and spiritual suffering in Christ sits rather awkwardly with our own anthropology, where the two are always connected. Certain commentators have doubted John's commitment to the humanity of Christ because of the conspicuous absence of the humanity of Christ in the darkest periods of the dark night, as described in the *Noche oscura*. In the *Noche*, John uses only Old Testament and Pauline models to speak of the soul's suffering rather than the Passion of Christ, in the most severe part of the night, which leads Karl Rahner to conclude that the humanity of Jesus is accidental to John's mysticism. (Karl Rahner, "The eternal significance of the humanity of Jesus for our relationship with God," *Theological Investigations* [London, 1967], 3:35–46, quoted in Matthew, 271. Matthew also notes that Morel makes the same accusation in *Le sens de l'existence*, 2:194–212.) Matthew counters Rahner and Morel by pointing out that John is using these references as a device to speak of the absence of God that is *felt* at the darkest times of the night, where the soul's *perception* of its relationship with Christ is severely impaired, while in actuality the "absence" that the soul feels is the presence of God in Christ. The soul has here reached the zenith of Jesus' own yes when at the nadir of his annihilation on the cross, where it loses all perception

of the divine company. Further, Matthew argues that John is using these Old Testament references to signify the soul's *journey* from the suffering of the "old" to the joy of the "new," as union has not yet been reached. One might add that, as John never completed the *Noche*, he may simply not have reached the part where he intended to treat the Passion. In the *Cántico espiritual*, John could not have signaled the soul's solidarity with Christ in his humanity more strongly. As we have seen, he says that the soul attains a union "corresponding [to] . . . the hypostatic union of the human nature with the divine Word" (C 37:3). Matthew further points to the *Romances* as a focal point of John's Christology. Here, the Bride and Bridegroom are joined in the *incarnation*; union is understood as the birth of Christ, where the tears of the Bride in her suffering become the tears of the baby "God in the manger," linking the humanity of the soul (the Bride's tears) seamlessly to the humanity of Christ (the tears of the baby Jesus) (R 9:4–5, quoted in Matthew, 190).

37. "El padecer le es medio para entrar más adentro en la *espesura* de la deleitable sabiduría de Dios; porque el más puro padecer trae más íntimo y puro entender y, por consiguente, más puro y subido gozar, porque es de más adentro saber." C 36:12 (549/882). For this reason, John does not think that the loss of forms and images of Christ means that we lose the humanity of Christ, but that, on the contrary, the suffering of this loss enables us to know the humanity of Christ from "further within": see Paul Russell, "The Humanity of Christ in St. John of the Cross," *Spiritual Life* 30 (1984): 143–56.

38. ". . . unir al género humano por gracia con Dios. Y esto fue, como digo, al tiempo y punto que este Señor estuvo más anihilado en todo." 2S 7:11 (124/311). The most intense phase of this transformation of our humanity into the humanity of Christ occurs in the passive night of the spirit. John says, "The divine extreme strikes [the soul] in order to renew and divinize it. . . . It suffers an anguish comparable to Jonah's when in the belly of the whale. It is fitting that the soul be in this sepulchre of dark death in order that it attain the spiritual resurrection for which it hopes." 2N 6:1 (337/529–30).

39. Vej 6, 7. See chap. 4, pp. 67–68, esp. n. 38.

40. Slade, *St. Teresa of Avila,* 58.

41. V 22:8, q.v. chap. 5, n. 57.

42. Contrast Teresa's use of "annihilation" in V 38:19 with the christological/ trinitarian context in the sixth and seventh dwelling places of the *Moradas*: 6M 6:5; 9:18; 7M 3:14. This is more like John's use of the term: see 2S 4:2; 7:11 (as above); 24:8; 2N 6:5; 8:2; 9:2, 5; 19:1; L 3:34; 4:16. On the cross in union, see chap. 5, p. 88, and chap. 6, pp. 99–100.

43. 3M 1:8; 2:6, 8, 9 (2:308–13/489–92). Here, however, Teresa does not use the word "annihilation," but these other words, "being abandoned" (*dejado*) and "nakedness" (*desnudez*), which possibly convey a less strong sense: she may intentionally reserve the word "annihilation" for the passive stages, rather than applying it to these active stages prior to union.

44. MC 7:8; 7M 3:15; 4:8, 10.

45. As noted in chap. 7: John and Teresa both regard the soul's humanity as fully included in the final union, through the christological vision in the center of the soul. In the *Moradas*, Teresa notes that the highest "imaginative" vision that she has of the humanity of Christ occurs in as deep a part of the soul as the place where she had her intellectual vision of the Trinity. She reveals some confusion over the distinction between imaginative and intellectual visions here, but her point is that the humanity of Christ is fully seen in the highest kind of vision, reflected in our

own humanity in the spiritual marriage, and is not confined to the lower sensory part of the soul. 7M 2:1–2.

46. These two strands in the history of Christian ideas of spiritual sensation are traced in Gordon Rudy, "Mystical Language of Sensation in the Later Middle Ages" (Ph.D. diss., University of Chicago, 1999). The two strands are characterized as the intellectualist, on the one hand, following Origen's theory of spiritual sensation, and the bodily, on the other hand, following Bernard of Clairvaux's theory.

47. Bernard of Clairvaux's idea of the "carnal love of Christ" (*amor carnalis Christi*) is of key importance here; Rudy's dissertation (ibid.) sees this bodily type of spiritual sensation as further developed in the late medieval mystics Hadewijch and Ruusbroec.

48. Her most powerful image is of the death of the silkworm, so that the butterfly of union may come forth from the cocoon which is Christ (5M 2:1–7). Teresa's image of dying and rising with Christ here is very similar to John's image of Jonah (which is itself taken from the Gospels), who was in the belly of the whale before emerging onto dry land and to new life (2N 6:1, as quoted above, n. 38). Like John, Teresa regards this as a death (the death of *mors mystica*): she says of the soul in this state, "Don't think, daughters, there is any exaggeration in saying that she dies. As I have said, it indeed happens that love sometimes operates with such force that it rules over all the powers of the natural subject." MC 7:2 (2:256/464). Teresa describes this as "annihilation," like John, in 6M 6:5; 9:18; 7M 3:14. For John's description of this death, see (in addition to the quotations cited above) C 7:4; L 1:29–30.

49. 6M 7:5–15.

50. "If they [souls at this stage] lose the guide, who is the good Jesus, they will not hit upon the right road." 6M 7:6 (2:400/549). Teresa acknowledges that as soon as the soul enters into union it is generally unable to meditate discursively; but it is still able to use the intellect to enkindle the will, using images of Christ, until the final dwelling place (6M 7:7). The remedy for "absorption" is to seek the companionship of Christ in his humanity by remembering the mysteries of faith and the example of the saints and, if necessary, to engage in active works of service (6M 7:13–15).

51. "Cuanto más el alma se quiere oscurecer y anihilar acerca de todas las cosas exteriores e interiores que puede recibir, tanto más se infunde de fe y, por consiguente, de amor y esperanza en ella, por cuanto estas tres virtudes teologales andan en uno." 2S 24:8 (192/379) (see also para. 7).

52. See n. 36 above.

53. "Anyone whom the Lord places in the seventh dwelling place rarely, or hardly ever, needs to make this effort [remembering the humanity of Christ using images]." 6M 7:9 (2:401/550).

54. John agrees with Teresa on the positive benefit of the use of the bodily senses in the final union: he says that the bodily senses can mediate spiritual goods by turning their sensory gratification "immediately and in the first movement" to "the thought of God," rather than allowing the gratification to remain in the bodily senses ("*luego al primer movimiento se pone la noticia y afección de la voluntad en Dios dándole más gusto aquella noticia que el motivo sensual que se la causa*"): 3S 24:5 (255/444). He is not adopting the bodily tradition of spiritual sensation instead of the intellectualist here; he remains clear that the soul's primary connection to God is through the interior, and that any spiritual light received through the bodily

senses is "out-shone" by the light in the spirit (C 26:16, q.v. chap. 3, n. 79). The same is true for Teresa.

Notes to the Appendix

1. For reasons of space I am unable to go into the differences between the redactions of these works in detail. All of John's major works were written within a relatively short period, between about 1582 and 1587, but the "A" redaction of the *Cántico* comes at the beginning of this period and the "B" redaction at the end, so that there are considerable differences between the redactions. The *Llama* also exists in two redactions showing some important differences (though they are not nearly as great). I have considered only the "B" redactions of both works in what follows, because they are the most commonly used and represent the full maturity of John's thought. The overall order of works and their approximate dates of composition is thought to be as follows:

Cántico espiritual A	1582–1584 (though the poem probably goes back to 1577);
Subida del Monte Carmelo	Completed 1582–1585 (fragments of plans for it go back to 1578–1580);
Noche oscura	1584–1585;
Llama de amor viva A	1582–1584 (poem), 1585–1586 (commentary, written in 15 days);
Cántico espiritual B	1585–1586;
Llama de amor viva B	1591 (revisions during last months of John's life at La Peñuela).

The most useful recent scholarship on the composition of the writings is by Eulogio Pacho, and it is his chronology that I have followed here: see, in order of importance, his *Iniciación a San Juan de la Cruz* (Burgos: Monte Carmelo, 1982); *San Juan de la Cruz y sus escritos* (Madrid: Ediciones Cristianidad, 1969); "El 'Gemido Pacífico de la Esperanza'. Síntesis definitiva del pensamiento Sanjuanista," *Studies in Spirituality* 6 (1996): 153–67; *San Juan de la Cruz. Temas Fundamentales*, 2 vols (Burgos: Monte Carmelo, 1984), translated under the title *The Art of Reaching God according to St. John of the Cross. Exposition of the Basic Themes of Sanjuanist Spirituality* (Jyothir Bhavan, Kalamassey: Jyothir Dhara pub., 1990). On the development of the *Cántico* and its different redactions, see Colin P. Thompson, *The Poet and the Mystic*.

2. "La primera noche o purgación es de la parte sensitiva del alma, . . . y se tratará en la primera parte de este libro, y la segunda es la de la parte espiritual, . . . y désta también trataremos en la segunda y tercera parte cuanto a lo activo, porque cuanto a lo pasivo será en la cuarta." 1S 1:2 (73/258–59).

3. Trueman Dicken, *The Crucible of Love*, 219. Eulogio Pacho cautions against integrating the *Subida* and the *Noche* in too unitary a way: the *Noche* is an independent and autonomous work which complements and amplifies the active and passive aspects of the *Subida*. See, for instance, Eulogio Pacho, "El 'Gemido Pacífico de la Esperanza'. Síntesis definitiva del pensamiento Sanjuanista," *Studies in Spirituality* 6 (1996): 155.

4. See chap. 2, pp. 27–29.

5. "Aquí comienza Dios a comunicársele . . . por el espíritu puro, en que no cae discurso sucesivamente, comunicándosele con acto de sencilla contemplación." 1N 9:8 (315/505).

6. John introduces two nights, corresponding to the senses and the spirit, and then subdivides them into four; now he divides a single night into three—making one, two, three, and four divisions of the nights! But this kind of multiplicity is typical of many mystical itineraries.

7. "Dios, el cual ni más ni menos es noche oscura para el alma en esta vida. (1) . . . La primera [noche], que es la del sentido, se compara a prima noche, que es cuando se acaba de carecer del objeto de las cosas; y la seguna, que es la fe, se compara a la medianoche, que totalmente es oscura; y la tercera, al despidiente, que es Dios, la cual es ya inmediata a la luz del día. (5)" 1S 2:1, 5 (74–75/260–61).

8. "Vía del espíritu, que es de los aprovechantes y aprovechados, que por otro nombre llaman *vía iluminativa* o de *contemplación infusa.*" 1N 14:1 (327/518).

9. N Prol. 1.

10. Trueman Dicken, *The Crucible of Love*, 216–17. Trueman Dicken speculates that the *Subida* is the most systematic of John's treatises because he wrote it over a long period of time, unlike his other treatises. It was written "over the course of no less than five or six years," whereas the *Llama de amor viva* was written in less than two weeks, and "it would not be surprising to find that the *Night* had been written in a still shorter space of time." See also n. 1.

11. "Unión del alma con Dios . . . entendido esto, se dará mucha luz en lo que de aquí adelante iremos diciendo." 2S 4:8 (115/301).

12. "Como pase adelante, irá entendiendo mejor lo primero, porque con lo uno se va declarando lo otro." S Prol. 8 (72/257).

13. 2N 3:1-2; 2N 14:3.

14. "No porque sea siempre necesario guardar este orden de primero y postrero tan puntual como eso . . . eso es como Dios ve que conviene al alma." 2S 17:4 (157/343).

15. The "A" redaction of the *Cántico* was written before the *Llama*—indeed it was the first of the treatises: see n. 1. The "B" redaction quotes the *Llama* (C 31:7) and significant parts of it were written later than the "A" redaction of the *Llama*, but nevertheless the *Llama* represents a development and certainly a clarification of the *Cántico.*

16. "La intensión de esta purgación y cómo es en más y cómo en menos, y cuándo es según el entendimiento y cuándo según la voluntad, y cómo según la memoria y cuándo y cómo también según la sustancia del alma, y también cuándo [todo y] según todo, y la purgación de la parte sensitiva, y cómo se conocerá cuándo lo es la una y la otra, y a qué tiempo y punto o sazón de camino espiritual comienza, porque lo tratamos en la *Noche oscura de la Subida de el Monte Carmelo* y no hace ahora a nuestro propósito, no lo digo." L 1:25 (589/932).

17. "Pues ya no solamente no me eres oscura como antes, pero eres la divina luz de mi entendimiento, que te puedo ya mirar. Y no solamente no haces desfallecer mi flaqueza, mas antes eres la fortaleza de mi voluntad con que te puedo amar y gozar, estando toda convertida en amor divino; y ya no eres pesadumbre y aprieto para la sustancia de mi alma, mas antes eres la gloria y deleites y anchura de ella." L 1:26 (589/933).

18 "En el desposorio sólo hay un igualdo 'si' y una sola voluntad de ambas partes y joyas y ornato de desposada, que se las da graciosamente el desposado; mas en el matrimonio hay también comunicación de las personas y unión." L 3:24 (619/985).

19. "No es sino una fuerte y copiosa comunicación y vislumbre de lo que El es en sí." C 14&15:5 (464/792).

20. "Estotro es en más subida manera, por intervenir en ello el ejercicio de la voluntad." L 3:77 (640/1022). John's view of cooperative grace here shows his Thomistic background.

21. See chap. 2, pp. 35–37. Contrast the final stage of the *Noche*: "the spiritual part of his soul is withdrawn and alienated from the lower and sensory part." 2N 23:14 (386/579).

22. See chap. 1, pp. 12–13; 3S 2:13 (218/407).

23. "Como ascua en que tanto se afervora el fuego, que no solamente está encendida, sino echando llama viva"; "De donde el alma que está en estado de transformación de amor, podemos decir que su ordinario hábito es como el madero que siempre está embestido en fuego, y los actos de esta alma son la llama que nace del fuego del amor." L 1:16 (585/925); 1:4 (580/917).

24. "Esos gozos y suavidades accidentarias . . . no . . . en lo que es sustancial comunicación de espíritu se le aumenta nada." C 20&21:13 (493/823). (Something parallel to the actual union of the *Llama* is clearly described here in the *Cántico*.)

25. L 1:6.

26. C 24:6.

27. "Si estuviese siempre en ella recordado, comunicándose las noticias y los amores, ya sería estar en gloria." L 4:15 (649/1038). God is only "*as though* awake" in the soul because properly speaking God does not change and cannot be said to be awake or asleep (see L 3:11); but nevertheless he brings about a change of state in the soul, like his awakening.

28. When these "awakenings" are not happening, the soul continues to "feel and enjoy" God, although this takes place "as though with a loved one who is asleep, for knowledge and love are not communicated mutually while one is asleep." ("*Aunque [el alma] le [Dios] sentía y gustaba, era como al amado dormido en el sueño; y, cuando uno de los dos está dormido no se comunican las inteligencias y amores de entrambos hasta que ambos están recordados.*") L 4:14 (648/1037). The awakenings are thus particularly associated with knowledge rather than with love, as love continues without them.

29. "It is not secret to the soul itself that it has attained this perfection, for within itself it feels this intimate embrace." L 4:14 (648/1037).

30. L 2:9.

31. "Dando Dios la riqueza y valor a las cabezas en las primicias del espíritu, según la mayor o menor sucesión que habían de tener en su doctrina y espíritu." L 2:12 (599/950). John mentions St. Paul and St. Francis as examples of these founders (*cabezas*); but his juxtaposition of this with a description of an experience closely resembling Teresa's transverberation (L 2:9–10) suggests that he thinks that she also belongs in this category, and that she would qualify as a founder of the Carmelite Reform.

32. See chap. 3, pp. 52–53.

33. Brief statements about the positive role of the senses in union at the end of the *Subida* do not explain how the division between the senses and spirit is overcome, only that they finally work together harmoniously (3S 24:4–7).

34. As above, L 2:10 (599/948): "Engolfada . . . [en] un mar de amor."

35. 1N 9:8; 2N 1:2.

36. "Muy semejante al de la otra [la beatífica vista de Dios en la otra vida]." L 1:14 (584/924).

Bibliography

A. John of the Cross

Bibliographies

"Bibliographia Carmeli Teresiani." In *Carmelus*. Rome: Institutum Carmelitanum, 1954– (annual).

Ruano, Lucinio. "Guion bibliográfico." In *Obras de San Juan de la Cruz*, ed. Lucinio Ruano, 14th ed. Madrid: Biblioteca de Autores Cristianos, 1994. Pp. 1043–80.

Concordance

Astigarraga, J. L., A. Borrell, F. J. Martin de Lucas. *Concordancias de los escritos de San Juan de la Cruz*. Rome: Teresianum, 1990. Edición electrónica, con texto contínuo de *Obras Completas* de José Vicente Rodríguez (Editorial de Espiritualidad), edita y distribuye por Centro Internacional Teresiano-Sanjuanista, Avila.

Texts

Obras Completas de San Juan de la Cruz. Ed. Lucinio Ruano. 14th ed. Madrid: Biblioteca de Autores Cristianos, 1994.

The Collected Works of John of the Cross. Translated and introduced by Kieran Kavanaugh and Otilio Rodriguez. Washington D.C.: Institute of Carmelite Studies, 1979.

The Complete Works of John of the Cross. Translated by E. Allison Peers. 3 vols. London: Burns & Oates, 1934–35.

John of the Cross. The Living Flame of Love. Versions A & B. Translated and introduced by Jane Ackerman. New York: Pegasus, 1995.

The Poems of St. John of the Cross. Translated by Roy Campbell. London: Penguin, 1951.

Studies

Actas del Congreso Internacional Sanjuanista (Avila 23–28 Sept. 1991). Volumen I, *Filología;* Volumen II, *Historia;* Volumen III, *Pensamiento*. Valladolid: Junta de Castilla y León, Consejería de Cultura y Turismo, 1993.

Alberto de la Virgen del Carmen. "Naturaleza de la memoria espiritual según san Juan de la Cruz." *Revista de espiritualidad* 11 (1952): 291–99 and 12 (1953): 431–50.

Balthasar, Hans Urs von. "St John of the Cross." In *The Glory of the Lord: A Theological Aesthetics*. Vol. 3. *Studies in Theological Style: Lay Styles*. Edinburgh: T. & T. Clark, 1986. Pp. 105–71.

Baruzi, Jean. *St. Jean de la Croix et le problème de l'expérience mystique*. Paris: F. Alcan, 1931.

Bord, André. *Mémoire et espérance chez Jean de la Croix*. Biblioteque de Spiritualité 8. Paris: Beauchesne, 1971.

Brenan, Gerald. *St. John of the Cross: His Life and Poetry*. Cambridge: Cambridge University Press, 1973.

Castro, Secundino. "La Experiencia de Cristo: Foco Central de la Mística." In *Experiencia y pensamiento en San Juan de la Cruz*, ed. Federico Ruiz Salvador. Madrid: Editorial de Espiritualidad, 1990. Pp. 169–93.

Centner, David. "Christian Freedom and The Nights of St. John of the Cross." *Carmelite Studies* 2 (1982): 3–80.

Cepeda, José, ed. *Antropología de San Juan de la Cruz*. Institución Gran Duque de Alba, Diputación Provincial de Avila, 1988.

Cerezo Galán, Pedro. "La Antropología del Espíritu en Juan de la Cruz." In *Actas del Congreso Internacional Sanjuanista (Avila 23–28 Sept. 1991)*. Volumen III, *Pensamiento*. Valladolid: Junta de Castilla y León, Consejería de Cultura y Turismo, 1993. Pp. 126–53.

Collings, Ross. "Passivity in the Spiritual Life from the Writings of St. Thomas Aquinas and St. John of the Cross." D.Phil. dissertation, University of Oxford, 1978.

——. *John of the Cross*. The Way of the Christian Mystics 10. Collegeville, Minn.: Liturgical Press, 1990.

Crisógono de Jesús Sacramentado. *San Juan de la Cruz: su obra científica y su obra literaria*. 2 vols. Madrid: Mensajero de Santa Teresa y de San Juan de la Cruz, 1979.

——. *Vida de San Juan de la Cruz*, 12th ed. Madrid: Biblioteca de Autores Cristianos, 1991. Translated by Kathleen Pond, under the title *The Life of St. John of the Cross*. London: Longmans, 1958.

Diez Gonzalez, Miguel A. *Pablo en Juan de la Cruz: sabidura y ciencia de Dios*. Burgos: Editorial Monte Carmelo, 1990.

Edwards, James Denis. "The Dynamism in Faith: The Interaction between Experience of God and Explicit Faith: A Comparative Study of the Mystical Theology of John of the Cross and the Transcendent Theology of Karl Rahner." S.T.D. dissertation, Catholic University of America, 1979.

Efrén de la Madre de Dios y Otger Steggink. *Tiempo y Vida de San Juan de la Cruz*. Madrid: Biblioteca de Autores Cristianos, 1992.

Garrigou-Lagrange, Réginald. *Christian Perfection and Contemplation According to St. Thomas Aquinas and St. John of the Cross*. Translated by Sr. M. Timothea Doyle. London: B. Herder Book Co., 1937, 1958.

Giovanna della Croce. "Johannes vom Kreuz und die deutsch-niederländische Mystik." *Jahrbuch für Mystiche Theologie* 1 (1960).

Huot de Longchamp, Max. *Lectures de Jean de la Croix: Essai d'anthropologie mystique.* Paris: Beauchesne, 1981.

——. "Les Mystiques Catholiques et la Bible." In *Bible de Tous les Temps.* Vol. V, *Le temps des Réformes et la Bible,* ed. Guy Bedouelle and Bernard Roussel. Paris: Beauchesne, 1989. Pp. 586–612.

——. *Saint Jean de la Croix: pour lire le Docteur mystique.* Paris: FAC Editions, 1991.

Maritain, Jacques. *Distinguish to Unite, or The Degrees of Knowledge.* Translated by Gerald B. Phelan (from 4th French ed.). Notre Dame: University of Notre Dame Press, 1995. Originally published as *Distinguer pour unir, ou les degrés du savoir,* 1932.

Matthew, Iain. "The Knowledge and Consciousness of Christ in the Light of the Writings of St. John of the Cross." D.Phil. dissertation, University of Oxford, 1991.

——. *The Impact of God: Soundings from St. John of the Cross.* London: Hodder and Stoughton, 1995.

Morel, Georges. *Le sens de l'existence selon Saint Jean de la Croix.* Aubier, Paris: Editions Montaigne, 1960, 1961.

Orcibal, Jean. *La Rencontre du Carmel Thérésian avec les Mystiques du Nord.* Paris: Presses Universitaires de France, 1959.

——. "Le Rôle de l'intellect possible chez Jean de la Croix: Ses sources scolastiques et nordiques." In *La Mystique Rhénane,* ed. Phillipe Dollinger et al. Paris: Presses Universitaires de France, 1963. Pp. 235–79.

——. *Saint Jean de la Croix et les mystiques rhénoflamands.* Bruges, Belgium: Desclee de Brouwer, 1966.

Pacho, Eulogio (de la Virgen del Carmen). "La antropología Sanjuanistica." *El Monte Carmelo* 69 (1961): 47–70.

——. *San Juan de la Cruz y sus escritos.* Madrid: Ediciones Cristianidad, 1969.

——. *Iniciación a San Juan de la Cruz.* Burgos: Monte Carmelo, 1982.

——. *San Juan de la Cruz. Temas Fundamentales.* 2 vols. Burgos: Monte Carmelo, 1984. Translated under the title *The Art of Reaching God according to St. John of the Cross: Exposition of the Basic Themes of Sanjuanist Spirituality.* Jyothir Bhavan, Kalamassey: Jyothir Dhara pub., 1990.

——. "El hombre, Aleación de Espíritu y materia." In *Antropología de San Juan de la Cruz,* ed. José Cepeda. Avila: Institución Gran Duque de Alba, 1988. Pp. 23–35.

——. "El 'Gemido Pacífico de la Esperanza'. Síntesis definitiva del pensamiento Sanjuanista." *Studies in Spirituality* 6 (1996): 153–67.

Patron, Joseph. "Christ in the Teaching and Life of St. John of the Cross." *Mount Carmel* 30 (1982): 94–110.

Payne, Steven. *John of the Cross and the Cognitive Value of Mysticism: An Analysis of Sanjuanist Teaching and Its Philosophical Implication for Contemporary Discussions of Mystical Experience.* Dordrecht/Boston/London: Kluwer Academic Publishers, 1990.

Rodríguez-San Pedro Bezares, Luis Enrique. *La formación universitaria de Juan de la*

Cruz. Valladolid: Junta de Castilla y León, Consejería de Cultura y Turismo, 1992.

Ruiz Salvador, Federico. *Introducción a San Juan de la Cruz: El hombre, los escritos, el sistema.* Madrid: Biblioteca de Autores Cristianos, 1968.

——. *Místico y maestro: San Juan de la Cruz.* Madrid: Editorial de Espiritualidad, 1986.

——, ed. *Experiencia y Pensamiento en San Juan de la Cruz.* Madrid: Editorial de Espiritualidad, 1990.

Russell, Paul. "The Humanity of Christ in St. John of the Cross." *Spiritual Life* 30 (1984): 143–56.

Sanson, Henri. *L'Esprit humain selon Saint Jean de la Croix.* Paris: Presses Universitaires de France, 1953.

Stein, Edith. *The Science of the Cross: A Study of St. John of the Cross.* Translated by Hilda Graef. Chicago: Henry Regnery Co., 1960.

Thompson, Colin P. *The Poet and the Mystic: A Study of the Cantico Espiritual of San Juan de la Cruz.* Oxford: Oxford University Press, 1977.

Tillyer, D. *Union with God: The Teaching of St. John of the Cross.* London: Mowbray, 1984.

Wilhelmsen, Elizabeth. *Knowledge and Symbolization in Saint John of the Cross.* Frankfurt am Main/New York: Peter Lang, 1993.

——. "La memoria en Juan de la Cruz." *Carmelus* 37 (1990): 88–145.

Williams, Rowan. *The Wound of Knowledge*, 2nd ed. London: Darton, Longman and Todd, 1990.

——. "Butler's *Western Mysticism*: Towards an Assessment." *Downside Review* 102 (1984): 197–215.

——. "Language, Reality and Desire in Augustine's *De Doctrina*." *Journal of Literature and Theology* 3 (1989): 138–50.

B. Teresa of Avila

Bibliographies

"Bibliographia Carmeli Teresiani." In *Carmelus.* Rome: Institutum Carmelitanum, 1954– (annual).

"Bibliografía Teresiana." In *Obras Completas de Santa Teresa de Jesús*, ed. Efrén de la Madre de Dios and Otger Steggink, 9th ed. Madrid: Biblioteca de Autores Cristianos, 1997, pp. xxxvii–cxvii.

Concordance

San José, Luis de. *Concordancias de los obras y escritos de Santa Teresa de Jesús.* Archivo silveriano de historia y espiritualidad carmelitana, 9. Burgos: El Monte Carmelo, 1945, 1965, 1982.

Texts

Obras Completas de Santa Teresa de Jesús. Ed. Efrén de la Madre de Dios and Otger Steggink, 9th ed. Madrid: Biblioteca de Autores Cristianos, 1997.

The Collected Works of St. Teresa of Avila. Translated and introduced by Kieran Kavanaugh and Otilio Rodriguez. 3 vols. Vol. 1: 2nd ed.; Vols. 2 & 3: 1st ed. Washington D.C.: Institute of Carmelite Studies, 1980–87.

The Complete Works of St. Teresa of Jesus. Translated by E. Allison Peers. 3 vols. London: Sheed & Ward, 1946.

The Letters of St. Teresa of Jesus. Translated by E. Allison Peers. 2 vols. Westminster Md.: Newman Press, 1951.

Studies

Ahlgren, Gillian. "Teresa de Jesús: A Case Study in Mystical Creativity and Inquisitional Censure." Ph.D. dissertation, University of Chicago, 1991.

——. *Teresa of Avila and the Politics of Sanctity.* Ithaca: Cornell University Press, 1996.

Alvira, Maria Isabel. *Vision de l'homme selon Thérèse d'Avila: Une philosophie de l'heroïsme.* Paris: F.X. de Guibert, O.E.I.L., 1992.

Auclair, Marcelle. *St. Teresa of Avila.* Translated by Kathleen Pond. New York: Pantheon Books, 1952/53.

Barrientos, Alberto, ed. *Introducción a la lectura de Santa Teresa.* Madrid: Editorial de Espiritualidad, 1978.

Bilinkoff, Jodi. *The Avila of St. Teresa; Religious Reform in a Sixteenth-Century City.* New York: Cornell University Press, 1989.

——. "St. Teresa of Avila and the Avila of St. Teresa." *Carmelite Studies* 3 (1982): 53–68.

Burrows, Ruth. *Interior Castle Explored: St. Teresa's Teaching on the Life of Deep Union with God.* London: Sheed & Ward, 1981.

Efrén de la Madre de Dios and Otger Steggink. *Tiempo y vida de Santa Teresa.* Madrid: Biblioteca de Autores Cristianos, 1968, 1977.

Egido Martínez, Teófanes. "The Historical Setting of St. Teresa's Life." Translated by Steven Payne and Michael Dodd. *Carmelite Studies* 1 (1980): 122–82.

Fernández Alvarez, Manuel, et al. *Teresa de Jesús y Juan de la Cruz. Convergencias, Divergencias, Influencias.* Burgos: Ed. Monte Carmelo, 1989.

Frohlich, Mary. *The Intersubjectivity of the Mystic: A Study of Teresa of Avila's* The Interior Castle. Atlanta: Scholars Press, 1993.

Lopez Diaz-Otazu, Ana Maria. *Aproximación a San Juan de la Cruz de la mano de Santa Teresa.* Madrid: Narcea, 1990.

Quitsland, Sonya A. "Elements of a Feminist Spirituality in St. Teresa." *Carmelite Studies* 3 (1982): 19–50.

Slade, Carol. *St. Teresa of Avila: Author of a Heroic Life.* Berkeley and Los Angeles: University of California Press, 1995.

Tomás de la Cruz (Alvarez). "Santa Teresa de Jesús Contemplativa." In *De contemplatione in schola teresiana.* Ephemerides Carmeliticae. Rome: Apud Teresianum, 1962. Pp. 9–62.

Weber, Alison. *Teresa of Avila and the Rhetoric of Femininity.* Princeton: Princeton University Press, 1990.

Williams, Rowan. *Teresa of Avila.* London: Geoffrey Chapman, 1991.

C. General

De Certeau, Michel. *The Mystic Fable: The Sixteenth and Seventeenth Centuries.* Chicago: Chicago University Press, 1992.

Dupré, Louis. *Transcendent Selfhood: The Loss and Rediscovery of the Inner Life.* New York: Crossroad, Seabury Press, 1976.

——. *Passage to Modernity: An Essay in the Hermeneutics of Nature and Culture.* New Haven: Yale University Press, 1993.

Elliott, J. H. *Imperial Spain 1469–1716.* London: Pelican, 1963.

Groult, Pierre. *Les mystiques des Pays-Bas et la littérature espagnole du seizième siècle.* Louvain: Librarie universitaire, Uystpruyst, 1927.

Hadewijch: The Complete Works. Translated by Mother Columba Hart. New York: Paulist Press, 1980.

Hamilton, Alastair. *Heresy and Mysticism in 16th Century Spain: The Alumbrados.* Toronto: University of Toronto Press, 1992.

Howells, Edward. "Mystical Experience and the View of the Self in Teresa of Avila and John of the Cross." *Studia Mystica* XVIII (1997): 87–104.

——. "Mystical Consciousness and the Mystical Self in John of the Cross and Teresa of Avila." Ph.D. dissertation, University of Chicago, 1999.

Ivánka, Endre von. *Plato christianus: Übernahme und Umgestaltung des Platonismus durch die Väter.* Einsiedeln: Johannes Verlag, 1964.

Kamen, Henry. *Inquisition and Society in Spain in the Sixteenth and Seventeenth Centuries.* Bloomington: Indiana University Press, 1985.

Leclercq, Jean. *The Love of Learning and the Desire for God.* New York: Fordham University Press, 1961.

Lonergan, Bernard. *Verbum: Word and Idea in Aquinas.* Ed. Frederick E. Crowe & Robert M. Doran. Toronto: University of Toronto Press, 1997.

——. *Method in Theology.* New York: Herder & Herder, 1972.

McGinn, Bernard. *The Presence of God. A History of Western Christian Mysticism.* Vol. 1, *The Foundations of Mysticism: Origins to the Fifth Century.* New York: Crossroad, 1992.

——. *The Presence of God. A History of Western Christian Mysticism.* Vol. 2, *The Growth of Mysticism: Gregory the Great through the Twelfth Century.* New York: Crossroad, 1994.

——. *The Presence of God. A History of Western Christian Mysticism.* Vol. 3, *The Flowering of Mysticism: Men and Women in the New Mysticism—1200–1350.* New York: Crossroad, 1998.

——, ed. *Meister Eckhart and the Beguine Mystics.* New York: Crossroad, 1994.

——. "Love, Knowledge and *Unio Mystica* in the Western Christian Tradition." In *Mystical Union and Monotheistic Faith: an Ecumenical Dialogue*, ed. Moshe Idel and Bernard McGinn. New York: Macmillan, 1989. Pp. 59–86.

——. "Ocean and Desert as Symbols of Mystical Absorption in the Christian Tradition." *Journal of Religion* 74 (1994):155–81.

——. "The Changing Shape of Late Medieval Mysticism." *Church History* 65 (1996): 197–219.

McIntosh, Mark. *Mystical Theology: The Integrity of Spirituality and Theology*. Oxford: Blackwell, 1998.

Pettas, William. *A Sixteenth-Century Spanish Bookstore: The Inventory of Juan de Junta*. Transactions of the American Philosophical Society 85/1. Philadelphia, 1995.

Price, James R. "The Reintegration of Theology and Mysticism: A Dialectical Analysis of Bernard Lonergan's Theological Method and the Mystical Experience of Symeon the New Theologian." Ph.D. dissertation, University of Chicago, 1980.

——. "Lonergan and the Foundation of a Contemporary Mystical Theology." TMs owned by Professor Bernard McGinn, Divinity School, University of Chicago. Also published in *Lonergan Workshop*, vol. 5. Ed. Fred Lawrence. Chico, California: Scholars Press, 1985, p. 163.

Rudy, Gordon. "Mystical Language of Sensation in the Later Middle Ages." Ph.D. dissertation, University of Chicago, 1999.

Sells, Michael A. *Mystical Languages of Unsaying*. Chicago: University of Chicago Press, 1994.

Toulmin, Stephen. *Cosmopolis*. Chicago: University of Chicago Press, 1992.

Trueman Dicken, E. W. *The Crucible of Love: A Study of the Mysticism of St. Teresa of Jesus and St. John of the Cross*. New York: Sheed and Ward, 1963.

Turner, Denys. *Eros and Allegory: Medieval Exegesis and the Song of Songs*. Kalamazoo, Mich.: Cistercian, 1995.

——. *The Darkness of God: Negativity in Christian Mysticism*. Cambridge: Cambridge University Press, 1995.

Index